HEIDEGGER
and the
PROBLEM of KNOWLEDGE

HEIDEGGER

and the

PROBLEM of KNOWLEDGE

CHARLES B. GUIGNON

HACKETT PUBLISHING COMPANY

Publication of this book was assisted
by a grant from the Publications Program
of the National Endowment for the Humanities,
an independent federal agency.

Interior design by James N. Rogers
Cover design by Jackie Lacy

For further information, please address
Hackett Publishing Company, Inc.
Box 44937
Indianapolis, Indiana 46204

Library of Congress Cataloging in Publication Data
Guignon, Charles B., 1944–
Heidegger and the problem of knowledge.

1. Heidegger, Martin, 1889–1976—Knowledge, Theory of.
2. Knowledge, Theory of—History—20th century.
I. Title.
B3279.H49G79 1983   121′.092′4   83–279
ISBN 0-915145-21-9
ISBN 0-915145-62-6 (pbk.)

For my mother,

Veronica Burke Guignon

Table of Contents

Preface

Few works from continental Europe have aroused so much interest and controversy as Heidegger's *Being and Time.* Yet this book has also proved to be unapproachable to many English-speaking readers. Part of the difficulty results from the fact that Heidegger's thought is rooted in a tradition that has been foreign to us since the time of Russell and Moore: that of Hegel. It is true that resonances between *Being and Time* and more familiar ideas have sometimes been heard. Sidney Hook reports, for instance, that John Dewey, after hearing a summary of *Being and Time,* remarked "that it sounded as if a German peasant were trying to render parts of *Experience and Nature* into his daily idiom,"[1] But the common historical roots that account for these similarities have generally been overlooked. Hook seems surprised to find that certain "positions" in Heidegger's major work are "reminiscent of points of view taken *independently* by other Western philosophers" (*ibid.* 6; my emphasis). Such a coincidence appears less remarkable, however, when we recall the shared Hegelian background of Heidegger and Dewey and note that Dewey's friend and mentor, George Herbert Mead, was studying under Wilhelm Dilthey in Berlin during the revival of interest in Hegel at the turn of the century.

Part of what is needed in order to assimilate Heidegger's thought, then, is the rediscovery of a way of seeing things that has been closed off to us to a large extent in this century. But the difficulty of understanding *Being and Time* also has a deeper source in Heidegger's unfamiliar conception of philosophy. The Anglo-American tradition generally tends to see philosophy as a set of current topics or problems that are to be discussed within pre-given frameworks. The method is argument and counterargument along tacitly agreed-upon guidelines. In contrast, Heidegger maintains that it is these frameworks themselves that are the source of traditional philosophical problems. As a result, he is concerned not so much with presenting arguments and defending theses as with completely re-evaluating and overhauling our inherited ways of understanding ourselves and the world. And this in turn means

---

1. Sidney Hook, "The Map Was Redrawn to Make Man's Agony a Part of the Geography," *The New York Times Book Review,* Nov. 11, 1962, p. 6. I am indebted to Kah Kyung Cho for pointing this passage out to me.

1

developing a new *vocabulary* of description and interpretation that will by-pass the prejudices built into our historically conditioned "common sense." Heidegger's new language, intractable as it already is in German, has practically defied translation into English. The result has tended to be a standoff between those who can bandy about the Heideggerian jargon and those who find the whole business elitist and incomprehensible.

In the meantime it has become increasingly difficult to ignore Heidegger. A well-respected American philosopher who has proved his mettle in the analytic tradition, Richard Rorty, tells us that Heidegger (along with Wittgenstein and Dewey) is one of "the three most important philosophers of our century."[2] Outside the academic discipline of philosophy, there is a growing interest in the kind of hermeneutic approach to human phenomena that Heidegger has helped to define in its modern form. And in literary circles there has been an increasing clamor over the writing of such post-structuralists as Derrida and Foucault, whose works can best be understood as responses to Heideggerian philosophy. The ever-widening impact of Heidegger's thought makes it pressing for philosophers to come to terms with his contributions.

One of my central aims in undertaking this work has been to make *Being and Time* more readily accessible to non-Heideggerians. Starting from Heidegger's critique of traditional epistemology, I have tried to work out a detailed analysis of the major themes of *Being and Time* while also exposing the kinds of tensions that run through his major work. My method has been to focus on a familiar problem that cuts across the Anglo-American and continental traditions: the problem of skepticism about the external world. This narrow puzzle provides a key which opens up a wide range of problems and presuppositions built into the Cartesian tradition.[3] By examining Heidegger's treatment of these problems, I hope to show that *Being and Time,* despite its inimical style and vocabulary, has profound consequences for a broad spectrum of topics of interest in the English-speaking world.

In the course of working out this explication, however, I came to realize that there is a dangerous counter-risk to jargonizing, and that is the temptation to trivialize what Heidegger says by making it

2. Richard Rorty, *Philosophy and the Mirror of Nature* (Princeton, N.J.: University Press, 1979), p. 5.

3. For my appreciation of the importance of the problem of skepticism, as well as my characterization of the stages of the skeptic's inquiry and the structure of epistemological arguments, I am deeply indebted to Thompson Clarke's lectures and seminars at Berkeley in 1970-1972.

too familiar. There is an inclination to conflate Heidegger's ideas with those of whoever is popular at the moment in the Anglo-American world, a tendency which distorts his thought as much as esotericism conceals. Such an attempt at assimilation often masks the fact that *Being and Time* is profoundly alien in many respects. Though Heidegger's debt to the existentialist and phenomenological movements in Europe has been noted in most interpretations and the religious motifs in his writings are now being brought to light, other crucial influences on his work have been overlooked. The result is that we have a rather one-sided and warped picture of this extremely eclectic philosopher.

There are two tributaries in particular which have to be understood if we are to grasp fully the novelty and uniqueness of *Being and Time*. The first is the hermeneutic tradition which extends from Schleiermacher through Dilthey to Heidegger and such contemporaries as Gadamer, Ricoeur, and Habermas. In its windings and turnings since its origins in biblical exegesis, this tradition has come to regard all human expressions as "text-analogues" which must be handled in a way similar to the reading of literary texts. The influence of the hermeneutic point of view has important implications for Heidegger's ontology of being human and his methodology in *Being and Time*. Since human existence is regarded as like a meaningful text, Heidegger is led to portray our everyday life-world as a holistic field of "internal relations" in which we find ourselves most originally as place-holders in a wider field of significance relations. And, insofar as philosophy itself has a hermeneutic structure, Heidegger's method breaks with traditional philosophy to the extent that it is concerned less with discovering obvious truths and providing proofs than with unearthing an underlying meaning in what is manifest in our normal lives.

A second influence on *Being and Time* which should not be overlooked is that of the nineteenth-century historical school represented by figures like Ranke, Droysen, and Dilthey. With the collapse of the Hegelian faith in Reason guiding the course of history to its culmination, a wave of historicism infected certain German intellectual circles, eventually leading to widespread historical relativism by the turn of the century. According to this historicist orientation, all values and interpretations are seen as embedded in the historical epoch in which they emerge, so that no *trans*historical judgments are possible. Each historical period is unique and can be evaluated only in terms of the values immanent in that period.

One of Heidegger's primary goals in *Being and Time* is to overcome this sort of historical relativism. While he recognizes the "historicity" of all human endeavors, he also hopes to circumvent the consequences of historicism by positing an underlying thread of meaning that weaves the whole course of historical events into a unified narrative. For this reason he characterizes being human as a "happening" (Geschehen) that flows into the greater stream of world-history and therefore always has access to some deeper sources of understanding beneath the transience of finite existence. Since a recognition of the historical situatedness of all inquiry is now emerging in the Anglo-American world, it will be profitable to examine the way that Heidegger tries to escape historical relativism through what I will call *transcendental historicism*. And it will also be instructive to see exactly why this attempt fails and how the failure motivates the shift or "turn" (Kehre) in Heidegger's later writings.

By raising to prominence the historicist and hermeneutic dimensions of *Being and Time,* my reading of Heidegger marks a shift in emphasis from the standard interpretations of his thought as mainstream existentialism. It takes seriously Heidegger's later claims that he had fully overcome subjectivism in *Being and Time,* and it attempts to show a deep level of continuity throughout his writings in his historical approach to philosophical problems. It should also help to clarify the effect his thought has had on his heirs, such as Hans-Georg Gadamer, and on such critics as Derrida and Foucault. From the standpoint of interpretations of Heidegger as an existentialist, the criticisms of this new wave of writers seem oblique and irrelevant. Only when Heidegger's historicist and hermeneutic orientation has been brought to light can the moves they make be seen as significant in a larger philosophical context.

In quoting, I have generally relied on the existing translations, occasionally making revisions where there are errors or for the sake of uniformity. Certain technical terms in *Being and Time* (such as 'Befindlichkeit' and 'Seinkönnen') have been consistently retranslated, since the standard translations are misleading. I have found Joan Stambaugh's new translation of the Introduction to *Being and Time,* which is available in David F. Krell's edition of Heidegger's *Basic Writings,* quite helpful in unraveling some of the convoluted sentences in the opening sections of the work. I retain the now standardized convention of leaving 'Dasein' untranslated. This term, a perfectly ordinary German word meaning "existence," is to some extent a dummy word which gains its meaning (in German as well as in English) only through contextual definition.

The original research for this work was made possible by a Fulbright grant for study at the University of Heidelberg from 1974 to 1976, and the final rewrite was aided by a Summer Research Award from The University of Texas in 1981. I would like to thank Thomas Bridges, Karsten Harries, Douglas Kellner, H. L. Dreyfus, and Charles Taylor for making their unpublished manuscripts available to me. My infrequent citations do not convey my reliance on these works. I am deeply indebted to my teachers who shaped my philosophical outlook: Thompson Clarke, Dorothea Frede, Hans-Georg Gadamer, Piotr Hoffman, Hanna Pitkin, Richard Rorty, Hans Sluga, Barry Stroud, Charles Taylor, and Ernst Tugendhat.

I also owe special thanks to colleagues and friends who over the years have discussed the ideas in this book and have made helpful comments on earlier versions: Douglas Browning, Kah Kyung Cho, Robert Causey, John Haugeland, Douglas Kellner, Noreen Kornmann, Louis Mackey, Al Martinich, Robert Palter, Thomas Seung, Robert Sokolowski, and Robert C. Solomon. I have benefited from their suggestions far more than the imperfect product would suggest. Most of all, I want to express my deepest gratitude to my teacher and friend, H. L. Dreyfus, who not only introduced me to Heidegger and laid the foundation for my interpretation, but also instilled in me a sense of the urgency and excitement of philosophy which is the greatest gift of the teacher to a pupil. Finally, and not least, I would like to thank Colleen Kieke for her excellent typing, Leigh S. Cauman for her painstaking editing, and my wife Hiromi for her assistance and endurance.

Abbreviations

(Page numbers in parentheses refer to *Sein und Zeit* (Tübingen: Max Neimeyer, 1972), twelfth edition. Translated by John Macquarrie and Edward Robinson as *Being and Time* (New York: Harper and Row, 1962). The English translation contains the German pagination.)

Works by Heidegger:

AWV	"The Age of the World View." Trans. Marjorie Grene. *Measure* 2 (1951), pp. 269–284.
BW	*Basic Writings.* Ed. David F. Krell. New York: Harper & Row, 1977.
EGT	*Early Greek Thinking.* Trans. D. F. Krell and F. A. Capuzzie. New York: Harper & Row, 1975.
EM	*Einführung in die Metaphysik.* Tübingen: Max Niemeyer, 1953.
EP	*The End of Philosophy.* Trans. Joan Stambaugh. New York: Harper & Row, 1973.
ER	*The Essence of Reasons.* Trans. Terrence Malick. Evanston: Northwestern University Press, 1969.
FD	*Die Frage nach dem Ding.* Tübingen: Max Niemeyer, 1962.
FS	*Frühe Schriften.* Frankfurt a. M.: Klostermann, 1972.
GP	*Die Grundprobleme der Phänomenologie. Gesamtausgabe,* vol. 24. Frankfurt a. M.: Klostermann, 1975.

HW	*Holzwege.* Frankfurt a. M.: Klostermann, 1963.
IM	*An Introduction to Metaphysics.* Trans. Ralph Manheim. Garden City, N.Y.: Anchor Books, 1961.
KPMe	*Kant and the Problem of Metaphysics.* Trans. James S. Churchill. Bloomington / London: Indiana University Press, 1968.
KPMg	*Kant und das Problem der Metaphysik.* Frankfurt a. M.: Klostermann, 1973.
LH	"Letter on Humanism." Trans. E. Lohner. In *Philosophy in the Twentieth Century: An Anthology.* Vol. 3. Ed. William Barrett and Henry Aiken. New York: Random House, 1962.
LL	*Metaphysische Anfangsgründe der Logik im Ausgang von Leibniz. Gesamtausgabe,* vol. 26. Frankfurt a. M.: Klostermann, 1978.
LFW	*Logik: Die Frage nach der Wahrheit. Gesamtausgabe,* vol. 21. Frankfurt a. M.: Klostermann, 1976.
OWL	*On the Way to Language.* Trans. Peter D. Hertz. New York: Harper & Row, 1971.
PLT	*Poetry, Language, Thought.* Trans. Albert Hofstadter. New York: Harper & Row, 1971.
PT	*The Piety of Thinking: Essays by Martin Heidegger.* Trans. James G. Hart and John C. Maraldo. Bloomington / London: Indiana University Press, 1976.
PuT	*Phänomenologie und Theologie.* Frankfurt a. M.: Klostermann, 1970.
QCT	*The Question Concerning Technology and Other Essays.* Trans. William Lovitt. New York: Harper Colophon, 1977.

SD	*Zur Sache des Denkens.* Tübingen: Max Niemeyer, 1969.
SvG	*Der Satz vom Grund.* Pfullingen: Neske, 1957.
TB	*On Time and Being.* Trans. Joan Stambaugh. New York: Harper & Row, 1972.
US	*Unterwegs zur Sprache.* Pfullingen: Neske, 1975.
VA	*Vorträge und Aufsätze.* Vols. 1–3. Tübingen: Neske, 1967.
WCT	*What Is Called Thinking?* Trans. J. Glenn Gray and F. Wieck. New York: Harper Torchbooks, 1972.
WhD	*Was heisst Denken?* Tübingen: Max Niemeyer, 1954.
WM	*Wegmarken.* Frankfurt a. M.: Klostermann, 1967.
WT	*What Is a Thing?* Trans. W. B. Barton, Jr. and Vera Deutsch. Chicago: Henry Regnery, 1969.

Works by Dilthey:

Aufbau	*Der Aufbau der geschichtlichen Welt in den Geisteswissenschaften.* Frankfurt a. M.: Suhrkamp, 1974.
GS	*Gasammelte Schriften.* Leipzig: Teubner, 1914–58. Vol. 1: *Einleitung in die Geisteswissenschaften;* vol. 4: *Die Jugendgeschichte Hegels;* vol. 5: *Die geistige Welt;* vol. 7: *Der Aufbau der geschichtlichen Welt in den Geisteswissenchaften.*
PM	*Pattern and Meaning in History.* Ed. H. P. Rickman. New York: Harper Torchbooks, 1962.
WD	*W. Dilthey: Selected Writings.* Ed. and trans. H. P. Rickman. Cambridge: Cambridge University Press, 1976.

I

Heidegger's Program and the Cartesian Model

At the heart of the enterprise of traditional epistemology lies the standard argument for skepticism about the existence of the external world. The point of this argument is to lead us to question the grounds for our most commonplace beliefs and practices. Underlying our everyday practical affairs, we are told, there is a web of beliefs about the world and our place in it. Picking up this pen and beginning to write, for instance, I might be said to believe there is a pen here, that there is paper in front of me, that the pen will make marks on the paper, and so forth. Of course, if saying that I have a "belief" is interpreted as meaning that I am explicitly entertaining some proposition in my mind, then I probably have no such beliefs. What is "in my mind" as I begin to write is not usually the pen and paper, but the subject matter I plan to write about. In a looser sense of the word 'belief', however, it might be said of me that I believe that there is a pen and paper before me. Under certain circumstances I would tend to assent to propositions like "There is a pen here" or "There is paper here," even though these thoughts are not part of the mental commentary that accompanies my activity. It seems plausible, then, to say that our practical affairs are made possible by a generally implicit background of beliefs about the external world which can be make explicit under appropriate circumstances.

Traditional skeptical arguments are designed to insinuate doubts into these mundane and seemingly self-evident beliefs. The skeptic asks whether our ordinary beliefs are really as well grounded as our assurance in acting would tend to suggest we think they are. The types of doubt raised are familiar. I feel confident there is a pen in my hand at this moment, but the only evidence I have for my belief is certain sensory data. I see the pen before me, I feel its firm pressure against my fingers, I hear it scratching across the page. But I also know such sensory experiences can turn out to be illusory. There have been occasions when I have thought I was seeing, feeling, and hearing things when actually there was nothing there. In fact, it is argued, I might still be in bed dreaming all of this, or I might be hallucinating. When taken seriously, such doubts can produce a certain giddiness. The skeptic can lead us to

11

think that we do not *really* know that our most mundane and trivial beliefs about the world are true. The results are counterintuitive and shocking: since all I really know is that I am conscious of certain images and ideas, I have no reason to believe anything actually exists outside my mind. For all I know, what I call "reality" may be nothing other than this play of mental contents dancing through my consciousness.

In the second edition of the *Critique of Pure Reason* Kant addresses the consequences that seem to emerge from this skeptical puzzle. He claims that "it still remains a scandal to philosophy and to human reason in general that the existence of things outside us . . . must be accepted merely on *faith,* and that if anyone thinks good to doubt their existence, we are unable to counter his doubts by any satisfactory proof."[1] To redress this scandal to philosophy he undertakes a "refutation of idealism" which will reply to both the "*dogmatic* idealism" of Berkeley and the "*problematic* idealism" of Descartes (B274). Berkeley's idealism is easy to deal with, Kant thinks, but Cartesian skepticism is worthy of special consideration. According to Kant, Descartes holds that "there is only one empirical assertion that is indubitably certain, namely, that 'I am'," so that "the existence of objects in space outside us" is "merely doubtful and undemonstrable" (B274). The proof that objects exist "outside us" is supposed to be achieved by showing that "inner experience is possible only through outer experience in general" (B278/9). The goal is to demonstrate the existence of an external world by showing that the discovery of the certain and indubitable "I am" is possible only if there is knowledge of things in the external world.

That Kant is concerned with what he calls Descartes's "problematic idealism" is indicative of the emerging centrality of skepticism and the problem of knowledge in eighteenth-century philosophical thought. The question is posed whether what is given in "inner experience" — the ideas, perceptions, and representations found inside consciousness — in fact provides us with true knowledge about what is "outside of us" — the objects we believe to exist in the external world. The demand for a proof of the existence of objects outside our minds Kant regards as "reasonable and in accordance with a thorough and philosophical mode of thought" (B275). The critical philosophy of the *Critique* cannot rest content with naive faith in an external world. A rational proof is warranted and must be provided if the scandal of philosophy is to be

---

1. *Critique of Pure Reason,* trans. Norman Kemp Smith (London: Macmillan, 1963), Bxxxixn.

remedied. Although the common man may blithely drift through life without ever facing the possibility that everything might in fact exist only in his mind, the philosopher has the obligation to determine with certainty whether an external world exists and how we come to know it.

In *Being and Time* Heidegger turns Kant's conception of the scandal of philosophy on its head. What is scandalous, in Heidegger's view, is the very idea that philosophy must reply to the skeptic and that this should be its first order of business. "The 'scandal of philosophy' is not that this proof has yet to be given," Heidegger says, "but that *such proofs are expected and attempted again and again*" (205). The real scandal of philosophy is the unquestioned centrality and sovereignty of epistemology in recent philosophy. The theory of knowledge is supposed to be "critical" in the sense of providing the grounds and limits for metaphysics. But Heidegger thinks that the theory of knowledge is itself shot through with dogmatic metaphysical assumptions. It is taken as obvious and beyond question by Kant and others that we can draw a clear distinction between the "inner experiences" that are in the mind or consciousness on the one hand, and things or objects in the external world on the other. Given this unchallenged metaphysical assumption, the natural question to ask is how we can "transcend the sphere of immanence" of our minds to gain knowledge of the external world. Heidegger hopes to rectify this scandalous situation by restoring metaphysics to its rightful place at the center of philosophy. In his view, the modern fascination with epistemology is a short-lived aberration in the history of philosophy which must be diagnosed and overcome.

My concern in what follows is to examine and evaluate Heidegger's radical approach to the traditional skeptical argument and to epistemology in general. The modern form of the skeptical argument has come down to us from Descartes. Although the problem of skepticism in its most recent form has parted company with many of Descartes's original aims and assumptions, it nevertheless retains an underlying structure which can be traced back to Descartes. In Heidegger's words:

> Descartes's interpretation of entities and truth first creates the presupposition underlying the theory of knowledge and the metaphysics of knowledge. Through Descartes, realism is first put in the position of having to prove the reality of the outer world (QCT 119, HW 91).

The Cartesian legacy includes a conception of the world as

consisting of minds and matter, a picture of truth as correct representation, and a belief that intelligibility is to be rooted in rationality. In what follows I will refer to this structure as the *Cartesian model*, even though its characterization does not always accord with the details of Descartes's thought. My goal is to present a version of the standard skeptical argument which will be familiar to readers of recent philosophy and to suggest how the assumptions that underlie it have their origins in Descartes. It is the Cartesian legacy we have appropriated in our times and not the actual fabric of Descartes's thought which the expression 'Cartesian model' is supposed to capture.

Heidegger's examination of the Cartesian model is part of the greater project of "fundamental ontology" in *Being and Time*. Since the treatment of skepticism can be understood only in the context of the work as a whole, the first section of this chapter will sketch out the program of *Being and Time* and locate the discussion of the skeptical puzzle in the framework of Heidegger's broader aims. In the second section my concern will be to identify three stages that make up the standard skeptical argument. It should become clear that, if certain assumptions are granted at the outset of the Cartesian inquiry, then the skeptic's conclusions are unassailable and inescapable. If we are to avoid the shocking results of the skeptic's argument, then, it appears that we must expose and examine the basic presuppositions that structure the argument. This will be the aim of the third section.

§1. *The "Question of Being" and the Problem of Skepticism*

The problem of our knowledge of the external world occupies only a small part of *Being and Time* (§43), and the main thrust of Heidegger's brief discussion there is to show that it is a misguided "pseudo-problem" not worthy of extended consideration. In order to understand this apparently cavalier treatment of the pivotal question of epistemology, we must see it in its relation to the overall goals of the work as a whole. The guiding aim of *Being and Time,* Heidegger says, is "to work out the question of Being in general [Seinsfrage überhaupt]" (436). Heidegger believes he can turn directly to this ancient metaphysical question and ignore modern epistemology's injunction to first clarify our mode of access to Being, because he maintains that "the question of Being" is prior to any other area of philosophical concern. As we shall see in Chapter II, Heidegger holds that every field of inquiry always works from some prior conception of the Being of the entities it deals with and therefore remains "precritical" and "opaque" until an account of the "meaning of Being in general" has been provided. This is especially true of epistemology with its picture of reality as a "context of things (*res*)" (201) which are to be known by "subjects" collecting data about them. Heidegger suggests that epistemology begins from uncritical prejudices which bar the way to true ontological understanding.

It might sound strange to say that the theory of knowledge, which came into its modern form as a safeguard against precritical flights of metaphysical speculation, is itself rife with uncritical ontological prejudices. Heidegger's point will be clearer if we consider his conception of the source of certain kinds of philosophical problem. The philosophical questions taken up and dwelt on by a culture are not, in Heidegger's view, timeless puzzles that naturally and inevitably arise from any encounter with the world. Generally the questions that seem "natural" and pressing to an age emerge out of a world-view that has been inaugurated by key historical transformations in that culture. In the background of *Being and Time* is the assumption that the whole history of Western thought has been set on the wrong track by the Greek interpretation of Being as *ousia* or *parousia* (25/6). Beginning "explicitly with Parmenides" (100), there was a tendency to cover up the deepest and earliest sense of reality by interpreting Being as mere "presence" (Anwesenheit). Given this initial epochal event, the later emergence of the Cartesian model appears to be almost an inevitable twist in the unfolding of Western thinking. The unpublished parts of *Being and Time* were to have traced our modern understanding of Being back to these early Greek roots. [2]

In the published part of the work Heidegger focuses primarily on the world-view that emerged in the sixteenth and seventeenth centuries and culminated in the rise of modern science. This world-view, which Heidegger sees as having been wrought by heroic, innovative individuals "out of the earliest passion of thinking,"[3] has become crystallized into a sort of template that determines in

---

2. Otto Pöggeler notes that the young Heidegger, recently having turned from theology to philosophy, interpreted the deepest understanding of time and Being in terms of the model of primitive Christianity. What is central in *Being and Time* is the notion of the *kairos,* the "moment" (Augenblick), and the Greek philosophical interpretation of Being as "presence" is seen as an essential error that has led Western thought astray ever since. See his " 'Historicity' in Heidegger's Late Work," *The Southwestern Journal of Philosophy*, IV (Fall 1973): 53–73, p. 56.

3. WT 42, FD 32.

advance the paths our thought can follow and the kinds of result we can achieve. Heidegger sees the establishment of a world-view as having both a revealing and a concealing function. It opens previously unimagined possibilities for understanding and contributes to the enrichment of human life. But it simultaneously tends to conceal older and more original possibilities of understanding ourselves and our world. When a world-view becomes firmly entrenched, it tends to perpetuate a set of problems that are taken as natural and obvious. The possibilities of thought become calcified; the same questions and the same types of futile answer are repeated along the guidelines laid out by the grid that structures our thought. We come to think that our framework of thought is the only right one, and that "we are such terrific people, the Lord must have given it to us in our sleep."[4]

With the epoch-making transition that culminated in the rise of modern science and the Enlightenment, a constellation of ideas and ways of thinking became firmly impressed in the West. Ever since, Heidegger says, this framework has provided us with "a universal way of thinking along certain basic lines" which "holds us captive and makes us unfree in the experience and determination of things."[5] When a world-view becomes rigid and calcified, it becomes necessary to distance ourselves from it and re-evaluate it. Since there is no external, neutral vantage point to which we can step back and view our framework, Heidegger believes that such a distancing can be achieved only by retrieving the forgotten possibilities of our heritage. Although these historical possibilities are always present in our horizon of understanding by virtue of the fact that our understanding is shaped by history, they are concealed or distorted by the prevailing world-view. Heidegger's goal in posing the "question of Being," then, is to "reawaken an understanding of this question" (1) by bringing us back to older and deeper possibilities for interpreting ourselves and the world. When these historical possibilities have been made accessible, the problem of skepticism and the assumptions that buttress it will be seen as the outgrowth of a world-view that holds no special claim on us.

Part of the project of *Being and Time* therefore consists in diagnosing the prevailing world-view of the modern age. Heidegger exposes the knots that bind together the net of our present understanding of Being and attempts to account for the surface plausibility of the whole in terms of an ingrained human tendency

4. WT 42, FD 32.

5. WT 51, FD 38.

to misread our actual situation in the world. By tracing this mesh of ideas back to its historical roots, he hopes to free us from our "one-sided orientation to Being" (201) and thereby open us to what he calls the more "primordial" (ursprünglich) possibilities of understanding that are implicit in our heritage.[6] The brief treatment of the venerated "problem of the external world" is part of this over-all attempt to release us from our fascination with the assumptions built into the Cartesian model.

It should be clear from this account of Heidegger's project in *Being and Time* that we will have to grasp the main outlines of the whole of the work before the impact of the critique of skepticism will be fully clear. For this reason I have left the discussion of Heidegger's explicit treatment of skepticism for the last chapter. It should also be clear, however, that Heidegger's challenge to skepticism will have consequences that ripple out beyond the confines of this particular puzzle. For the problem of skepticism seems to encapsulate perfectly many of the assumptions of the world-view that structures our ways of thinking today. Two clusters of ideas in particular are subjected to Heideggerian diagnoses. First, there is the modern tendency toward subjectivism and individualism which Heidegger traces back to Descartes's "discovery" of the mind. And, second, there is the technological orientation of the modern world which has originated from the new conception of the grounds for intelligibility of modern science.

Heidegger sees the modern picture of man as a "subject of experience" — as essentially a mind or consciousness — as originating in Descartes's thought. Starting with Descartes, a clear distinction is drawn between what is given in the mind in perceiving, willing, imagining, desiring, and other mental acts, and what exists in the external world and is represented by such mental acts. The subject becomes the center around which all other entities revolve as "objects" of experience: the self is the "*sub-jectum*" — that which is "thrown under" and underlies beings. The *res cogitans* discovered by Descartes's methodological doubt comes to replace God as the essential substance that determines the Being of beings. Through Descartes, "man is transformed into an exceptional being, into a subject which, as the first true (i.e., certain) being, has priority over all other beings."[7] Man is "the representer of all representing, and

---

6. As we shall see in section 6, Heidegger believes that the two distinct senses of the word primordial — "early" in time and "fundamental" or "underlying" — in fact amount to the same thing.

7. QCT 150, HW 101.

therewith the realm of all representedness, and hence of all certainty and truth."[8]

Descartes's discovery of the mind was bound up with the intensely individualistic interpretation of Christianity in Erasmus and Luther, to generate the modern form of individualism. What makes a person unique is now seen as the hidden, private riches of his innermost mental realm. Understanding myself as essentially a mind only accidentally hooked up to a body, I can distinguish "that within which passeth show" — my emotions, feelings, perceptions, and thoughts — from the masks I wear and games I play in the world. This kind of dichotomy existed at earlier times, of course, but what is new in the Cartesian turn is a picture of the inner self as completely self-defining, with no essential bonds to anything else in the cosmos. Lionel Trilling identifies three traits of the form of individualism that arose in the sixteenth and seventeenth centuries. The new individual has an increasing awareness of his "internal space"; he begins to think of himself as playing various roles, as someone who stands "outside or above his own personality"; and he sees himself as an object of interest to his fellow man not because of his achievements, "but simply because as an individual he [is] of consequence."[9]

With the rise of this subjective individualism, a transformed understanding of what is at stake in being human appears on the scene. The true self is to be found by a kind of inner concentration which draws together the different strands of the subjective life. There is a growing concern with being "integrated," "centered," "fulfilled," and this is understood as attainable only by severing one's accidental ties to one's community and history. Since I am self-defining and autonomous, my family, religion, occupation, and national origins are appendages or decorations that may be cast off in my search for integration. My ethical and social relations are contrived, conventional devices superimposed over me through the demands of expedience. With this picture of what it is to be human, the central question of recent times comes to prominence: the issue of being "true to oneself," of being "authentic." To achieve self-integration I must be faithful to my innermost impulses, needs, aspirations, and feelings. The ideal of authenticity in turn leads to the problem of identifying this elusive and ephemeral point of the inner self: "How can we know the dancer from the dance?"

8. QCT 150, HW 100/1.

9. Lionel Trilling, *Sincerity and Authenticity* (Cambridge, Mass.: Harvard, 1974), p. 24.

One of Heidegger's goals in *Being and Time* is to diagnose and deflate the picture of the self as a substantial subject distinct from an external world of things. Although the issue of authenticity has gained currency among contemporary intellectuals through Heidegger as mediated by Sartre, we will find that the ideal of authenticity as presented in *Being and Time* does not involve being true to one's feelings, impulses, instincts, or any other "mental" possessions. Heidegger defines being human, or Dasein, as essentially Being-in-the-world, that is, as being contextualized in equipmental contexts, in a culture, and in history. These contexts *define* the self without residue—the Cartesian mind as a center of experiences divides out without remainder. What makes us unique as individuals is not an "internal space" or substantial self distinct from our roles in the world. Heidegger diagnoses modern individualism by showing the origins of our sense of uniqueness without reference to an inner reality distinct from our participation in the world. In this way he attempts to retrieve from oblivion an earlier understanding of the self as inextricably woven into the wider context of a community and a cosmos.[10]

The second cluster of ideas that Heidegger diagnoses is rooted in the new sense of man as the center around which all other entities revolve. When the subject is interpreted as the ground of all beings, Being comes to be understood as something merely at man's disposal. Nature and the world are regarded as something on hand for fulfilling our utilitarian ends. In this process, Being loses its gravity and weightiness. We become quiescent and complacent in our assurance that with science and technology we will achieve full mastery and dominance over all beings. Heidegger calls this worldview of modern times the "age of technology." Since Cartesian foundationalism is only a part of modern technology, Heidegger's diagnosis of the Cartesian model is comprehended within a wider re-evaluation of the aims and methods of modern science in general. For this reason Heidegger's diagnosis of Cartesianism is more radical than the familiar attacks on "the myth of the given" or the "dogmas of empiricism." It is aimed at the most general assumption of technology: that we can gain final control over Being by making it fully explicit and intelligible. Heidegger's goal is to shift the center of gravity from the subjectivism and instrumen-

---

10. The Greek understanding of the self as having fluid boundaries and as being indistinguishable from the *oikos* or *polis* has been developed by Bruno Snell, *The Discovery of the Mind* (New York: Harper Torchbook, 1960), John Jones, *On Aristotle and Greek Tragedy* (London: Chatto & Windus, 1962) and M. I. Finley, *The World of Odysseus* (New York: Viking Press, 1965).

talism of modern technology back to a more primordial sense of Being.

By examining his treatment of the standard problem of skepticism, then, we can bring to light the more far-ranging consequences of Heidegger's thought for our contemporary world-view. But in order to evaluate the impact of *Being and Time* on our modern framework, it will be necessary also to examine Heidegger's method and to question the success of his project. It is well known that *Being and Time* remained frustratingly incomplete. Heidegger says at the outset of the work that "our provisional aim is the interpretation of *time* as the possible horizon for any understanding of Being whatsoever" (1). Yet at the end of the published part not even this "provisional" aim has been carried out. Even in the final pages of the book Heidegger tells us that the analysis so far has been only "*a path*" (436) and that "the *question* of the meaning of Being remains unformulated and unclarified" (437). The over-all project of *Being and Time* is, as Heidegger suggests in his later writings, an illuminating—and perhaps unavoidable—failure.

If Heidegger himself regards *Being and Time* as unsuccessful, we will have to try to identify the reasons for this failure and ask whether anything of value remains after the wider goals of the work are abandoned. In the course of tracing the collapse of fundamental ontology it should become clear that Heidegger's project of finding *the* meaning of Being, or *the* correct representation of the nature of reality falls victim to the same sorts of challenge he raises against the Cartesian model in general. I will try to suggest, however, that even when the grandiose aims of this early approach to the "Seinsfrage" collapse, Heidegger's diagnosis of the Cartesian model has a lasting value and interest. To show this, it will be necessary to disentangle the more limited achievements of *Being and Time* from the bolder goals of the work as a whole.

§2. *Three Stages of the Cartesian Inquiry*

The Cartesian quest for certainty must be understood as a response to the shattering blows dealt to the relative stability of Medieval Europe in the sixteenth century.[11] During much of the

---

11. My account of this transition draws on Richard Popkin, *The History of Scepticism from Erasmus to Descartes* (Assen: Van Gorcum, 1960) and Theodore K. Rabb, *The Struggle for Stability in Early Modern Europe* (New York: Oxford, 1975).

late Middle Ages and Renaissance we find a picture of the world as a *liber naturae,* a structure of symbols which expresses the divine plan in external creation. The universe is grasped as a text in which the "great chain of Being" manifests the harmonious intentions of the Creator. Different regions of the whole are made intelligible by discovering the hidden analogies, sympathies, and correspondences that express the meaningful order emanating from the *Verbum.* The key to intelligibility is to be found in divine revelation as this is made accessible in Church doctrine. The task of the interpreter, guided by God's grace and by the inspired texts of the ancients, is to uncover the hidden meanings embodied in the text of the world.

A series of bewildering changes during the sixteenth century brought an end to this vision of the source of intelligibility. The revolutionary advances in science and technology, new discoveries abroad, abrupt shifts in demographic patterns, the breakdown of traditional political and economic structures, and, in the beginning of the seventeenth century, the devastation of warfare on the scale of the Thirty Years' War—all these proved to be incomprehensible within the traditional framework of medieval thought. Most significant among these dislocations was the protest launched by Luther in 1517. Luther challenged the authority of the Church and the traditional conception of reason, insisting on the absolute authority of individual conscience in interpreting Scripture. As a result of these sudden transitions, the traditional standards for knowledge had been undermined by the beginning of the seventeenth century, and there was no longer any universally binding criterion that could provide assurance for beliefs in science, morality, or religion.

One consequence of this shift was a wave of skepticism and relativism unprecedented in the previous centuries. The movement toward relativism reached its pinnacle in the *Essays* of Montaigne. Montaigne found that even the most cherished beliefs could be subjected to doubt. With a simple question, for instance, he casts doubt on the formerly undisputed supremacy of man in the chain of being: "When I play with my cat," he asks, "who knows if I am not a pastime to her more than she is to me?"[12] Even the natural superiority of Christianity could be challenged. "Compare our morals with a Mohammedan's, or a pagan's"; Montaigne suggests, "we always fall short of them" (*ibid.* 56). Instead of seeing the universe as a more or less fixed structure of symbols that can be intelligible to man, Montaigne argues that all things are in a constant

---

12. Montaigne, *Selections from the Essays,* trans. D. M. Frame (Northbrook, Ill.: AHM Publishing, 1973), p. 60.

state of flux. Since nothing can ever be grasped with certainty in the turbulence of the world, he is led to a full-blooded Pyrrhonism summed up in his famous slogan: "Que sais-je?"

What scandalized readers of Montaigne's *Essays* was his tolerant attitude toward religious and moral relativism. He holds, for example, that reason neither is nor should be the basis for our religious beliefs:

> Our faith is not of our own acquiring. . . . It is not by reasoning or by understanding that we have received our religion; it is by external authority and command. The weakness of our judgment helps us more in this than its strength, and our blindness more than our clear-sightedness (*ibid.* 61).

The sole foundation for our beliefs and practices is found to lie in the culture and historical epoch in which we are thrown. Right and wrong, truth and falsity are relative to the accidents of the time and place of our birth. Montaigne asks,

> What am I to make of a virtue that I saw in credit yesterday, that will be discredited tomorrow, and that becomes a crime on the other side of the river? What of a truth that is bounded by these mountains and is falsehood to the world that lives beyond? (*ibid.* 67)

Lacking any criterion that will guarantee our beliefs, Montaigne recommends that we turn inward and seek inner peace: "I advise moderation and temperance, and avoidance of novelty and strangeness" (*ibid.* 64).

The intellectual upheaval that occurred between the posting of Luther's ninety-five theses and Montaigne's *Essays* had effectively laid siege to the traditional foundations of understanding and intelligibility. Descartes's writings, which appeared in this atmosphere of the collapse of the old criteria, must be understood as an attempt to overcome relativism. In the *Discourse on Method* we can sense his anguish in the face of the prevailing uncertainty and lack of grounds.

> I had recognized in my travels that those who have feelings very contrary to ours are not, for that alone, either barbarians or savages, but that many of them use reason as much or more than we do; and I had considered how the same man, with the same mind, being raised from childhood among the French or Germans, becomes different from what he would be if he had

always lived among the Chinese or cannibals; and how, regarding the style of our clothes, the same thing which pleased us ten years ago, and perhaps will please us again ten years hence, now appears extravagant and ridiculous to us, so that we are more persuaded by custom and example than by certain knowledge. . . . Therefore I was unable to choose anyone whose opinions were preferable to those of others, and I found myself forced to undertake to guide myself.[13]

What is needed in order to overcome the ravages of relativism is a method that will lead us to certain and indubitable truths. Thus Descartes resolves "to rid myself of the opinions which I had formerly accepted, and commence to build anew from the foundation."[14]

When the confidence that man can attain a global understanding of himself and his world through authority or through discovering analogies between the macrocosm and microcosm is no longer tenable, it becomes necessary to find a criterion that will assure us that our understanding is firmly grounded, that it is based on genuine knowledge and not mere prejudice or superstition. Descartes's search for a foundation for our beliefs leads him to look for a basis that is certain and indubitable, a "self-grounding ground." The transition occurs, according to Heidegger, when man "frees himself from obligation to Christian revelational truth and Church doctrine," and is thereby obliged to "guarantee for himself the certainty of what is known."[15] The crucial decision made by Descartes is to determine the ground of understanding as lying in the *self*-certainty of the knowing subject. With this shift in the conception of the source of true understanding, the anthropocentrism and subjectivism of the modern age begins.

Heidegger sees this conflation of the quest for intelligibility and the quest for certainty as the origin of modern metaphysics. "The metaphysics of the modern age begins and has its essense," he says, "in the fact that it seeks the unconditionally indubitable, the certain and assured, certainty."[16] In a world in which the old foundations

13. *Discourse on Method, Optics, Geometry and Meteorology,* trans. P. J. Olscamp (Indianapolis: Bobbs-Merrill, 1965), pp. 14/5.

14. *Meditations* in *The Philosophical Works of Descartes,* vol. I, trans. Haldane and Ross (New York: Cambridge, 1968), p. 144.

15. QCT 148, HW 99.

16. QCT 82, HW 220.

of understanding are crumbling, Descartes makes the decisive move of identifying self-certainty as the self-grounding ground of all knowledge and understanding.

Descartes's methodological doubt is designed to pave the way for this complete certainty by freeing us from the prejudices we arrive at through "custom and example" in our everyday lives. The method of doubt "delivers us from every kind of prejudice, and sets out for us a very simple way by which the mind may detach itself from the senses."[17] We must reject "shifting earth and sand," he says, "in order to find rock or clay."[18] The image that recurs throughout Descartes's writings is that of finding a "firm foundation" on which to build the edifice of our beliefs. The process of doubt is to clear away the "vulgar" assumptions that run through our ordinary lives in order to uncover a ground for our beliefs based on pure intellection. The first prerequisite Descartes lays out for his method of inquiry, then, is that we disengage ourselves from our active involvement in the world in order to achieve the vantage point of an unprejudiced spectator. Descartes says he has prepared himself for his meditations by always wandering "here and there in the world, trying to be a *spectator* rather than an actor in all the dramas that are played there."[19] At the outset he assures himself that he has achieved the standpoint of pure contemplation: "I have delivered my mind from every care and am happily agitated by no passions."[20] Only in the rarified atmosphere of such a disengaged standpoint, stripped of all its ties to the cares and concerns of the world, can one achieve the "objectivity" of the contemplative attitude.

Having achieved this purified, objective standpoint, Descartes begins his investigation into the true sources of understanding. It will be helpful to divide this Cartesian inquiry into three stages and examine each in detail. Stage I is supposed to be a straightforward, commonsensical statement of what we believe in our everyday lives and how we come to hold these beliefs. In stage II, skeptical doubts are cast on those beliefs, resulting in a revised understanding of our epistemic situation. In the first stage we had believed ourselves to be embodied agents interacting with objects; we now find that, for all we actually know, we are merely minds with certain ideas or

17. *Meditations,* 140.

18. *Discourse,* 24.

19. (*Ibid.,* my emphasis).

20. *Meditations,* 144.

representations that may or may not be related to things in the world. Finally, in stage III an attempt is made to rationally reconstruct the set of common-sense beliefs we found in stage I on the basis of what is given in the new understanding of our epistemic predicament.

Stage I of the Cartesian inquiry is apparently the most innocuous and unproblematic. The Cartesian begins by cataloguing the types of beliefs we hold in our daily lives: "For example, there is the fact that I am here, seated before the fire, attired in a dressing gown, having this paper in my hand and other similar matters."[21] In our everyday epistemic predicaments we are seen as fundamentally observers collecting data about the world through the senses and forming beliefs about objects on that basis. Descartes also provides a plausible account of how we arrive at our everyday beliefs. In our normal affairs we perceive various features of things and then make "inferences" about what it is we see. "When looking from a window and saying I see men who pass in the street," Descartes says, "I really do not see them, but *infer* that what I see is men. . . . And yet what do I see from the window but hats and coats which may cover automatic machines? Yet I *judge* these to be men."[22] Our everyday beliefs about the objects we encounter in the world are grounded in the sorts of ad hoc inference we make from the observed features of things to conclusions about the things themselves.

The stage I account of our ordinary epistemic situation is designed to pave the way for the skeptical challenge in stage II of the inquiry. In this second stage the skeptic assesses the grounds we have for our beliefs and finds them to be inadequate. Since our beliefs are based on the evidence of the senses and the senses are not always trustworthy, our beliefs about the external world are not as secure as we would tend to think they are. Descartes notes, for example, that "those towers which from afar appeared to me to be round, more closely observed seemed square . . . and so on in an infinitude of other cases I found error in judgments founded on the external senses."[23]

But Descartes is not content with raising doubts on a piecemeal basis. He devises global counterpossibilities that can be applied to any of our beliefs about the world around us. He suggests that in any case in which I think I am observing something, I might actually be dreaming. Or, alternatively, it is always possible that an evil

21. *Meditations,* 145.

22. *Ibid.,* (my emphasis).

23. *Ibid.,* 189.

demon might be deceiving me into thinking something is the case when it is not. The skeptical pressure exerted by such global counterpossibilities is devastating to common sense. For if my belief in a proposition is based on some sort of evidence and if that evidence is always consistent with another proposition that entails the falsity of my belief, then it follows that I do not really know—cannot really be certain—that my belief is true.

It should be noted that the skeptic's arguments in stage II seem to be harmonious with our ordinary ways of assessing our beliefs in everyday life. Under the pressures of normal practical affairs we are sometimes compelled to accept certain things as true without much consideration of the grounds we have for our assumptions, and in this respect we may be seen as being ordinarily somewhat rash and negligent. In challenging our everyday beliefs, it seems that the skeptic is only being more wary and circumspect than we can normally afford to be. But though he is more scrupulous in considering possibilities, it does not appear that his *method* of considering possibilities is radically different from our ordinary techniques of reflection. The skeptic's cross-examination of our beliefs seems to be a natural extension of the mundane investigations we conduct in everyday life when we are forced to be more thorough than we usually are. For instance, we can normally overlook the effects of poor lighting or lack of sleep on our identification of an acquaintance. For all practical purposes, I can say that I saw Smith last night because I saw someone who looked very much like Smith get out of a car that looked like Smith's car and enter Smith's house. But if something important hangs on my claim I might have to be more guarded in what I say. If I am testifying at Smith's murder trial and the defense attorney asks me if I am certain I saw Smith, I would be inclined to hedge my claims. I might say, "Well, it *looked* like Smith in that lighting, but I can't really be sure." Under such circumstances I have to take into account counterpossibilities that the demands of daily life usually make me overlook. This is the sort of mundane way in which we tend to minimize our claims under oath in a court of law: I cannot say I *know* something unless I have ruled out all genuine counterpossibilities. And there does not seem to be any break between such circumspect minimizing of claims in ordinary situations and the more extreme caution and rigor of the skeptic's assessment of his beliefs.

It seems, then, that the stage II challenge to our everyday beliefs is on the same plane as mundane investigations in everyday life. The skeptic's stringent requirements are already built into our common-sense conception of knowledge and justification. If it is part of our concept of knowledge that we cannot say we know something to be the case unless we have ruled out all counter-possibilities, then the skeptical conclusions that follow from stage II seem to be unavoidable. The account of our epistemic predicament in stage I now appears to be dubious. If I ask whether I really know that I am seated before the fire with this paper in my hand "and other similar matters," I must answer that all I *really* know is that certain sensory perceptions and ideas are present to my consciousness that seem to originate from objects outside me but may be a product of dreams or hallucinations. My understanding of my epistemic situation, therefore, has to be reduced and contracted if it is to cover only what I know with certainty.

In stage III of the Cartesian inquiry an attempt is made to rationally rebuild our former beliefs on a more secure foundation. What is necessary, the Cartesian suggests, is to find a more secure basis for the edifice of our beliefs. This involves at first a redescription of our epistemic predicament based on the findings of the second stage of the inquiry. In stage I we saw ourselves as observers forming beliefs about the objects around us on the basis of their perceived characteristics. As a result of the reduction of stage II, however, we are now left with nothing but the certainty of the *ego cogito* and its *cogitationes*. The reduction has yielded a picture of the self as a kind of receptacle or container in which a collection of ideas is given immediately and indubitably. This last stronghold of certainty—the thinking self within its veil of ideas—must provide the foundation for rebuilding our former beliefs. If the structure of our everyday beliefs is to have a solid basis, we must find the machinery to convert the incorrigible data found in consciousness into the full richness of our ordinary view of the world.

The stage III redescription of our epistemic situation seems to provide us with the kind of self-grounding ground we hoped to find for our everyday beliefs. But this new picture of our epistemic predicament also appears to present us with an insoluble problem. It is not at all clear how the thinking subject can get out of the circle of its own ideas to gain knowledge of objects in the external world. In fact, it is arguable that this project is in principle bound to fail. For if the ideas immediately given to consciousness are subject to various interpretations (including the dream and evil-demon hypotheses), then such ideas can never be sufficient to guarantee the truth of our common-sense interpretation as opposed to alternative interpretations. It seems that our everyday beliefs are essentially underdetermined by the data present in consciousness.

Descartes's *deus ex machina* attempt to salvage our beliefs in terms of a beneficent God need not be discussed here since it hardly suits our modern taste for immanent explanations. Two more recent attempts to reinstate our common-sense beliefs might be mentioned. The first is the attempt, shared by both phenomenalism and Husserl's *Cartesian Meditations,* to show that we actually mean much less in our claims to know things about the world than we thought we meant. These theories try to overcome the impasse reached in stage II by bringing our beliefs down to the level of the data rather than by constructing mechanisms that will raise the data to the level of our beliefs. We are told, for example, that all we really mean in saying there is a pen on the desk is that certain data are present to consciousness, or that certain actions will lead to certain future data, or that a particular meaning is being constituted within consciousness. The flaw in such attempts to devalue our ordinary epistemic claims lies in their stipulation of the meaning of 'meaning.' It seems clear that our ordinary claims to know things about the external world carry more weight than is contained in propositions about the data present to consciousness or propositions about the constituting activity of consciousness. Theories of language that attempt to buttress such views of meaning usually seem cooked up for this special purpose.

The second type of attempt to salvage common sense argues that the "hypothesis" or "theory" of the existence of an external world is more reasonable than the dream or evil-demon hypotheses. According to this view, scientific canons of theory selection determine that the common-sense hypothesis should be favored by any rational individual: it is said to be more simple, parsimonious, elegant, and so forth. There are a number of difficulties with this suggestion, however. First, it is not at all clear that our common-sense understanding of the world constitutes a theory in the requisite sense. But, second, even if our everyday beliefs *are* regarded as a theory, we cannot be sure that the best case has been made for the alternative theories. Nor is it clear that all the possible alternatives are in yet; so it is always possible that a previously undetected hypothesis might better satisfy the criteria of theory selection. Although it may be more rational in some sense to adopt the common-sense view, then, we cannot strictly speaking say we *know* it is right. Theories of rationality that are developed *solely* in order to escape the consequences of skepticism seem fainthearted and artificial when regarded from the standpoint of the skeptic's unflinching concern with reason.

The Cartesian inquiry starts from a common-sense conception of the conditions for knowing something and then presses this common-sense approach in a way that is more careful and thorough than our daily practices permit. As a result of the stage II reduction, we are led to see ourselves as thinking subjects within a veil of ideas. Since any hypothesis about the nature of reality is underdetermined by these ideas, there seems to be no way to transcend the sphere of what is given in consciousness to gain knowledge of the external world. Descartes's achievement was to win an intrinsically intelligible ground in the *ego cogito*. But, in spite of this achievement, it appears that the quest for certainty that motivates Cartesian foundationalism ends in frustration. There is no way for me to gain certain and indubitable knowledge of the physical objects outside of me. Moreover, following the same line of reasoning, I cannot even know that there are other people in the world or that I existed five minutes ago. The reduction that was to lead us to an ultimate founding level for rebuilding all our beliefs turns out to provide us with nothing more fruitful than a "solipsism of the present moment."[24]

§3. *The Structure of Traditional Epistemological Arguments*

We have seen that the stage II challenge to our ordinary beliefs is continuous with certain ordinary forms of inquiry in which our claims to know things about the world are assessed from a more rigorous and detached standpoint. We have also seen that the stage III redescription of our reduced epistemic predicament in terms of a knowing subject equipped with certain types of data follows quite naturally from the reduction of the stage II challenge. The entire Cartesian inquiry appears to be based on methods of rationally evaluating beliefs which are dictated by common sense. Nevertheless, the results of the inquiry seem to undermine common sense: the beliefs we are normally inclined to take as obvious and self-evident turn out to be ungrounded. The Cartesian's findings that we do not really know — cannot really be *certain* — seem to be inescapable.

Traditional attempts to escape the impasse reached by the skeptical inquiry have tended to focus either on the stage II challenge or on the prospects for rational reconstruction that seem to become available in the stage III redescription of our epistemic predicament. The stage I description of our ordinary beliefs and how we come to arrive at them is generally accepted as unproblematical. It is possible, however, that the supposedly "common-sense" description of our everyday predicament in stage I might *already* embody

24. For this way of describing the outcome of the Cartesian enterprise I am indebted to Richard Rorty's lectures at Princeton University in 1977.

certain philosophical assumptions that are in need of examination. Since the second and third stages of the inquiry seem to be in order and since the counterintuitive results of the inquiry suggest that something is going wrong at some stage in the Cartesian inquiry, it is reasonable to focus on the stage I description of our everyday situation. In particular, we can ask with Thompson Clarke, "What is the skeptic examining: our most fundamental beliefs, or the product of a large piece of philosophizing about empirical knowledge done before he comes on stage?"[25] It may be the case that the plain, common-sense description of our lives at the very outset of the Cartesian inquiry is already infected by philosophical assumptions that misrepresent our everyday situations in the world. The picture of the quiescent observer contemplating the world around him might be a distorted portrayal of our actual epistemic predicament.

In fact, we shall see that Heidegger regards the common-sense description of our lives as a distorting lens that warps our deepest understanding of ourselves and our world. The "self-evidence" and "obviousness" of common sense is, in his view, the product of a historical shift that culminated in the Enlightenment. "Common sense," Heidegger says, is "the shallow product of that manner of forming ideas which is the final fruit of the eighteenth-century Enlightenment."[26] What is at issue in Heidegger's approach to the Cartesian model, then, is not engaging in arguments and counterarguments *within* the framework of the common-sense view of our epistemic predicament, but rather re-evaluating the assumptions underlying that framework itself.

If the common-sense picture of stage I is a philosophical construct, it will contain from the start certain philosophical presuppositions that pave the way for the skeptic's findings and prescribe in advance the plausibility of the stage III redescription of our epistemic predicament. We may distinguish two central assumptions built into this portrayal of our daily epistemic situations. The first assumption is the picture of ourselves as subjects distinct from a world of objects about which we come to have beliefs. The second has to do with a particular conception of justification or grounding which is imputed to be the condition for the possibility of understanding our beliefs and practices in the world. It is necessary to expose these assumptions if we are to grasp Heidegger's con-

25. "The Legacy of Skepticism," *Journal of Philosophy,* LIX, (1972): 754–769, p. 754.

26. WCT 66, WhD 64.

tribution to the problem of skepticism.

The first assumption that structures the Cartesian inquiry is the subject/object model of our everyday epistemic predicament. This assumption seems so commonplace it hardly needs explicit formulation. It seems obvious that we can draw a distinction between ourselves and our interests, needs, and aims on the one hand, and a world of objects on the other. These objects exist independently of us: they are what they are regardless of our beliefs or interests. At a basic level we are subjects ascribing concepts to objects outside of us. Each concept has a determinate extension that is legislated by necessary and sufficient conditions built into the meaning of that concept. The concept "tree," for instance, ranges over a unique and more or less fixed set of items regardless of how we happen to use the concept in particular cases. It is part of the meaning of the concept "tree" that it cannot be correctly ascribed in its normal sense to something that sings and dances or to something that is inorganic. Our position in our everyday lives is therefore that of trying to ascertain whether objects in the world are in fact of the types legislated by the concepts we employ. I am in a position to say I *know* that a particular item is a tree only if I have been able to determine that the item satisfies the conditions for identifying it as a tree.

If we accept this subject/object picture of our everyday situations, it appears that we are condemned to skepticism from the outset. For it seems that, no matter how many characteristics of an item we are able to discover, it is always possible that all these observable features might be present in an item that was nevertheless not of the type legislated by the concept in question. In other words, what we perceive of objects can never be sufficient to guarantee that a concept has been used correctly. This is the case in part because our ordinary situations are in a certain sense "open-ended" or "porous." There are always additional factors that might arise after even the most painstaking examination of an object which would tend to defeat our ascription of the concept to that object. If the object I have always thought of as a tree in my garden suddenly blinks out of existence or begins speaking, then all my past ascriptions of the concept "tree" to this object are undermined, and I am compelled to admit that my past claims to *know* that this item was a tree were simply mistaken. Since such situations might always arise, my knowledge claims are always on shaky grounds.

It seems, then that if we grant the common-sense assumption that we are to be understood as subjects identifying items solely on the basis of perceived traits and characteristics of things, skepticism will be unavoidable. The stage II reduction only makes explicit what was implicit in stage I. The question therefore arises whether this subject/object picture of our ordinary lives is a faithful reflection of our actual, everyday epistemic predicament or whether it is not rather a portrayal of a highly refined and specialized way of operating in the world. We might draw a distinction between the "philosophical epistemic situations" characterized in the philosopher's "common-sense" description of our lives and the "plain epistemic situations" of our actual ordinary involvements in the world prior to philosophical reflection. If it can be shown that the Cartesian philosophical epistemic situation does not mirror the structure of our everyday plain lives, then the idea that the Cartesian model has important consequences for our everyday beliefs and practices will be deflated.

Heidegger suggests that the subject/object picture of our ordinary epistemic predicament draws its plausibility from what we might call a "name-and-object" model of the workings of language. According to this name-and-object view, language consists of a set of lexical items that are on hand for our use in making assertions or statements about the world. The paradigmatic unit of meaning is the simple predication in which the subject term refers to or picks out some object in the world and the predicate term ascribes some property to it. This picture of language leads us to see the world as made up of so many self-identical things with attributes—the "substance/accident" ontology. In our everyday lives we understand ourselves as language users employing a "subject-predicate" language to identify and form beliefs about things. Our epistemic predicament is then portrayed in terms of subjects more or less explicitly formulating beliefs on the model of the simple predication. In Chapters III and IV we will see how Heidegger attempts to undermine this name-and-object model of language. He argues, first, that the sharp distinction between word and world presupposed by this model cannot be drawn, and, second, that language use as predication or statement-making is derivative from a more original linguistically articulated way of encountering the world, so that our plain epistemic situation cannot be understood in terms of subjects formulating beliefs on this model. When the name-and-object model of language is disarmed, the aura of self-evidence that surrounds the subject/object model also tends to dissolve.

Whereas the first assumption of the Cartesian model concerns the ontological structure of our plain, everyday situations, the second assumption has to do with a specific conception of what is involved in rationally grounding our beliefs and practices. In the course of our lives we act in the familiar world with competence and assurance, for the most part handling our daily tasks with confidence. The Cartesian rationalist asks: What is the *ground* for our everyday grasp of things? Is our confidence and assurance really warranted? The Cartesian inquiry seems to be motivated from the outset by the assumption that there is something obscure or unclear about our daily affairs which requires a special sort of philosophical clarification. It inquires into the grounds and justification for the plain, mundane grasp of things we have in our day-to-day involvement in the world. Our ordinary activities seem to "go by too fast," as it were, so that we need to detach ourselves from the whirlwind of our practices to inquire into their foundations. When the stage I "common-sense" account of the grounds for our beliefs is found to be inadequate, the road is paved for providing the special sort of grounding that is promised by the stage III rational reconstruction.

What can possibly count as a rational clarification of our beliefs and practices is already laid out in advance to some extent by the common-sense understanding of a cluster of concepts having to do with reasons, grounds, foundations, and justifications. The Cartesian's approach seems to be a natural extension of the ways we justify our claims in ordinary discourse. Just as we overcome disagreements in conversation by adducing reasons and justifications, the philosopher is trying to reply to the skeptic by providing a *global* foundation for our beliefs and practices in general. Common sense already dictates a certain conception of what justification is. The Cartesian is not concerned merely with how we actually happen to arrive at the beliefs we hold. This factual question—the *quaestio facti*—is irrelevant, since it might be the case that we believe certain things by virtue of our genetic coding or through some other causal chain totally extraneous to the truth of the belief. What is of interest to common sense and the Cartesian alike is not the story of how we have come to hold our beliefs, but what justifies us in holding those beliefs—the *quaestio juris*. Only when this sort of question is answered will the fog that surrounds our daily lives be dispelled.

The correct method for making our beliefs and practices intelligible is also implicit in the stage I account of how we come to hold our beliefs about things in the world. We have seen that Descartes first notes the perceived features of things—e.g., the hats and coats he sees passing below his window—and then draws an *inference* from these features to the nature of the things themselves—that men are passing by. This common-sense method of first isolating the units of experience and then looking for an inference that will justify the step from these units to larger claims reflects a broad conception of method shared by both science and the more rigorous ideal of rational construction in stage III of the inquiry. What is implicit from the outset in common sense is a conception of our understanding of the world as rooted in the familiar method of analysis and synthesis or resolution and composition.

Since, as we shall see in Chapter IV, Heidegger suggests that both the common-sense and the Cartesian conceptions of method are extrapolations from the method of science, it will be helpful to characterize the Cartesian conception of justification in a manner broad enough to display its roots in the ideals of the early scientists. According to the method of resolution and composition, the way to understand a phenomenon is to divide it up into its basic components in order to see how these elements contribute to the workings of the whole. This is the method Hobbes is advocating when he says that

> everything is best understood by its constitutive causes. For as in a watch, or some such small engine, the matter, figure and motion of the wheels cannot be well known, except it be taken asunder and viewed in parts; so as to make a more curious search into the rights of states and duties of subjects, it is necessary, I say, not to take them asunder, but yet that they be so considered as if they were dissolved.[27]

The method of taking things apart in order to understand their constitutive causes is reductivist and atomistic. Its immense and undisputed success in dynamics and physics resulted in its being taken as the model toward which all sciences aspire. To appreciate Heidegger's critique of the applicability of science in accounting for our everyday lives, it will be helpful to lay out the method of resolution and composition in detail. I will refer to the two components of this method as unitizing and generalizing.

The first component of the ideal method, unitizing, begins by regarding reality as dissolved into basic units. The concern of unitizing is to find the discrete, simple "bits" that make up the world. This is accomplished by a method of abstraction: we overlook the complex interrelationships and sensory richness that are first apparent in nature in order to isolate the underlying elements from which this complexity is composed. The ultimate goal is to develop a systematic picture of nature in which the

---

27. *De Cive,* in *Man and Citizen,* ed. Bernard Gert (Garden City: Anchor, 1972), p. 98. Quoted by Charles Taylor in his "Language and Human Nature" (unpublished), p. 15.

unitized terms of the theoretical matrix (the words, concepts, representations, or ideas) correctly map onto the abstracted bits or units projected by the theory. True intelligibility can be achieved only when the systematically interrelated elements of thought correctly represent the actual configuation of units that make up the world. What can count as a unit will vary, depending on historical stages of development and areas of investigation: they may be thought of as, for instance, primary qualities, bare particulars, brute objects, or constitutive causes. What is common to all these conceptions of unitizing is the belief that what is investigated by any inquiry must consist of discrete, isolable units.

Descartes's "first philosophy" also begins with a process of unitizing. His concern is to identify the elements upon which our knowledge is grounded. In the stage I common-sense account of what we know, the units were taken to be the traits and characteristics of things we perceive: e.g., the hats and coats passing below the window. In the more rigorous stage III reconstruction, however, a clear distinction is drawn between units that are intrinsically simple and the complexes built up from them. Here the basic units are simple *not* relative to the *actual* order of discovery; rather they are simple relative to the *rational* order of justification. Descartes says that he has resolved to direct his thinking

> in an orderly way, by beginning with the objects that were simplest and easiest to understand, in order to climb little by little, gradually, to the knowledge of the more complex. . . . and *even for this purpose assuming an order among those objects which do not naturally precede one another* (*Discourse* 16; my emphasis).

In the Cartesian legacy that has come down to us, these units are interpreted as representations, ideas, sense data, perceptions, impressions, sensibilia, or whatever is taken as immediately and incorrigibly given to consciousness.

The second component of this ideal method involves a process of generalizing. The goal of generalizing is to find regular, orderly relations among the units arrived at by unitizing, in order to show how they are combined into the organized whole of nature. Once again, what can count as a generalization varies with what is taken as a "normal form" for providing intelligibility at any time: generalizations may be found intelligible if they are "first causes," principles, causal laws, statistical correlations, or "structures." The method of Euclidean geometry often serves as the paradigm for such generalizations: the goal is to generate a system of knowledge by showing how the regularities existing in nature can be accounted for in terms of the axioms, corollaries, and principles of the theory.

The process of generalizing over units is implicit in the stage I ad hoc inferences Descartes makes from the perceived marks and features of things to the things themselves. For the more sophisticated reconstruction of stage III, however, generalizing is to be achieved by uncovering a few intrinsically intelligible principles from which the totality can be rationally reconstructed. For Descartes these principles are to be found through the *lumen naturale:* on the basis of the "seeds of truth which are naturally in our souls," he says, we can "discover the general principles, or first causes, of all that is in the world."[28] The rational reconstruction must show both how the units of experience are woven together to make up a coherent totality of experience and that this totality in fact correctly mirrors the nature of reality. Because of this second demand, there must be some privileged representations that break out of the veil of ideas and can be known with certainty actually to hook up with reality. This is the role of the Cartesian *cogito, ergo sum.*

The Cartesian ideal of intelligibility lies in the background of the common-sense account of how we come to hold our beliefs and what justifies them. The main difference between common sense and Cartesian foundationalism is that whereas common sense is content with assorted inferences suitable for specific situations, the Cartesian seeks intrinsic and global intelligibility for the whole fabric of our beliefs and practices. If the rational reconstruction is to find a "firm foundation" for our lives, it cannot be framed in terms of theories or views that are themselves ungrounded, since this might generate an endless regress of justification with no prospect of finding a firm foundation. The rationalist enterprise can therefore make our beliefs and practices fully intelligible only if it shows them to be grounded in a ground that is itself immediately intelligible. It must also aim for a global, all-encompassing intelligibility. It seeks not piecemeal clarifications, but a set of basic principles or first causes that will apply to all regions of our lives. Ultimate intelligibility is achieved when the entire range of our activities and practices can be shown to be answerable to the tribunal of reason.

The ideal of achieving global intelligibility places certain restrictions on what can count as the elementary units that compose reality. First, the basic units should be of the fewest possible *homogeneous* types of particular. The requirement of ontological

28. *Discourse* 52.

homogeneity follows from the goal of making our over-all system of knowledge intellectually manageable by basing it on a limited number of principles. We seek a unified science in which the generalizations found to be true in one domain of investigation can be expected to hold for other regions as well. Our ability to achieve global intelligibility therefore demands that we regard the universe as like a grid with slots which are filled with uniform types of unit. Newton could account for the extraterrestrial in terms of terrestrial laws, for example, only by rejecting the Aristotelian notion of the qualitative differences of the spheres. Because of this requirement of ontological parsimony the Cartesian tradition has postulated the existence of only two types of substance, mind and matter, and the dream of unified science has been to reduce all explanations to the physical.

Secondly, there is a tendency to see the basic units that make up reality as being only externally or contingently related to one another. The method of abstraction and generalization presupposes that we will be able to decontextualize entities from their places in specific situations in order to grasp them as interchangeable bits that can occur in a wide variety of law-governed combinations. Heidegger points out that Galileo's famous thought-experiment in the *Discourses*, where he imagines bodies moving without any resistance ("Mobile . . . mente concipio omni secluso impedimento"), is possible only where there is a capacity to abstract things from their actual contexts and see them as behaving in uniform ways in a variety of real or imagined contexts.[29] Generalizations can range over a wide assortment of units only if those units are understood as having determinate properties independent of the particular contexts into which they happen to enter. In contrast, where the universe is thought of as a symbolic structure expressing the intentions of a Creator, *what* any thing is is determined by its *place* in the whole, and understanding is restricted to grasping the actual relations among things as they express the plan of the whole.

I have tried to isolate two basic assumptions which are implicit in the Cartesian inquiry from the outset and serve to structure the Cartesian model: an ontological assumption about our plain epistemic situations, and a rationalist assumption about the conditions for making those situations fully intelligible. Heidegger's challenge to the Cartesian model may therefore be seen as two-pronged. First, he undermines the common-sense assumption that our plain epistemic situations are structured according to the

29. WT 90/1, FD 69/70.

subject/object schema. This is accomplished by carrying through the stage I description of our everyday lives in a way that by-passes the presuppositions of common sense and focuses instead on our actual involvements in the world. From the standpoint of this redescription we come to understand our daily lives in a way that is holistic and nondualistic, with the result that there is no role to be played by the contemplative subject set off from a world of objects that are to be known. Second, Heidegger diagnoses and deflates the assumption that our everyday lives can be made fully intelligible only through the method of unitizing and generalizing. In the picture that emerges in *Being and Time*, we come to see that the background of intelligibility that permeates our everyday practices is prior to, and a condition for there being anything like, scientific or rationalist forms of grounding. It becomes apparent that a global explanation of our lives is neither possible nor necessary. There can be no self-grounding ground that will make our horizon of practices untimately intelligible. But, at the same time, the very idea that we need such a grounding is found to be an illusion.

II
Epistemology and Metaphysics

Heidegger's examination of the Cartesian legacy may be seen as unfolding with both a narrow and a wider scope. With respect to the narrow puzzle of skepticism, he criticizes the Cartesian tendency to take "knowing" as our primary way of interacting with things. If we begin by focusing on knowing, Heidegger suggests, we will imagine ourselves as subjects, and "the problem [will] arise of how this knowing subject comes out of its inner 'sphere' into one which is 'other and external' "(60). Knowledge on this view is understood as a "procedure" in which we begin by passively perceiving things and forming mental "representations" of them. On this basis we then come to formulate statements or propositions for ourselves about reality. Perception is interpreted as "a process of returning with one's booty to the 'cabinet' of consciousness after one has gone out and grasped it" (62). Given such an initial model of our situation, I have argued, skepticism is a foregone conclusion.

In response to this traditional picture, Heidegger tries to show us that "knowing" is a "founded mode" of Being-in-the-world (59). Like Hegel before him,[1] he suggests that "critical" philosophy and its implicit ontology beg the question as to our human predicament and predetermine both the "problem" of knowledge and its possible outcome. According to Heidegger,

> If one formulates the question "critically" with such an ontological orientation, then what one finds on hand as proximally and solely certain is something merely "inner." After the primordial phenomenon of Being-in-the-world has become shattered, an isolated subject is all that remains, and this has to be the basis on which a hookup with the world is brought along (206).

"Critical" philosophy is uncritical and dogmatic because, in beginning with the problem of knowledge, "the question of the kind of Being which belongs to the knowing subject is left entirely

---

1. See the Introduction to *The Phenomenology of Spirit*.

39

unasked" (60). For this reason the puzzle of skepticism can be dealt with only by an investigation that is *metaphysical,* beginning directly with an inquiry into the Being of the self and the world. But the critique of traditional epistemology also has a wider scope. The problem of justifying our beliefs about the external world is only a part of a much larger enterprise of providing rational grounding for our activities in general. The Cartesian tradition sees philosophy's central task to be that of determining a framework for rational inquiry which will enable us to identify grounds, foundations, and justifications for every aspect of our lives. This Cartesian concern with rationality, which is the common ground of both the Empiricist and Rationalist traditions, pervades all areas of philosophy to such an extent that doing philosophy seems indistinguishable from the sorts of inquiry dictated by this concern. To be a philosopher just *is* to be interested in providing rational grounds and clarifications for our logical inferences, aesthetic judgments, ethical precepts, scientific theorizing, religious beliefs, mathematical calculations, linguistic practices, and so forth.

The preoccupation with rational grounding, which I will refer to as *epistemology in the broad sense,* seems so central to philosophy that to question its validity would be to shatter the very discipline of philosophy itself. Yet this is precisely what *Being and Time* does. By turning directly to the question of Being, Heidegger by-passes the whole concern with rational, critical inquiry into the grounds for our beliefs and practices. As a result, the project of *Being and Time* might at first appear as mysticism or irrationalism.

Since *Being and Time* must necessarily seem alien when viewed from the standpoint of traditional philosophy, it will be helpful to clarify Heidegger's motives for denying the primacy of epistemology in the broad sense. In the first section of this chapter I will attempt to locate Heidegger's thought within the context of the gradual disaffection with epistemology that characterized German philosophy in the early part of this century. The key figure in this story is Wilhelm Dilthey, whose seminal work had an immeasurable impact on the young Heidegger. In section 5, I will discuss the genesis of *Being and Time,* tracing Heidegger's own intellectual development from the epistemological orientation of his early writings on logic to his concern with metaphysics. Finally, in section 6, I will examine the new conception of philosophy and philosophical method that appears in *Being and Time,* and consider some of the difficulties involved in attempting to set aside the methods and ideals of epistemology.

§4. *Rationalism and Life-Philosophy*

It is perhaps insufficiently recognized today that while Hegelian philosophy continued to flourish in England and America until the end of the nineteenth century, it had virtually disappeared in Germany by the 1850's. As a result of advances in the natural sciences, the intellectual scene in the second half of the century was dominated by a materialistic naturalism represented not by academic philosophers, but by natural scientists such as Büchner, Vogt, and Moleschott. Given the increasing capacity of zoology, physiology, and evolutionary theory to account for human nature, it seemed natural to assume that a purely materialistic and mechanistic account of all aspects of human experience could eventually be provided. It was this faith in the power of naturalism to provide a total explanation of human life that led Vogt to say, "Thoughts stand in roughly the same relation to the brain as gall to the liver or urine to the kidneys."[2] According to Hermann Lübbe, the various movements of criticism that dominated the German universities from the 1870's onward must be understood as responses to this "cryptometaphysical materialism" of the sciences (*ibid.*). The critical reaction was *not* against Hegelianism, as the developments in the Anglo-American world might suggest. Bertrand Russell's rebellion against the British Hegelians had quite different roots.

The turn of the century was characterized by a rationalist backlash to the prevailing naturalism. These rationalist movements shared a common goal: "the overcoming of metaphysics." The question that materialism seemed unable to answer was basically epistemological: How are we to account for the fact that the human organism is a subject that perceives, draws inferences, develops theories and, generally, has a grasp of the world outside of its own body? It was this question that was to lead scientifically oriented thinkers such as Helmholtz back to Kant. In order to understand the intellectual climate in which *Being and Time* emerged, it will be helpful to sketch out the goals of some of these rationalist schools of thought.

One response to the problem of accounting for the activities of the human subject was the Empirio-Critical School of Mach and Avenarius. This school attempted to take an intermediate position between naturalism and rationalism by developing the psychologism

---

2. Quoted in Hermann Lübbe, "Positivismus und Phänomenologie (Mach und Husserl)," in H. Höfling, ed., *Beiträge zu Philosophie und Wissenschaft: Wilhelm Szilasi zum 70. Geburtstag* (Munich: Franke, 1960), p. 170.

of Wundt and others while simply ignoring ontological issues. The method was to posit a realm of objects that are metaphysically neutral with respect to the mind/body distinction. The development of scientific laws and theories, on this view, is to be understood as a psychological process, but this process itself falls neither in the psychical nor in the physical realm. Drawing on evolutionary theory, Mach and Avenarius sought to ground the universality of reasoning in "thought-economical laws." The goal of this "neutral monism," which undoubtedly exerted a strong influence on the young Wittgenstein, was epistemological: to provide a theoretical basis for our beliefs, inferences, language, and scientific activity without being compelled to introduce any unprofitable metaphysical theses. For Mach, metaphysics is always a "red entry" in the account books of science, and objects are posited solely for the purposes of grounding and justification.

While the Empirio-Critical School tried to straddle the line between naturalism and rationalism, other thinkers of the late nineteenth century returned to more traditional forms of rationalism. A typical example of the priority given to epistemological aims is found in Frege's concern with grounding mathematics in pure reason. According to Frege, "the history of the discovery of a mathematical or natural law cannot replace the giving of justifying reasons."[3] Although some have suggested that Frege was interested in developing a realist metaphysics, his actual aim was to avoid metaphysics. The attempt to demonstrate that numbers are objects and the introduction of terms like 'Sinn' for ideal objects should be understood as purely epistemological moves designed to ground the possibility of engaging in certain sorts of activity. Just as a "thought" must exist throughout time, even when there are no thinkers, in order to make truth possible, so numbers must have some form of existence in order to justify mathematics. But, as for Mach, this "form of existence" does not involve any sort of ontological commitment. Frege's primary goal is to *by-pass* all metaphysical questions in favor of a pure epistemology.

A second movement oriented toward providing a rational ground for our beliefs and practices was the neo-Kantianism of Heidegger's teacher, Heinrich Rickert. Opposing even the metaphysically neutralized psychologism of Mach, Rickert draws a distinction between the *matter* of experience, the stream of actual psychological

3. Gottlob Frege, *Nachgelassene Schriften,* ed. H. H. F. Kambartel and F. Kaulbach (Hamburg: Meiner, 1969), p. 3. Quoted in Hans Sluga, "Frege as Rationalist," in M. Schirn, ed., *Studien zu Frege,* vol. I (Stuttgart: Fromann-Holzboog, 1976), p. 35.

events, and its *form,* the ideal content which organizes the data and is the same for all minds everywhere. The "intelligible world" constructed by the formative "consciousness in general" is supratemporal and suprahistorical. Rickert borrows the term 'validity' (Geltung) from Lotze to denote the a priori sphere which grounds the universal intelligibility of human experience. Rickert's concept of "validity" is a purely epistemological notion, as it was for Lotze before him. It is introduced to account for the ways that laws can be universally binding and is therefore supposed to be metaphysically neutral, beyond both realism and nominalism. Rickert also wants to leave the concept of the "transcendental subject" or "consciousness in general" metaphysically neutral. The subject is posited solely in order to justify the construction of cross-cultural and transhistorical values that are the a priori imperatives of thought.

The turn to rationalism and epistemology in the broad sense reached its culmination in the *epochē* of Husserl's writings in the period following the publication of the *Logical Investigations.* Although Husserl seems to brush aside the central puzzles of epistemology when he says that *"the right attitude to take"* in the sciences is *"to discard all skepticism together with all . . .'theory of knowledge',"* [4] he nevertheless maintains that the first concern of philosophy is to deal with the *quaestio juris* — the question of grounding experience and activities. Following Descartes (whom he sees as "the prototype of philosophical reflection"[5]), Husserl says that his guiding aim is to provide "an absolute grounding of science" based on the apodictic evidence found in transcendental subjectivity.[6] The *epochē* of the transcendental reduction is introduced to strip away all metaphysical posits, thereby opening a realm of certain and indubitable knowledge within what Husserl calls *"transcendental solitude,* the solitude of the ego."[7] At this level, all "meaning and validity" is found to be the product of the constituting transcendental ego:

I may owe much, perhaps almost everything to others, but

4. Edmund Husserl, *Ideas* (London: Collier Books, 1969), §26 (Husserl's emphasis).

5. Husserl, *Cartesian Meditations: An Introduction to Phenomenology* (The Hague: Nijhoff, 1969), p. 1.

6. *Cartesian Meditations,* "First Meditation."

7. Husserl, "Phenomenology and Anthropology," in R. Chisholm, ed., *Realism and the Background of Phenomenology.* (Glencoe, Ill.: Free Press, 1960), p. 135 (my emphasis).

even they are, first of all, others for me who receive from me, whatever meaning of validity they have for me. They can be of assistance to me as fellow subjects only after they have received their meaning and validity from me. As transcendental ego I am thus *the absolutely responsible subject* of whatever has existential validity for me (*ibid.* 138; my emphasis).

The bracketing of existence to arrive at the "transcendental solitude" of the *"de facto ego"* is supposed to be only preparatory for the " 'essential' or 'eidetic' analyses" that are fundamental to transcendental analysis.[8] In the eidetic method, I vary perceptual objects to "change the fact of this perception into a pure possibility" in order to find its essence (*ibid.*). In doing so, I also discover *"the all-embracing eidos,* transcendental ego as such" (*ibid.*), the essential structure of subjectivity in general. Whereas the eidetic reduction provides knowledge of what it is to be an object of a certain type, the phenomenological reduction discloses the constituting activity of transcendental consciousness as the source and ground of all objectivity. Husserl's ultimate intention is to do away with all metaphysical presuppositions in favor of grounding our experience of the world in the meaning-giving activity of a transcendental ego.

What these different rationalist movements have in common is a shared concern to avoid any ontological commitments in favor of a pure epistemology in the broad sense. Each school attempts to find the basic, intrinsically intelligible building blocks from which the rational reconstruction of our experience and practices can begin. Whether these are taken to be neutral objects, ideal objects, values, or meanings, what motivates the inquiry is a concern with justification and what generally appears to be a studied indifference to ontological affairs. Rickert and Husserl pursue the Cartesian quest even further in tracing the founding level back to the activities of a self-grounding "consciousness" or "transcendental ego." But both try to free these notions from their objectifying ontological import by neutralizing them into metaphysically noncommittal epistemological posits. As we shall see, Heidegger came to regard these attempts to avoid ontological commitment as tending more to obscure basic issues than to clarify. The epistemological trend of rationalism, which had labeled metaphysics as uncritical, comes to be seen by Heidegger as itself uncritical and in need of clarification.

Heidegger's own move toward metaphysics was mediated

8. *Cartesian Meditations* 70.

through the life-philosophy of Wilhelm Dilthey. Dilthey's philosophy is one of the most important influences on the composition of *Being and Time*. In the course of his long and complicated intellectual development, the paths Dilthey traversed covered almost all the main movements of the period. His starting point, like that of other thinkers of his time, was epistemological in the broad sense. The concern with grounding is seen in his life-long goal of completing Kant's enterprise with a "critique of historical reason" and is also reflected in his description of his project as seeking a "firm foundation" for the *Geisteswissenschaften*.[9] Nevertheless, under the influence of Fichte and the Romantics, he rejects the *res cogitans* or transcendental ego as the ultimate point of departure and turns instead to the whole active and creative human being. "No real blood flows in the veins of the knowing subject constructed by Locke, Hume and Kant," Dilthey writes, "but rather only the diluted juice of reason, a mere process of thought."[10]

Accordingly, in his *Ideas on a Descriptive and Dissecting Psychology* of 1894, Dilthey examines mental life as a holistic structure. "Mental life does not arise from parts growing together," he says, "it is not compounded of elementary units; . . . it is always an encompassing unity."[11] Although Dilthey describes his work in terms drawn from Cartesian foundationalism, then, his understanding of his subject matter already rules out the conception of atomistic unitizing which plays a central role in the Cartesian model.

The epistemological question from which Dilthey starts is the following: How is it possible for a knowing subject to gain knowledge of the thoughts and experiences of another subject from which it is seemingly separated by an impassable abyss? The crucial breakthrough for answering this question came as a result of his studies of the life of the young Hegel. In *Die Jugendgeschichte Hegels,* parts of which appeared as proceedings of the Prussian Academy in 1906, Dilthey examined the concept of "life" in Hegel's theological writings prior to 1800. The term 'life' is used in metaphysics to capture the idea of a dynamic process of becoming in contrast to more static conceptions of the universe as a collection of all that happens to be the case at any given time. The key concepts for Hegel's "pantheism" at this time are, in Dilthey's words, "life, the whole, the one that articulates itself in the manifold, the

9. WD 161, GS I xvii.

10. WD 162, GS I xviii.

11. WD 94/5, GS V 211.

organization of nature."[12] Drawing on Hegel's conception of life as a dynamic totality, Dilthey tried to account for our knowledge of others in terms of the shared participation of the knowing subject and the object of study within a field of common cultural systems. Even more important from a historical standpoint, however, with this work Dilthey recovered the world-view of Hegel which had been subjected to neglect in Germany for more than half a century.

The picture that emerges from Hegel's early writings is fundamentally at odds with the kind of atomistic and classificatory ontology that appears, for instance, in Aristotle's *Categories*. The difference between the two pictures may be seen in their radically different ways of conceiving of substance—that which endures through change and is self-sufficient in existing by itself. In the view found in the *Categories,* substance is generally thought of as the being of particular individuals, the "primary substances." Each primary substance has its own essence and exists without dependence on any other entity. Opposed to this view is the vision of the Eleatics and neo-Platonists, which holds that substance is the articulated totality, or whole of the universe. This holistic conception of substance has a long and dignified history, though it is now difficult to grasp—especially for empiricists who traditionally have tended to interpret reality as constructed from discrete and interchangeable bits of data.[13] Nevertheless, the Eleatic vision holds an important place in German philosophy, running through Spinoza, Hegel, Schopenhauer, and Schelling to Dilthey, Heidegger, and more recently Gadamer. It is therefore important to understand its significance and to try to make it plausible.

On the holistic view of substance, the being of an entity is determined by the totality of its relations to other entities within a whole field or system. Hence, there is no way meaningfully to pick out or identify an entity without at least implicitly referring to the entire context in which it finds its place. Such a holistic conception of substance forms the basis for Hegel's characterization of life. In Dilthey's words:

12. "des Lebens, des Ganzen, des Einen, das in Mannigfaltigen sich gliedert, der Organization der Natur" (GS IV 59).

13. For a brief discussion of the differences between the empiricist and Hegelian world-views, see Charles Taylor's "Marxism and Empiricism" in *British Analytic Philosophy,* ed. B. A. O. Williams and A. Montefiore (New York: Humanities, 1966). Taylor points out that, without being able to make sense of the tradition that reached its apex in Hegel, it is impossible to fully grasp such statements as Marx's Sixth Thesis on Feuerbach: "The human essence is no abstraction inherent in each single individual. In its reality it is the ensemble of social relations" (Taylor, p. 243).

> Life for [Hegel] is the relation of the parts to the whole according to which these can neither exist nor be thought isolated from the whole. . . . Out of this basic concept of life as the whole encompassed by the manifold in its unity, it follows that the concepts of totality, part, unity, separation, standing-over-against [Entgegensetzung] and unification dominate the thought of Hegel at that time (GS IV 138).

It is because substance is conceived of as a totality that Hegel defines the being of any entity in terms of its relation to what it is not, as "the negation of the negation" or as "the other of the other."

One consequence of this emphasis on the context of the whole is that relations are raised to prominence while the relata are dissolved into the network of relations in which they stand. The priority of relations over individuals leads to a "philosophy of internal relations"[14] in which each concept serves to pick out a nexus in a field rather than an object. If all relations are internal, then changes in any term in the network will have repercussions across the whole. A billiard ball, for instance, is thought of as only *externally* related to other balls on a table, since a change of location does not make any difference to the nature or being of that ball. Spatial relations are therefore thought of as external or contingent, because the being of an entity is independent of its momentary spatial location. For a number of other relations, however, the being of the entity is not independent of whether or not it has that relation. It is *internal* to being an aunt, for example, that one is related to the children of one's siblings. If one has no siblings, or if one's siblings have no children, then one cannot be an aunt. Thus an aunt is internally related to her sibling's children. Similarly, what it is to be a king in chess is totally defined by a network of relations to other pieces in the game as determined by the rules of chess. It makes no sense to speak of what a king is independent of these relations. A philosophy of internal relations maintains that, appearances notwithstanding, most or all of the relations in which an entity stands are internal to that entity. Since the being of any entity consists of its place in a totality, to imagine changes in that entity is to imagine changes in the entire system.

The concept of internal relations will be discussed in relation to Heidegger's thought in the next chapter, but a few general observations may be made here. First, it seems that claiming that a relation

---

14. This term has recently been revived by Bertell Ollman in *Alienation: Marx's Conception of Man in Capitalist Society* (New York: Cambridge, 1976), cf. pp. 26–40 and pp. 237–276.

is internal to an entity is always relativized to a particular description of that entity. Aunt Ethel is internally related to her nieces and nephews only under the description of her as an "aunt"; the plastic piece I am using as a king is internally related to the other pieces only under the description of it as a "king." Under another description, these relations would not appear to be internal. One very general line of objection to the idea of internal relations maintains, then, that the thesis involves a confusion which arises from reading the properties of language into things in the world. In different contexts of language use we may have to regard an entity under one description rather than another, but it is claimed that this does not show us anything about the *being* of entities in the world. For all we know, these may be "bare particulars" invested by us with certain types of values and properties.

Secondly, the philosophy of internal relations has generally been associated with a teleological conception of the universe. Usually it is because entities derive their nature from their place in a plan that their properties and relations are internal. Any change in a particular term would, in some sense, point to a change in the plan or design itself. In this way, items in the world are seen as being like words in a text or notes in a melody: they gain their meaning only through the purposes and intentions embodied in the plan for the whole. The philosophy of internal relations is generally conjoined with a picture of the world as evolving through time toward some final goal or state of fulfillment. Consequently, to make intelligible the being of any entity requires a prior grasp of the whole, and understanding the whole involves a grasp of the parts. This in turn leads to the final observation, namely, that the world cannot on this view be conceived of as reducible to a few homogeneous types of interchangeable particulars. If an entity's being is fully circumscribed by its place in a totality, then it is not clear that another entity could take its place without changing the meaning of the whole. As a result, the essence of any entity is inextricably bound up with its actual locus within the totality. It cannot be picked out or identified independently of its position in that context.

The impact of Dilthey's rediscovery of Hegel's concept of life and its field of relations can hardly be overestimated. It is manifest in the work of such writers who were influenced by Dilthey as George Herbert Mead, Ortega y Gasset, and the young Georg Lukàcs. On the basis of Dilthey's reappreciation of Hegel, Lukàcs developed a philosophy that closely resembled Marx's yet unknown early manuscripts.[15] For Dilthey, the discovery of Hegel's concept of life

15. In *History and Class Consciousness* (Cambridge, Mass.: M. I. T., 1971). The

made possible the development of his most mature thoughts on the human studies, *Der Aufbau der geschichtlichen Welt in der Geisteswissenschaften,* parts of which were first published in 1906 and 1910.[16] In this work, "life" plays the role of a medium in which the other is made accessible to the knowing subject by virtue of their shared forms of life in the historical culture in which they find themselves. This notion of life as the medium of shared intelligibility bears interesting similarities to Heidegger's conception of "meaning" (Sinn) and "historicity." It will be worth while, then, to review some of the main points in Dilthey's *Aufbau.*

The subject matter of the *Geisteswissenschaften,* according to Dilthey, is not the causal relation holding between a domain of objects. In contrast to the natural sciences, the human sciences study the temporal flow of "life-experiences" which are bound together by internal relations into a coherent whole. They are concerned with finding the "structure" (Struktur) of the psychic life.[17] For Dilthey, life-experiences always point beyond themselves to embrace past and future experiences in an organic temporal unity. Experience is essentially "fortgezogen," or "carried away": my present experience, which is "about" something, is carried away into a past "from" which it originates and a future "toward" which it is directed. Experience occurs only in the midst of memories and goals. For this reason the theme of the human sciences must be understood holistically, in terms of a dynamic temporal totality in which the present, past, and future are bound together.

All this "about," "from" and "toward" [*Uber, Von und Auf*],

---

remarkable similarities between this work and *Being and Time,* which have so often become a topic for debate, can be understood in terms of their common ancestor, Dilthey. In his Preface to the 1967 edition of the work, Lukàcs says that "the question of who was first and who influenced whom is not particularly interesting here," and that it is enough to note that "the problem was in the air" at the time (*History and Class Consciousness,* p. xxii).

16. Although the complete version of the *Aufbau* was not published until 1927, it is quite likely Heidegger had access to the manuscript through his friend and Dilthey's literary executor, Georg Misch. Heidegger refers to the *Aufbau* by name on page 376 of *Being and Time,* and on page 399 expresses his indebtedness to Misch's survey of Dilthey's thought in his editor's introduction to volume V of Dilthey's collected works.

17. Dilthey notes that the concept of "structure" is drawn from Husserl's *Logical Investigations,* a work he regards as "epoch-making" because it liberates inquiries from the idea that causal relations are the only relations that can be the object of study in the sciences (GS VII 13).

> all these relations to what has been lived and remembered or still lies in the future, carry me along backwards and forwards. . . . Thus, in this process, there arises a view of the continuity of mental life in time which constitutes the course of a life (WD 185, *Aufbau* 169/70).

The temporal unity of life is to be understood under the irreducible category of "meaning" (Sinn). Experience, as a "relation" or "comportment" (Verhalten) toward entities that "exist-for-me" (für-mich-Da-sein),[18] is possible only in the field of a unified whole of life which is bound together by meaning.

The ground for our knowledge of life is found in the basic triad: life-experience, expression, and understanding. These three aspects of human existence are always bound together and can be separated only in thought. In life-experience, a subject, who is involved in the world in representing, evaluating, and setting purposes and goals, encounters entities as being important or as mattering in some way in its "life-relations" (Lebensbezüge).

> There is not a person or a thing that is merely an object [Gegenstand] to me, which does not represent pressure or furtherance, the goal of some striving or a restriction on my will; everything is important, worthy of consideration, close or distant, resistant or strange (WD 178, *Aufbau* 158).

It is through the context of his life-relations that an agent, active in the world, experiences entities as *counting* or as having a *point* in his life.

For Dilthey, life-experiences always express themselves in some concrete form in the objective world. Since expressions leave a mark, experiences become concretely manifested in what Dilthey calls the "objectivations of life."[19] Life-experiences are given an objective form and are therefore always accessible in the intelligible world in which we live. Dilthey uses Hegel's concept of "objective mind" (objektiver Geist) to refer to this world:

> The great outer reality of mind always surrounds us. It is a manifestation of the mind in the world of the senses—from a

---

18. GS VII 26

19. "Objektivierung des Lebens." I translate '*Objektivierung*' as 'objectivation' and reserve 'objectification' for the German word '*Vergegenständlichung*'. My interpretation is indebted to Jürgen Habermas' excellent discussion of Dilthey in his *Knowledge and Human Interests,* trans. J. J. Shapiro (Boston: Beacon, 1971), chapters 7 and 8.

fleeting expression to the century-long rule of a constitution or code of law (WD 191, *Aufbau* 178).

Understanding the expressions of others is grounded in a "re-living" or "co-living" ("Nacherleben" and "Mitleben") of the inner lives of those who express themselves in objective mind.[20] Since language is the vehicle in which "human inwardness finds its complete, exhaustive and objectively comprehensible expression,"[21] the method of the human studies reaches its highest form in the interpretation of the enduring expressions of life found in literature.

Objective mind is the medium in which understanding of others is made possible.

> From this world of objective mind the self receives sustenance from earliest childhood. It is the medium in which the understanding of other people and their expressions takes place. . . . Every square planted with trees, every room in which the seats are arranged, is intelligible to us from our infancy because human planning, arranging and valuing—common to all of us—have assigned a place to every square and every object in the room. The child grows up within the order and customs of the family which it shares with other members and its mother's orders are accepted in this context. Before it learns to talk it is already wholly immersed in that common medium (WD 221, *Aufbau* 256).

The shared public world in a sense "speaks to us" of common interests, purposes, and goals. Each individual in that world is "a bearer (Träger) and representative (Repräsentant) of the common features interwoven in him."[22] As active agents who have been acculturated into the articulated social systems of a communal world, we are "the crossing-points of systems of relations"[23] of a culture and of history. Through our mastery of a public language and par-

---

20. WD 226, *Aufbau* 264. H. P. Rickman translates both 'Mitleben' and 'Sichhineinversetzen' as 'empathy', thereby adding fuel to the myth that Dilthey was committed to a crude "empathy theory" of understanding. Dilthey in fact draws a sharp contrast between these technical terms, and the terms 'Mitfühlen' and 'Einfühlen' which have a related but distinct sense. Cf. WD 227, *Aufbau* 265.

21. WD 249, GS V 319.

22. WD 195, *Aufbau* 184.

23. WD 197, *Aufbau* 187.

ticipation in the forms of life of our culture, Dilthey says, we have access to "the articulated order in the objective mind."[24]

Objective mind contains an "articulation" (Gliederung)[25] which organizes it into "types" corresponding to the different "systems" that structure the society. Each of us, by having taken over roles and holding a position in society, has a competence in dealing with economic, political, religious, and other sorts of systems. Understanding individuals, then, is a matter of grasping their expressions as tokens of the types of system *in which we all participate.* I encounter the other as a place-holder or exemplification in the same social systems in which I participate and which make me the person I am. Dilthey says that individuals differ only "quantitatively" in the degree to which they exemplify the structural types of the cultural world. They "are not distinguished qualitatively."[26]

> Just as objective mind is articulated into a structural order of types, so also is mankind, and this leads from the regularity and structure of general human nature to the types through which understanding grasps individuality (WD 225, *Aufbau* 263).

We understand the systems of our society not necessarily because we have all taken the same stand in those systems, but because we live in a world in which we must take some stand or other with respect to such systems. Since the ability to take a coherent stand implies a general grasp of what is at issue in a particular system, we must have some grasp of the whole range of possibilities built into it. For example, although I am not particularly religious, I have been brought up in an environment in which one has to take some stand with respect to religion. As a result, I can understand the religious behavior of others through my competence in the social system of religion precisely because in taking my irreligious stand I have understood what is at stake in the religious dimension of life. Opting for an irreligious life presupposes a competence in the articulated system that serves as the framework for making that decision. What guarantees my understanding of others in their individuality, then, is my mastery of the public pool of roles and functions that I take up or reject in gaining a concrete content for my life. Our knowledge of others is rooted in our shared

24. WD 222, *Aufbau* 257.

25. WD 194, *Aufbau* 183.

26. WD 225, *Aufbau* 263.

participation in these articulated regions of the social world. Life-experience, expression, and understanding serve to justify our knowledge of others through their reciprocal interaction in objective mind. The advertisement I receive in the mail directly expresses the solicitous attitude of the advertiser. It is an objectivation of life which I understand immediately by virtue of the fact that I participate in an economic system made up of producers and consumers. Through my role as a consumer I can understand this piece of paper as an expression of a life-experience of someone concerned to sell a product, that is, the profit motive. I first encounter the advertisement not as a brute object that I then invest with a significance. Rather, in the intelligible world of objective mind, I understand it immediately as an expression of human needs, interests, and goals. This is possible because of my mastery of the economic system from which the item comes to enter into my life. At the same time, however, I also discover *myself* as a consumer in relation to the economic system through my life-relations to this and similar objectivations of life. The advertisement contributes to my self-understanding as a consumer in relation to producers.

From the foregoing account of objective mind it would seem to follow that, since the individual is only a nexus of cultural systems, one's self-knowledge should also be fully determined through one's place in a cultural network. And indeed at times Dilthey seems to suggest that this is the case. He says, for instance, "Man knows himself only in history, never through introspection."[27] He also suggests that the ultimate given for any individual is the system of relations of the culture into which he is socialized:

> An individual wills national purposes as his own, experiences national experiences and knows the memories of such experiences as his own. . . . It is not possible to penetrate behind this reality . . . by means of problematical psychological reasoning (PM 154, *Aufbau* 355).

Yet Dilthey is reluctant to take this final step toward regarding the self as solely a place-holder in a web of social relations. The reason he is unable to follow his thoughts through to their logical conclusion is to be found in his epistemological starting point. In order to have a firm foundation for building the sciences of man, Dilthey feels he needs, as a grounding level, the life-experiences discovered in the "self-reflection" (Selbstbesinnung) of the knowing subject. As a result of this Cartesian orientation, he is unable fully to over-

27. PM 138, *Aufbau* 348.

come psychologism with its semi-substantial picture of the subject. As we shall see in Chapter III, it is exactly at this point, where Dilthey falters because of his concern with epistemology that Heidegger radicalizes Dilthey's insights into a new conception of the self.

In the course of the *Aufbau,* Dilthey presents various unsystematic groupings of "categories" to characterize life as a totality. Three of these categories are of interest because they shed light on Heidegger's "existentialia," or essential traits of being human. The first of these, "meaning," has already been mentioned. Meaning weaves life-experience into a coherent totality. Since each life-experience is "carried away" into the past and toward the future, experiences gain their significance only from the *whole* meaning of a life. Dilthey generally uses the concept of "meaning" (Sinn) to capture the unity and continuity of a life as a whole. The identity of individual experiences as well as the connections between experiences are determined by "significance" (Bedeutung).

The categories of "essence" and "development" embrace life under the aspects of the past and future, respectively. Seen under the category of development, life is always striving toward the achievement of stable "configurations" (Gestaltungen) of meaning. Life has a teleological structure: it is essentially goal-directed and purposive, striving toward some final, definitive realization or fulfillment of itself. In order to understand the life of an individual or a historical period, we must grasp it as projected toward a set of possibilities that will define it as a whole. Since life can be understood only in terms of its totality, it also has a hermeneutic structure. We understand ourselves in terms of the meaning of our lives as a whole, and that whole is constantly being reinterpreted in the light of the partial achievements and events that make it up. Dilthey says that to be alive is to be able "to move forward and to realize new possibilities in one's own existence."[28] Since life is constantly reinterpreting itself in terms of new possibilities, it follows that the meaning of life is always defeasible, subject to new interpretations of its meaning as a whole. The relationship of parts to whole in life is never ultimately determined as long as one is still alive. Only at the moment of death can life be said to have achieved a determinate and final meaning.

> One would have to wait for the end of life, for only at the hour of death could one survey the whole from which the relationship between the parts could be ascertained. One would have to wait for the end of history to have all the material neces-

28. WD 245, *Aufbau* 303.

sary to determine its meaning (WD 236, *Aufbau* 288).

To understand life under the category of "development" is to see it in terms of freedom and "the will to power." The counterpart of this sense of unbounded freedom and possibility in setting goals and seeking configurations of meaning is the sense of limitation and finitude in the category of "essence." Essence captures the totality of life in its finitude as this is contained in the weight of the past. In making choices at the crossroads of our lives, we always let some possibilities go by, and this fact limits our potentialities in the future. "When we look back at the past we are passive," Dilthey writes, "it cannot be changed; in vain does the man already determined by it batter it with dreams of how it could have been different."[29] Under the category of essence, life is seen in the "tragedy of its finitude": there are limits to what an individual can achieve, and these limits become increasingly oppressive with the passage of time. For Dilthey, as for Hegel, essence is what has been: "Wesen ist was gewesen ist."[30] But the fact of finitude embraced by the concept of "essence" is not something simply given. The "fact" of life is seen as a *task* that must be taken up and brought to fulfillment or accomplishment in the active aspect of development. The passive aspect of finitude and limitation impels us to transcend our limitations by taking a stand on our facticity.

Although the priority of epistemology held Dilthey back from fully re-evaluating the subject/object dichotomy, his penetrating study of life led him to see that the goals of epistemology in the broad sense could not be realized. Every expression and life-experience points beyond itself to other moments within the totality of life, but Dilthey sees that life itself does not point to anything beyond itself. To make this point, he draws an analogy with music. Although the individual notes in a melody point beyond themselves to the other notes and so are experienced as part of a piece of music only in the context of the melody as a whole, the melody itself does not point to anything beyond itself. Similarly, although the moments of life are intelligible only in the context of the whole, when Hegel's eschatology is discarded, there is no ultimate plan or point to life lying outside of life which can ground or justify it.

Life is the fundamental fact which must form the starting-

29. WD 209, *Aufbau* 238.

30. Rudolf A. Makkreel, *Dilthey: Philosopher of the Human Studies* (Princeton, N. J.: University Press, 1975), p. 390.

point for philosophy. It is that which is known from within, that behind which we cannot go [hinter welches nicht zurück-gegangen werden kann]. Life cannot be brought before the judgment seat of reason (PM 73, *Aufbau* 323).

Since life itself is the horizon that makes possible the intelligibility of moments within life, there is no way to make life itself intelligible. Achieving this intelligibility would require positing a horizon outside of life in terms of which life could be grasped. But without the transcendent standpoint of Platonic ideas, or the eschatological conception of historical design, there is no way to go back behind life in order to justify it or ground it. The constantly changing flux of life cannot be grasped in terms of some ultimately intelligible principle. This realization led Dilthey to adopt a form of relativism in which historical world-views are seen as unfolding with a dialectical drive but without a purpose or destination.

The finitude of every historical appearance, be it religion or an ideal or a philosophical system, as well as the relativity of every kind of human comprehension of the totality of things, is the last word of the historical world-view, all flowing in a process, nothing enduring (GS V 9).

There is no final foundation for our beliefs and practices outside the actual forms of life of the culture as these unfold through history. The individual, as bearer of the cultural systems handed down to him by history, is guaranteed knowledge of others in his own historical tradition. But beyond this grounding of our understanding of others in our common human history, there is no absolute, unchanging ground for life.

We can see, then, that Dilthey's epistemological starting point of seeking a firm foundation for knowledge in the human studies ends in relativism. The historical consciousness can catalogue and classify the passing show of world-views, but it cannot gain total clarity about life in terms of some intrinsically intelligible ground. Without Hegel's faith in the culmination of the world-spirit in history, we are left with an endless succession of epochal configurations of meaning which come to be replaced by new configurations. There is no transcendental ego or consciousness in general outside of history which can find atemporal meanings in history. In his last writings, Dilthey recommends that we give up the search for absolutes and turn to the contemplation of history and poetry which, he says, "make man more free and capable of resignation."[31]

§5. *The Genesis of* Being and Time

Heidegger's early writings on logic reveal his commitment to the antimetaphysical trends that characterized the late-nineteenth-century backlash to naturalism. Like Frege and Rickert, he is concerned in these writings solely with epistemology in the broad sense of justifying our beliefs and practices. He is lavish in his praise of Frege, who, he says, "fully overcame psychologism in principle" and whose work is "still not appreciated in its full significance."[32] He is also acquainted with Russell's *Principles of Mathematics* and refers to *Principia Mathematica,* but he feels that nothing is gained by what he refers to as Russell's method of "Logistik" in which "the deeper meaning of the principles remains in darkness."[33] For Heidegger, the function of logic is to provide grounds for such phenomena as "the 'unchangeable' direction of the relation between subject and predicate," and this is something he feels is "covered over" in Russell and Whitehead.[34] But Heidegger never questions the rationalist assumption that the foundations of logic must be independent of any naturalistic assumptions. In his dissertation of 1914, he employs Rickert's notion of a realm of "validity" to identify a metaphysically neutral foundation for the possibility of agreements in judgment. Since my psychological activity is distinct from the "something" I want to communicate when I speak or write, Heidegger argues, there must be a "form of existence next to the possible kinds of existence of the physical, the psychical and the metaphysical."[35] This timeless, rational realm grounds logic without reference to psychological processes.

Heidegger's position in his *Habilitationsschrift* (1916) is a continuation of this basically rationalist and antimetaphysical orientation. Like Frege, Heidegger argues that a doctrine of "logical grammar" must be possible without reference to its origins in "the physiological-psychical chain of causes running between sign and

31. WD 126, GS V 409.

32. "Neuere Forschungen über Logik," in *Literarische Rundschau für das katholische Deutschland,* 38 (Oct. 1, 1912), cols. 467/8.

33. "Neuere Forschungen," Dec. 1, 1912, col. 570.

34. "Neuere Forschungen," Dec. 1, 1912, cols. 570, 520.

35. *Die Lehre vom Urteil im Psychologismus,* in FS 111.

meaning" or in its "historical development.[36] But the conclusion of the *Habilitationsschrift* seems to mark a change in direction. Clearly under the influence of Husserl here, Heidegger argues that any analysis of the *modi significandi* leads us to the sphere of "acts in general," and the consideration of intentional acts in turn leads to an examination of "the direct life of subjectivity."[37] "Object and objectivity," Heidegger writes, "only have meaning as such *for* a subject."[38] But this means in turn that logic can be provided with a foundation only if the nature of the acting subject has been fully clarified. The attempt to provide justification and grounding for logic therefore leads Heidegger to a "translogical" inquiry into the nature of subjectivity. The conclusion he draws is that logic must be grounded in an investigation that is essentially metaphysical.

It is in part Heidegger's study of logic, then, that leads him to metaphysics. He sees that the attempt to provide epistemological grounding for our beliefs and practices cannot avoid dealing with the ontological status of the entities posited in such grounding. The need for ontological clarification cannot be ignored in the name of "overcoming metaphysics." *"In the long run,"* he writes, *"philosophy cannot dispense with its authentic instrument* [Optik], *metaphysics.* For the theory of truth, that means the project of a final metaphysical-teleological interpretation of consciousness."[39] When Heidegger says that the epistemological concern of providing foundations for logic leads us to the metaphysics of subjectivity, he does not mean that we are compelled to return to the Cartesian *cogito* or to a naive acceptance of psychologism. On the contrary, he promises that in his future works he will pursue the question of the acting subject in terms of the "living spirit" (lebendiger Geist) which is "essentially historical mind in the broadest sense of the word."[40] Logical and epistemological problems must be given an *"authentic conceptual foundation in the philosophy of culture"* which alone can guarantee "clarity, certainty and unity."[41] Following Dilthey's path, Heidegger asserts that the project requires a dialogue with "the most powerful system of a historical

36. *Die Kategorien- und Bedeutungslehre des Duns Scotus,* in FS 280.

37. FS 343.

38. FS 345.

39. FS 348 (Heidegger's emphasis).

40. FS 349.

41. FS 350 (Heidegger's emphasis).

Weltanschauung, . . . with Hegel."[42] As we know, this Hegelian "philosophy of culture," which provides a "metaphysical-teleological interpretation" of the "living spirit" as the ontological condition for the possibility of epistemology, was to become *Being and Time.*

The period following the first World War has been characterized as a period of "the resurrection of metaphysics" in German philosophy.[43] Heidegger's lectures and seminars during this period reveal the growing influence of Dilthey on his thought. By the early 1920's, Heidegger is using the term 'life' for what he later came to call "Dasein."[44] In his accounts of "factical life" or "Leben-in-der-Welt" during this period, Heidegger employs Dilthey's holistic conception of "meaning" as the basic category for characterizing life. According to Otto Pöggeler, Heidegger holds that

> meaning is not a world to itself which must be grasped as static and resting in itself; meaning is much more what is inherent in factical life, and its structure must be conceived according to life. [Life] is in its reality a context of significance [Bedeutsamkeitzusammenhang]. Certainly significance can be leveled off through the human tendency toward reification or "objectifying," . . . but the objectifying must be comprehended as the "denial of life" in life: through it life is deprived of its "living," of its "tendentious" structure, and of the relations of significance of its world.[45]

Like Dilthey, Heidegger sees life as striving toward the development of configurations of meaning that stand as its fulfillment. The meaning of life is determined by a constant drive toward "accomplishment" or "achievement" [Vollzug]: "The accomplishment of life itself stands over the coordination of 'contents' ['Gehalte']" (*ibid.*).

The teleological conception of life as a meaningful totality oriented toward accomplishment or fulfillment leads Heidegger to stress the whole or totality as prior to the parts of life. For this

42. FS 353.

43. See Ludwig Landgrebe, *Major Problems in Contemporary European Philosophy,* trans. K. Reinhardt (New York: Ungar Publishing Co., 1966).

44. For instance, in his lectures, "Einleitung in die Phänomenologie der Religion" of 1920/21, according to Ernst Tugendhat in his *Der Wahrheitsbegriff bei Husserl und Heidegger* (Berlin: Walter de Gruyter, 1970), p. 265.

45. *Der Denkweg Martin Heideggers* (Pfullingen: Neske, 1963), p. 27.

reason in *Being and Time* he constantly emphasizes total interacting fields. In his analysis of "worldhood," he focuses on the "totality of equipment" (Zeugganzheit) (68), the "totality of relations" (Bezugsganze) (87), the "totality of assignments" (Verweisungsganzheit) (76), and the "totality of significations" (Bedeutungsganzheit) (161). In each case, what is basic is not the primary substances of Aristotle and Locke, but an interrelated totality of internal relations. According to Heidegger, this "system of relations" (Relationssystem) "provides the basis on which [entities within-the-world] can for the first time be discovered 'substantially' 'in themselves' " (87/8).

Heidegger uses the technical term 'Dasein' to refer to human "life" or "existence." This term makes use of the same ambiguity between distributive and collective senses which is contained in the word 'life.' In the same way that Dilthey's "life" is something "behind which one cannot go" in giving justifications or grounds, it is also impossible to "go behind" Dasein in order to justify it: "Dasein never comes back behind its thrownness," Heidegger says (das Dasein komme nie hinter seine Geworfenheit zurück) (383, cf. 284). Dasein is always "thrown" into a world of cultural and historical meanings which makes up the horizon in which anything is intelligible, but which cannot itself be grounded by something beyond that horizon.

The fact that there is no way to go behind thrownness to justify it has the consequence that Dasein can no longer be conceived of as the "absolutely responsible subject" of Husserl's "transcendental solitude." Dasein is described as essentially "indebted" (Schuldig) for the possibilities it can take up. For Heidegger, the picture of an ego constituting the world out of its own monad leads to a distortion of our understanding of what it is to be human. Such a picture of man as an ego or subject is seen as motivated solely by epistemological interests and therefore as one-sided and misleading. In a primarily conciliatory letter to Husserl aimed at resolving their differences over an *Encyclopedia Britannica* article they were to co-author, Heidegger argues that any conception of man that starts solely from epistemological concerns, ignoring the "concrete totality of man," is unjustified as a starting point for phenomenology:

> The "one-sided" reflections of somatology and pure psychology are only possible on the basis of the concrete totality of man which as such primarily determines the mode of Being of man.
> The "purely mental" has certainly not developed with a view

to the ontology of man in totality, that is, not with psychology as its aim — rather, since Descartes it has originated at the outset from *epistemological* considerations.[46]

From Heidegger's standpoint, the concept of the knowing subject, trapped within its "veil of ideas" and constituting its world out of meaningless "hyletic data," is a highly specialized and refined way of understanding man which originates solely from epistemological interests and has no real counterpart in our actual lives. He therefore resolves to by-pass this tradition of order to describe human life in actual everyday contexts of action. What Heidegger focuses on is ordinary agents involved in mundane practical situations. The epistemologically motivated distinctions of subject and object, person and thing, inner and outer, and mental and physical are held in abeyance. In fundamental ontology, Heidegger says, "the idea of man as a subject is, to speak with Hegel, *pushed aside.*"[47] What emerges from this description of everyday practical context is a picture of being human in which the subject/object ontology tends to dissolve. And when the doubtful ontological assumptions that underlie the Cartesian model are called in question, the implications of skepticism for our plain epistemic situations are also deflated.

The interpretation of everyday life in terms of the concept of Being-in-the-world draws on Dilthey's insight into the nature of life and liberates it from the confines of psychologism and the epistemological orientation. Extreme forms of historical relativism are to be overcome by discovering an underlying "structure" of being human which will be present in all human phenomena at all times. Whereas our interpretations of reality are constantly shifting with different world-views, Heidegger believes that *the structure of interpreting itself* is something that remains constant and makes possible these defeasible interpretations. Like Dilthey, Heidegger takes this underlying structure to be temporal in nature: it is the unity of projecting toward goals, appropriating the past, and comportment (Verhalten) toward entities. But unlike Dilthey, Heidegger does not conceive of this structure as "psychic" in any sense. Instead he holds that the temporal modes of "ecstasis" or "ex-sistence" which make up what he calls Dasein's "transcendence" are prior to the distinction of psychic and physical. Dasein's very

---

46. Letter to Husserl dated 22 Oct., 1927, quoted in *Phänomenologische Psychologie,* ed. Walter Biemel, in *Husserliana,* v. IX (The Hague: Martinus Nijhoff, 1962), p. 602 (Heidegger's emphasis).

47. SvG, pp. 146/7 (my emphasis).

Being comes to be regarded as the "movement" (Bewegung) or "happening" (Geschehen) of interpreting, and this interpreting is found to have a deep structure that can be analyzed from the standpoint of the activity of interpreting itself. What Heidegger is seeking are the transcendental conditions for the possibility of any interpretation whatsoever.[48]

It seems, then, that Heidegger is trying to find a middle ground between Husserlian and neo-Kantian rationalism on the one hand and a naturalistic empirical anthropology on the other. His starting point is a description of our everyday situations in which we are involved in the world. But his reason for focusing on everydayness is to find "essential structures" that are the conditions for the possibility of any human existence whatsoever.

> In this everydayness there are certain structures which we shall exhibit — not just any accidental structures, but *essential ones* which, in every kind of Being that factical Dasein may possess, persist as determinative for its Being (16/7; my emphasis).

In seeking these a priori essential structures, Heidegger says he is using a method drawn from Husserl:

> Edmund Husserl has not only enabled us to understand once more the meaning of any genuine philosophical "empiricism"; he has also given us the necessary tools. "A-priorism" is the method of every scientific philosophy which understands itself. There is nothing constructivistic about it (50 n).

Understood in this way, the aim of *Being and Time* is not to discover attributes of man by empirical research, but to exhibit "transcendental structures" which "can neither be firmly established in anthropology nor derived from it through mere assumptions."[49] Since this project has nothing to do with developing a philosophical anthropology, the object of inquiry is not man but something more primordial than man: *"More primordial than man is the finitude of the Dasein in him."*[50]

A tension seems to arise in this conception of the role of the "existential analytic" in *Being and Time*. On the one hand, the descrip-

---

48. The difficulties involved in this transcendentalist motif of *Being and Time* will be taken up below in section 15.

49. KPMe 140, KPMg 128.

50. KPMe 237, KPMg 222 (Heidegger's emphasis).

tion of our everyday lives leads us to see ourselves as contextualized in a world and in history. From this standpoint it will appear that the Cartesian ideal of finding absolute grounds and foundations is out of order and based on a false idea of the conditions for intelligibility. Our interpretations are always finite and rooted in the context of the world in which we live. On the other hand, however, Heidegger is seeking the transcendental conditions for the possibility of any interpreting or understanding whatsoever. This broader undertaking of working out the essence of man as transcendence is in turn subordinate to the overriding goal of coming to terms with the question of Being. In *The Essence of Reasons,* which was published shortly after *Being and Time,* Heidegger writes,

> We might point out here that the portion of the investigations into "Being and time" published so far has as its task nothing more than a concrete, revealing projection of transcendence. . . . All concrete interpretations . . . should be evaluated solely as they aim at *making* the *question* of Being possible (ER 97n, WM 58n).

It is not clear, however, that these two projects are consistent. For the results of the description of everydayness seem to undermine the prospect of finding any sort of transcendental essential structures underlying interpretation in general. If all interpretations are rooted in finite and historical Dasein, then it seems natural to assume that the "interpretation of interpreting" which makes up the existential analytic will be in the same boat as any other interpretation: it will be a cultural and historical product, not the discovery of timeless, immutable structures. And Heidegger seems at times to recognize these consequences. In *Kant and the Problem of Metaphysics* he writes, "the explication of the essence of finitude required for the establishment of metaphysics must itself always be basically finite and *never absolute.*"[51] But is also seems clear that Heidegger's goal, at least during the period when *Being and Time* was composed, is in fact to find *trans*historical and *trans*cultural structures that underlie any possible interpretations. Seen in this way, the existential analytic is aimed at finding a firm foundation for ontology, and this goal strikes us as rather similar to that of Cartesian foundationalism. This tension in Heidegger's thought—which I will call *the problem of reflexivity*—will be taken up again in Chapter V.

---

51. KPMe 245, KPMg 229 (my emphasis).

§6. *The Conception of Philosophy and Method in* Being and Time

Almost every great philosophical work carries with it a more or less explicit reinterpretation of the nature of philosophy and the methods appropriate for fulfilling its aims. When Heidegger shifts his orientation from epistemology to metaphysics, he also transforms the modern understanding of philosophy's goals and methods. The "basic theme" of philosophy, he says, is Being (38). The question of Being has this central position because any inquiry into one of the areas of philosophy (e.g., epistemology, logic, ethics, aesthetics) operates within a tacit set of presuppositions about the Being of the entities with which it deals.

What is true of the discipline of philosophy holds for the sciences as well. Every science presupposes some conception of the Being of the entities that are the objects of its inquiry. The ontologies of the regional sciences, Heidegger says, have already been worked out "roughly and naively" on the basis of our prescientific ways of interpreting and experiencing domains of Being (9). Scientists work within frameworks that determine in advance what sorts of question are appropriate and what kinds of answer will make sense. Historians, for instance, have a generally tacit grasp of the subject matter of their investigations: they are interested mainly in historical events, not in neutrinos or transfinite numbers. Generally there is no need for scientists to question the ontological frameworks in which they work. During periods of crisis in the sciences, however, it is precisely these frameworks which are called in question. As examples of crises in the sciences in the early part of the century, Heidegger cites the debates between formalists and intuitionists concerning the nature of mathematics and between vitalists and mechanists about the nature of biological life.

When what is at issue in the sciences is no longer questions within the frameworks of those sciences but the very frameworks themselves, the ontological presuppositions of the regional inquiries must be made explicit. Heidegger believes that philosophy alone can fulfill such a service. Philosophy, which he sees as not itself bound by any framework, is the study of frameworks in general. Philosophy is not an underlaborer "which limps along after" the sciences trying to tidy up their methods and concepts. Rather, it has the responsibility of acting as a "productive logic" which first discloses an area of Being for a science and makes its structures transparent (10). The function of philosophy is to provide a *metaphysica generalis* that can illuminate the regional ontologies of the sciences. The inquiry into the Being of entities in general Heidegger calls "ontology taken in the widest sense" (11). It is a "science *of Being as such*" (230), and its task is to provide "a genealogy of the different possible ways of Being" (11). Ontology in the widest sense lays out the conditions for the possibility of any science.

> The question of Being aims . . . at ascertaining the *a priori* conditions not only for the possibility of the sciences which examine entities as entities of such and such a type . . . but also for the possibility of those ontologies themselves which are prior to the ontical sciences and which provide their foundation (11).

As ontology in the widest sense, philosophy is the "science of sciences." The ultimate aim of *Being and Time* is to provide such an ontology as a basis for all regional ontologies: as Heidegger says, "Our *aim* is to work out the question of Being in general" (436). But ontology as a science will be possible only if it is guided in advance by a grasp of what we *mean* by the term 'Being'.

> Ontological inquiry is indeed more primordial, as over against the ontical inquiry of the positive sciences. But it remains itself naive and opaque if in its researches into the Being of entities it fails to discuss the *meaning* of Being in general (11; my emphasis).

Ontology in the widest sense therefore requires a further subordinate investigation to serve as its foundation, namely, an inquiry into "what we really mean by this expression 'Being' " (11).

The inquiry into the *meaning* of Being, whose role is that of "preparing for the question of Being in general" (316), is called "fundamental ontology." Fundamental ontology therefore seems to be a propaedeutic to genuine ontology and not the fulfillment of the goals of ontology per se. Since fundamental ontology has to do with the *meaning* of Being, it must first deal with "the problem of the internal possibility of the *understanding* of Being, from which all specific questions relative to Being arise."[52]

> To lay bare the horizon within which something like Being in general becomes *understandable,* is tantamount to clarifying the possibility of having any understanding of Being at all — an understanding which itself belongs to the composition of the entity called Dasein (231; my emphasis).

52. KPMe 240, KPMg 255 (my emphasis).

Since Dasein is unique among entities in understanding what it is to be, the starting point for fundamental ontology is a fully worked out account of human understanding: *"Fundamental ontology, from which alone all other ontologies can take their rise, must be sought in the existential analytic of Dasein"* (13). The primary goal of the analysis of Dasein, which makes up the core of the published parts of *Being and Time*, is to "arrive at the horizon for the understanding of Being and for the possibility of interpreting it" (39). Heidegger sums up the role of the "existential analytic" as follows:

> The question of the meaning of Being becomes possible at all only if there *is* something like an understanding of Being. Understanding of Being belongs to the kind of Being which we call "Dasein." The more appropriately and primordially we have succeeded in explicating this entity, the surer we are to attain our goal in the further course of working out the problem of fundamental ontology (200).

It is not immediately evident in *Being and Time* whether the existential analytic is identical with or only preparatory for fundamental ontology. Heidegger says, for instance, that "the ontological analytic of Dasein in general is what constitutes fundamental ontology" (14). But he also says that "the analytic of Dasein . . . is to prepare the way for the problematic of fundamental ontology — *the question of the meaning of Being in general"* (183; 37). In a supplement to a series of lectures delivered in 1928, however, Heidegger suggests that the existential analytic is included in, but is not co-extensive with, the concept of fundamental ontology:

> By "fundamental ontology" we understand the foundation of ontology in general [die Grundlegung der Ontologie überhaupt]. To this belongs: (1) the demonstrative grounding of the inner possibility of the question of Being as the basic problem of metaphysics — the interpretation of Dasein as temporality [Zeitlichkeit]; (2) the laying out of the basic problems encompassed by the question of Being — the temporal [temporale] exposition of the problem of Being; (3) the development of the self-understanding of this problematic, its task and limits — the overturn [Umschlag].[53]

53. LL 196. The published portion of *Being and Time* deals only with the first of these three topics. The second was to have dealt with in the third division of the

The distinction Heidegger draws between "ontology in the widest sense" and "fundamental ontology" seems to lead to the same kind of tension in his thought that was noted at the end of the last section. For if the goal of *Being and Time* is limited to unfolding the meaning of Being "insofar as Being enters into the understandability [Verständlichkeit] of Dasein" (152), then it seems that the account should be subject to the same cultural and historical limitations that are found to shape Dasein's understanding in general. But if fundamental ontology is supposed to pave the way for a final determination of Being as such, independent of Dasein's conditional ways of understanding, then this aim will turn out to be at odds with Heidegger's most basic conclusions about the conditions for the possibility of any inquiry whatsoever. In fact, as should become clear in section 15, even the project that defines fundamental ontology — the enterprise of finding *the* meaning of Being — seems to be undermined.

The conception of philosophy as concerned with the question of Being carries with it a new conception of philosophical method. Since fundamental ontology is supposed to lay a foundation for the regional sciences, it cannot take over the frameworks of those sciences. But neither can it start from the intuition of meanings or essences presented to consciousness, since the very ideas of "intuition" and "consciousness" have become problematic. The question therefore arises of how we are to gain *access* to the theme of fundamental ontology. How is the inquiry into the meaning of Being to get under way? Heidegger suggests that, even though the assumptions of science, common sense, and the tradition are to be set aside, we nevertheless have a mode of access to the question of Being in our plain, prereflective sense of reality. In our everyday lives, Heidegger says, we already have some *"vague, average understanding of Being"* (5). By virtue of the fact that we have taken up the task of living and are already coping with the world, we have a "pre-ontological understanding of Being" (15) which can serve as the basis for a thematic and explicit conceptualization of the meaning of Being.

Fundamental ontology therefore begins with a description of the vague sense of what it is to be which is implicit in our "average everydayness." Our plain understanding is regarded as a text-

---

first part, to be entitled "Time and Being." It may be speculated that the third topic was to have been the subject matter of the second part of *Being and Time*, the "phenomenological destruction of the history of philosophy." The sense in which fundamental ontology requires an "overturn" or "turn" will be discussed below in section 17.

analogue which is to be laid out and made explicit. But this text of everydayness is also seen as, in a sense, "corrupt": it is shot through with distortions and misinterpretations from the tradition, though it nevertheless retains a deeper meaning which can be brought to light. In order to recover the hidden meaning of our ordinary ways of interpreting ourselves and our world, then, we must engage in a deep interpretation of this text, seeking the concealed meaning while revealing the source of the distortions that infect it. THe method of *Being and Time* may therefore be seen as having four stages: (1) a *descriptive* stage in which the text-analogue of everydayness is exhibited; (2) a *hermeneutic* stage in which the structure of everydayness is interpreted to find its deep underlying meaning; (3) a process of *dialectic* in which we are led to "remember" the primordial origins and springs of our pre-ontological understanding; and (4) a recurrent *diagnosis* of common sense, which exposes the source of its aura of self-evidence and thereby dissolves the pseudo-problems that arise from it.

The proximal goal of *Being and Time* is to develop a descriptive metaphysics. Heidegger is not interested in fanciful speculation about Being. He is concerned with what Being means to us, and this requires at the outset an understanding of the Being of that entity which understands what it is to be, namely, Dasein. The analytic of Dasein begins by working out the vague pre-ontological understanding of Being which we all have by virtue of our involvement in the world.

Dasein in the course of its everyday activities and practices is characterized as "Being-in-the-world." The descriptive component of Heidegger's method therefore begins with the attempt *"to work out the idea of a 'natural conception of the world'"* (52). His starting point is his own "factical" life as it is "thrown" into a cultural milieu with a background and history. This inquiry into the characteristics of a unique individual is called "existentiell" and is distinguished from the "existential" understanding of the essential structures of Dasein to which it leads. In a stylistically un-Heideggerian letter to Karl Löwith written in 1921, as the first sections on "worldhood" were being composed, Heidegger describes his method as follows:

> I work concretely and factically from my "I am"—from my
> spiritual and overall factical origin—milieu—contexts of life—
> and from that which is accessible to me as living experience—
> wherein I live—this facticity, as *e*xistentiell, is no mere blind
> Dasein—it lies therewith in existence—that means, however,

that I live it—this "I must" of which no one talks—with this *facticity* of Being-so.[54]

The description of everyday Being-in-the-world is not oriented toward a final "explanation" of life that reduces it to underlying physical processes. But neither is it aimed at finding the necessary and sufficient conditions for being human, as in traditional philosophical anthropologies. Heidegger's interest is in describing a more or less typical instance of Dasein as it is "proximally and for the most part" in normal, average situations. For this reason we should not expect an account of what it is to be human which will encompass infants, the comatose, the insane, or even momentary eccentricities among normal adults. The frequent emphasis on the words 'proximally and for the most part' indicates that Heidegger's concern is with describing a *core* case of being human—how "Dasein is 'manifest' in the 'with-one-another' of publicness," how it "shows itself for Everyman, not always, but 'as a rule' " (370).

The existentiell understanding of oneself must serve as the foundation for the analytic of Dasein if we are to avoid "free-floating constructions" and epistemological posits: "Unless we have an existentiell understanding," Heidegger says, "all analysis of existentiality will remain groundless" (312). But the methodological primacy of the individual does not indicate a return to Cartesianism with its faith in the self-transparency of consciousness. Heidegger cautions us against thinking that because the entity we are examining is immediately accessible (since *we* are it), it is also the case that "the kind of Being which it possesses is presented just as 'immediately' " (15). For Heidegger, there is no reason to presuppose that the self is immediately intelligible to itself in reflection, as even Dilthey was inclined to believe. A "thematic ontological reflection [Besinnung] on one's ownmost composition of Being" cannot guarantee us an "appropriate clue" to the Being of Dasein (15), because Dasein's "closest" self-understanding is generally a *misunderstanding*. This is the case because our self-understanding is generally mediated by the culture and historical tradition in which we find ourselves. As text-analogues, we are in a sense "commentaries" on the public text of the social world. But insofar as that social world will always embody certain distortions and concealments, what we discover by reflection is often deceptive. Heidegger thinks that we have a certain degree of "competence" in

54. Letter to Karl Löwith dated August 19, 1921, quoted in part in "Zur Heidegger's Seinsfrage: Die Natur des Menschen und die Welt der Natur," in K. Löwith, *Aufsätze und Vorträge* (Stuttgart: W. Kohlhammer, 1971) (Heidegger's emphasis).

Being that assures us that we will eventually be able to achieve a genuine grasp of what it is to be from our existentiell modes of activity in the world. But the deeper understanding of Dasein's Being
cannot be reached directly or immediately by self-reflection.

It is apparent, then, that although he borrows the label
'phenomenology' from Husserl to identify his descriptive method,
the term has undergone a considerable change in Heidegger's
hands. Husserl takes the maxim, "To the things themselves!" (Zur
den Sachen selbst!) to mean that we should start from "objec-
tivities" (Gegenständlichkeiten) given immediately in intuition. For
Heidegger, on the other hand, what is given immediately and self-
evidently is often an illusion mediated by the historical epoch in
which the self-reflection occurs.

What Heidegger wants to describe is not objects presented to the
mind; it is rather understanding itself.[55] The objects that show
themselves at the outset are therefore not the genuine phenomena
with which phenomenology deals. The "phenomena" of phenomenology are precisely what do *not* show themselves.

> What is it that must be called a "phenomenon" in a distinctive
> sense? . . . Manifestly, it is something that proximally and
> for the most part does *not* show itself at all: it is something
> that lies *hidden,* in contrast to that which proximally and for
> the most part does show itself, but at the same time it is some-
> thing that belongs to what thus shows itself, and it belongs to
> it so essentially as to constitute its meaning and ground
> [seinem Sinn und Grund ausmacht] (35).

The hidden "meaning and ground" of entities is the implicit
background of understanding which is the condition of the
possibility of encountering *anything* as given. The goal of the
description of everydayness, then, is to bring to light this
background "clearing" (Lichtung) which makes possible the
discovery of what "proximally shows itself."

Since the phenomena are defined as the "hidden meaning"
underlying entities, the descriptive stage of fundamental ontology
is necessarily coupled with a hermeneutic stage in which the text-
analogue revealed by the description of everydayness is interpreted
to uncover its deep meaning. "The phenomenology of Dasein is a
hermeneutic in the primordial signification of this word" (37).
"Hermeneutics" here is not a methodological technique or

55. I am indebted to Otto Pöggeler for this distinction. Cf. Pöggeler, *Der
Denkweg,* p. 70.

"Kunstlehre" for discovering the meanings embodied in the expressions of a "thou," as it was for Dilthey. In fact, hermeneutics in not a technique or device at all in Heidegger's philosophy. Insofar as the Being of Dasein is seen as understanding, 'hermeneutics' refers to the very constitution of being human. To be human is to care about the meaning of life, to try to be deep and coherent about what it is to be. In this sense the hermeneutics of *Being and Time* is merely a reflection of what we all do all of the time. Heidegger says that "the question of Being is nothing other than the radicalization of an essential tendency of Being that belongs to Dasein—the pre-ontological understanding of Being" (15). In our everyday lives we grasp entities in terms of a tacit understanding of what it is to be, and we are constantly driven to make that understanding explicit and revise it on the basis of passing encounters and collisions. The hermeneutic approach to fundamental ontology, far from being a technique for uncovering meanings in an alien text, is just a more rigorous and explicit version of the kind of movement toward clarity and depth which makes up life itself.

Like the interpretation of a text, the interpretation of Dasein must always be circular. There are no axioms or self-evident truths from which we can build up an edifice of knowledge about ourselves. As our lives always involve a back-and-forth movement between partial meanings and some sense of the whole, the method of fundamental ontology also moves back and forth between uncovering structural items of Dasein and a pre-understanding of the totality.

But Heidegger does not regard this circularity as a vicious circle that handicaps his investigation in any way. For we are not demonstrating unknown truths on the basis of known truths. Instead we are making explicit something that is in a sense already known in living itself. The hermeneutic circle is constitutive of Dasein's Being: "An entity for which, as Being-in-the-world, its Being itself is at issue, has ontologically a circular structure" (153). Fundamental ontology reflects this circularity. What we are trying to get clear about is not an external object, but our own self-understanding in the ongoing process of seeking clarity and depth about what it is to be in our lives. The inquiry into the meaning of Being is possible because we are *already under way* in such an inquiry. Heidegger says that it belongs to the essence of being human that we *are* ontologists: "Dasein is ontically distinctive in that it *is* ontological" (12).

Nevertheless, taking hermeneutics as the method of fundamental ontology raises certain difficulties for the over-all project of *Being and Time* which must be considered. These difficulties are characteristic of textual interpretation in general. First, there is the problem of determining the *closure* for the interpretation of Dasein. If there are no basic premises from which the propositions of *Being and Time* are deduced and if our interpretations may always uncover deeper levels of meaning, the question arises of how we can know we have reached the deepest or final interpretation of the text-analogue of everydayness. Second, there is the problem of a *criterion* for the correctness or adequacy of our interpretation. If we have two plausible but incommensurable interpretations of the meaning of Dasein's Being, how are we to decide which of them is correct? What justification can be adduced for accepting one interpretation over another? Since questions of this sort, when applied to textual interpretation, have often been thought to open the prospect of interpretive relativism, it is important to see how Heidegger answers them.

The problem of finding a closure for the hermeneutic of Dasein arises because of the circular structure of questioning in general. Heidegger points out that every question must be guided in advance by some prior understanding of the answer to that question. "Inquiry, as a kind of seeking, must be guided beforehand by what is sought. So the meaning of Being must already be available to us in some way" (5). In the question of the meaning of Being, we are to begin by examining an entity — Dasein — in order to discover its Being. But in order to pose this question, Heidegger says, we must already have some understanding of the Being of entities — for otherwise how would we know it is this entity's *Being* we were discovering in the investigation and not something else? We have seen that our pre-ontological understanding of Being can serve as a provisional and tentative basis for posing the question of Dasein's Being at the outset. Using this horizon of understanding, Heidegger says, we can then work out a "preparatory" analytic of Dasein as "Being-in-the-world."

But this initial characterization of Dasein is itself provisional and incomplete: "It merely brings out the Being of this entity, without interpreting its meaning" (17). What is required, then, is an interpretation of this text-analogue of everyday Dasein to uncover its deeper meaning. This interpretation will lead in turn to a more primordial horizon for understanding Being. But this is still not the end of the matter. For when we have reached this deeper horizon through interpreting the results of the initial analytic of Dasein, the "preparatory analytic of Dasein will have to be *repeated* on a higher and authentically ontological basis" (17; my emphasis). Yet when the analytic of Dasein has been repeated, a new text-analogue will become available for a new and still deeper interpretation of its meaning. And so on.

It seems, then, that the structure of the inquiry is not so much a circle as it is a "spiral." The analysis of Dasein always presupposes a prior understanding of Being which guides the description. Yet every description of Dasein will open the possibility of arriving at a deeper horizon of understanding of Being. The fact that we are already *in* this spiral assures us of the possibility of undertaking an inquiry into the meaning of Being: since "pre-ontological understanding" defines our Being, such an inquiry is in fact already under way. What is uncertain here is whether the inquiry can ever be terminated. As Heidegger says,

> In any investigation in this field . . . one must take pains not to overestimate the results. For in such an inquiry one is constantly compelled to face the possibility of disclosing an even more primordial and more universal horizon from which we may draw the answer to the question, "What is *'Being'*?" (26)

If the possibility always remains open of finding a "more primordial and universal horizon," however, how can we know there is a closure for the cycle of interpretations?

The second problem in the application of hermeneutics to fundamental ontology—the problem of finding a criterion for the correctness and adequacy of the interpretation—arises because of Heidegger's conception of the nature of understanding in general. Interpretation, according to Heidegger, always operates within a "fore-structure" of presuppositions that are projected in advance over what one is interpreting. There can be no such thing, he says, as a "presuppositionless apprehending of something presented to us" (150). Every interpretation is shaped and regulated by a set of assumptions and expectations about the meaning of the whole which is sketched out beforehand in understanding. Even when one is engaged in precise textual interpretation and one wants to appeal to what just "stands there" in the text, "one finds that what 'stands there' in the first instance is nothing other than the obvious undiscussed assumption of the person who does the interpreting" (150). There are no bare facts, no things themselves that can be encountered independent of the presuppositions outlined by the understanding.

It follows, then, that the interpretation of Dasein will also operate within the framework of such a fore-structure of presuppositions. Heidegger calls the "totality of 'presuppositions' " that guides the existential analytic "the *hermeneutical situation*" (232). The hermeneutical situation contains a "formal idea of existence" that "illuminates" the inquiry as a whole (314).[56] But if fundamental ontology always " 'presupposes' an idea of Being in general" and is "already illumined by the 'presupposed' idea of existence" (313), the problem arises of justifying what has been presupposed from the outset. Heidegger therefore asks, "where are ontological projections to get the evidence that their 'findings' are phenomenally appropriate" (312)? "Where does this [presupposed] idea get its justification" (313)?

The solution to both of the problems built into the method of hermeneutics is to be found in the notion of "primordial and authentic truth." Heidegger says that

> truth which is primordial and authentic must guarantee the understanding of the Being of Dasein and of Being in general. The ontological "truth" of the existential analysis is developed on the ground of the primordial existentiell truth (316).

In the context of *Being and Time*, it seems that this "existentiell truth" is uncovered when one *becomes authentic*. If we become authentic, Heidegger claims, we will be able to clear away the concealments and obscurities that block our access to a genuine self-understanding, and we will thereby achieve "transparency" about Being-in-the-world and "*all* of the constitutive items which are essential to it" (146). When Dasein has achieved authentic transparency, it will recognize the most fundamental horizon for understanding its own Being, and it will be able to "*decide for itself whether, as the entity which it is, it has that composition of Being which has been disclosed in the projection of its formal aspects*" (315).

What is "primordial and authentic truth," and how does it "guarantee the understanding of the Being of Dasein and of Being in general"? If the concept of authenticity is to satisfy the methodological demands placed on it, it seems that becoming authentic must provide us with some new "information" or "facts" that were previously not available. But, at first sight at least, it does not seem that authenticity involves coming to have any new information. In fact, as we shall see in section 10 below, authenticity is more a matter of the *style* of one's life than of a particular content of understanding. In his last Marburg lectures, for instance, Heidegger speaks of authenticity as an "art of existing" which involves not self-reflection but a special way of acting:

---

56. See section 7 for a discussion of the "formal" characterization of Dasein.

> Only he who understands this art of existing, that which is grasped at any time as the absolutely single thing to be dealt with in his actions [Handeln], and is clear thereby just as much about the finitude of these activities, only he understands finite existence and can hope to achieve something in this. This art of existing is not self-reflection, . . . but is rather solely the clarity of action itself, the pursuit of genuine possibilities (LL 201).

If the authentic life is a particular art or style of existing, however, in what sense does it give us access to "primordial and authentic truth"?

To understand how authenticity can provide a thematic content for fundamental ontology, we must see that Heidegger's method is also "dialectical" in a Platonic sense. Its goal is not to give us new information, but to lead us to "remember" something that lies concealed in our ordinary interpretations of ourselves and our world. Everydayness is characterized by "forgetfulness" or "oblivion" (Vergessenheit). In our normal involvements in the world, we are not so much ignorant as we are misled about our own Being. As Heidegger says in his Marburg lectures of 1927,

> The covering over of transcendence is not total ignorance, but, what is much more portentous, a misunderstanding, a misinterpretation. These misinterpretations and misunderstandings obstruct the path to authentic knowledge much more obstinately than total ignorance (GP 458).

Fundamental ontology is dialectical, then, in the way it tries to lead us through the darkess and opacity surrounding our everyday lives to the light of the authentic knowledge that underlies our ordinary misinterpretations.[57]

The source of our forgetfulness is a tendency to "fall" into the world of our day-to-day preoccupations. As involved agents in the world, we generally throw ourselves into routine tasks and chores and act according to the norms and conventions laid out for us in the social context in which we find ourselves. For the most part we are dispersed and adrift; we forget the deeper origins and significance of the guidelines that regulate and govern our

---

57. Unlike Plato, of course, Heidegger does not believe that the "primordial truth" lies in a realm of "ideas" distinct from everydayness. Just as the meaning of a text might be said to lie in the text itself, there is a meaning in everydayness that is generally disguised and covered over. I am indebted to Thomas Seung for this comparison with Plato.

behavior. Like Nietzsche, Heidegger sees forgetting as a positive phenomenon (339). We can be normal participants in the contemporary world only if we can draw a horizon around ourselves and shut out our awareness of the sources of our possibilities of acting.[58] Our forgetful involvement in ordinary practical affairs first discloses our "situatedness" in an intelligible life-world and makes it possible for us to be open to the past as "having-been" (Gewesenheit). For this reason Heidegger says that forgetfulness is *prior to* remembering:

> ... *remembering* [is possible only] on the basis of forgetting, *and not vice versa;* for in the mode of forgetfulness, one's having-been "discloses" primarily the horizon into which Dasein, lost in the "superficiality" of its concerns, can bring itself by remembering (339).

What we forget under the pressure of daily life is something that "is indeed known, but at the same time is not conceptualized."[59]

The interpretations we take over in our everyday forgetfulness are drawn from what Heidegger calls the "tradition" (Tradition). In its ordinary understanding of itself, Dasein is inclined to

> fall back upon its world . . . and to interpret itself in terms of the world by its reflected light, but also . . . Dasein simultaneously falls prey to the *tradition* of which it has more or less explicitly taken hold (21; my emphasis).

The tradition provides us with the common-sense grid of categories and schematizations through which we encounter ourselves and the world. According to Heidegger, the tradition is the medium from which we draw all our possibilities of understanding. But it transmits these possibilities in a warped and distorted form which conceals their true significance.

> When tradition thus becomes master [in everyday forgetfulness], it does so in such a way that what it "transmits" is made

---

58. The idea that a "healthy," normal life requires the ability to "draw a horizon around oneself" and "the power of forgetting, . . . the capacity for feeling 'unhistorically' " is found in Nietzsche's *The Use and Abuse of History* (New York: Liberal Arts, 1949), pp. 14/5. Heidegger's use of this essay will be discussed in section 16.

59. KPMe 241, KPMg 226.

so inaccessible, proximally and for the most part, that it rather becomes concealed. Tradition takes what has come down to us and delivers it over to self-evidence; it blocks our access to those primordial "wellsprings" ["Quellen"] from which the categories and concepts handed down to us have been in part quite genuinely drawn. Indeed it makes us forget that they have had such an origin, and makes us suppose that the necessity of going back to these sources is something which we need not even understand (21).

The goal of fundamental ontology, then, is to lead us to remember our forgotten "roots" and "origins": "the basic, fundamental-ontological act of the metaphysics of Dasein is, therefore, a *'remembering'* ['Wiedererinnerung'].''[60]

It seems, then, that achieving authenticity is supposed to enable us to overcome the forgetfulness of everyday life so that we can remember what is handed on to us in a distorted form by the tradition. What we remember in the dialectical stage is what Heidegger calls the "springs," "origins," "sources," "roots," or "soil" on which our everyday understanding is nurtured. It is important to see that, whereas for Husserl such "origins" were to be found in trans-cendental subjectivity, for Heidegger they are *historical.* The tradition, which opens a range of possibilities for our lives, is conceived of as a commentary on a primordial "ur-text" or "primal text" of possibilities opened up at the dawn of Western history. In this sense the understanding of Being that governs our current interpretations of self and world is just a variation on certain basic themes that emerged at the outset of Western history.

If this interpretation of the notion of origins is correct, then it follows that, by becoming authentic, we are able to see through the distortions and concealments in the tradition in order to retrieve the "primordial experiences in which we achieved our first ways of determining Being—the ways which have guided us ever since" (22). What the dialectical stage reveals is not some ahistorical *eidos* or *ratio,* but rather the deep historical sources of our ways of understanding Being. "Fundamental ontology," Heidegger says, "is always only a repetition and retrieval of these old and early things."[61]

Since the "tradition" is seen as merely a commentary on a primal text that emerged at the origin of history, to recover this original

60. KPMe 242, KPMg 227 (my emphasis).

61. LL 197.

understanding is also to reveal the conditions for the possibility of our contemporary interpretations. This explains what appears to be an equivocal use of the term 'primordial' (ursprünglich: literally, "original") in *Being and Time*. The term 'primordial' has both a transcendental and a historical signification. First, to say that "*A* is more primordial than *B*" can mean that *A* is a condition for the possibility of *B* in the sense that *B* is grounded in and parasitic on *A*. Thus Heidegger says that encountering a hammer in hammering is "more primordial" than merely perceiving a "hammer-thing" (69) because "mere seeing" is a special derivative case of our involvement with equipment in practical activities, whereas those activities cannot be accounted for in terms of sense impressions of mere things. Second, "*A* is more primordial than *B*" can also mean that *A* is "earlier" or "more ancient" than *B* in the sense of being closer to a "primordial experience" of Being that appeared in the earliest times. These kinds of "basic experience" (Grunderfahrung; 232) are still accessible to us (in anxiety, for instance). But they are found in their most concrete form in the aboriginal language of what Heidegger calls our "heritage" (Erbe).[62] What must be understood is that, for Heidegger, these two senses of 'primordial' *amount to the same thing*. Since all our ways of encountering the world are just variations on ancient themes, to discover the conditions for the possibility of our encounter with the world *just is* to recover or "remember" the primal possibilities opened by our heritage.

It should be clear, then, that the ultimate content arrived at in fundamental ontology lies in history. We achieve closure and confirmation for our interpretations when we have reached "the origin of our basic ontological concepts by an investigation in which their 'birth certificate' is displayed" (22). Primordial and authentic truth is discovered not by transcending our historical context to reach a vantage point of pure reason or intuition of essences, but by remembering the historical origins embedded in our contemporary interpretations. Since our Being is characterized by "historicity" (Geschichtlichkeit), we are "bearers" of history and, therefore, always have access to the implicit historical understanding that underlies our traditional ways of interpreting ourselves and the world. The "bedrock" of the interpretation of everydayness lies in the primordial possibilities flowing through history.

We are now in a position to see how Heidegger's concept of

---

62. For instance, Heidegger claims that the Greek word *alētheia* embodies a "prephilosophical way of understanding truth" (220) as "un-concealment" or "disclosedness." To understand what truth is, we should by-pass the confusions of the tradition and return to this primal meaning.

historicity is supposed to overcome historical relativism by making *history itself* the ultimate ground of all intelligibility. Whereas Dilthey tends to regard history as an endless pageant of incommensurable world-views, Heidegger sees history as having an underlying core of meaning which gives it continuity and coherence. Beneath the swirling eddies of contemporary fads and competing world-views there is a deep, constant undercurrent of understanding which is the basis for our changing interpretations. For Heidegger, history is the *logos* that unites our "heritage" and "destiny" into a cohesive narrative with a beginning and an end. The task of the dialectical stage of fundamental ontology is to recapture the elemental understanding that lies at the wellsprings of our heritage and directs us toward the realization of our sending or destiny (Geschick). Since we are all participants in this "world-historical happening" (19), we always have access to the sources of intelligibility of our heritage.

This picture of history as a story with an underlying meaning may seem like a bizarre throwback to theology, but it is important to see that it is not gratuitous. In fact, the conception of history as a meaningful totality is necessitated by a hermeneutic understanding of history. Hans-Georg Gadamer has traced the reasoning that led the nineteenth-century historical school to posit the existence of a "world-history" or "universal-history."[63] When history is understood as a text-analogue, the hermeneutic circle comes into play: although the whole of history can be understood only from its parts, it is also the case that the parts of history can be understood only in terms of the whole. If history must be conceived of as a whole, however, it is necessary to posit the existence of a "world-history" in the light of which individual events or epochs may be understood as significant. But this conception of history seems paradoxical, since the "whole" of history is incomplete and still outstanding. If we reject Hegel's conception of the culmination of history in "absolute knowing," then, we must find some other way to posit a completion for world-history.

Ranke and Droysen tried to make sense of the idea of a historical totality by viewing history as a "growing aggregate" whose over-all point could be discovered by purely empirical methods. As Gadamer makes clear, however, the conception of history as a growing aggregate does not seem to be something that can be simply discovered by empirical research. For events and occurrences that are qualitatively different cannot simply be added up to obtain a sum. On the contrary, finding a unified meaning in disparate events

63. *Truth and Method* (New York: Seabury, 1975), pp. 182–187.

presupposes that "the unity, in terms of what they are grouped together, is already the criterion for that grouping" (*ibid.* 183). In other words, a concrete conception of history as a meaningful totality is a "regulative idea" that makes historiography possible. When there is no conception of the point of history as a whole, there is no historical understanding.

The groundwork for Heidegger's later conceptions of "heritage" and "destiny" already appears in his 1915 lecture to the Freiburg faculty on the concept of time in historical science.[64] In that early work Heidegger argues that the historian is not interested in just registering all the "objectivations of human spirit" that have occurred in the past. Instead he is concerned with what is "historically effective," and this requires that the historical be *selected* in terms of the interests of the *present*. What we count as historical is what has proved "effective" in bringing the present into being: we see past events as the "results of development." But this means that the historical is selected according to the norms and values of the present.

> The selection of the historical from the plethora of what is given is therefore grounded in relations to values. The goal of historical science is thus to present the context of effectiveness and development (Wirkings- und Entwicklungszusammenhang) of the objectivations of human life in their uniqueness and singularity as this is made intelligible by their relation to cultural values (FS 369).

When history is seen as a cohesive context of effectiveness and development pointing toward cultural values and when these values are understood as projections of a historical people into the future, we have the foundation for the conception of heritage and destiny in *Being and Time*.

Heidegger's picture of history as a continuous narrative with a beginning and an end is therefore rooted in his hermeneutic understanding of the historical. Unlike Hegel's eschatological conception of world-history, however, there is no predetermined *telos* that will make the whole course of events finally rational and fully intelligible. But neither is there a pre-given, factual *archē* that determines a plan for the whole from the outset. Instead, what Heidegger's conception of history gives us is a sense of an underlying ground-rhythm of intelligibility in which we participate and which we constantly reshape and transform in our decisions. This

---

64. *Der Zeitbegriff in der Geschichtswissenschaft* in FS 355–375.

undercurrent of history is the ultimate *ground* of all of our possible ways of understanding Being, but it is not a "self-grounding ground" in the Cartesian sense. As with Dilthey's "life," there is no way to "go behind" history in order to "bring it before the judgment seat of reason." Yet, as the source of all possibilities of our understanding, it cannot be contrasted with an ideal, unconditioned vantage point of reason, since that ideal standpoint itself is constituted by interpretations that are a product of history.

The dialectical stage of *Being and Time* was to have been carried out in the unpublished second half of the work: the "phenomenological destruction of the history of ontology" (39). The goal there was to "de-structure" the sediment and accretions of misunderstandings that make up the tradition in order to expose the original sources and springs of our understanding of Being. "If the question of Being is to have its own history made transparent, then this hardened tradition must be loosened up, and the concealments which it has brought about must be dissolved" (22). The image of peeling off the hardened crust of traditional misinterpretations in order to expose the hidden core of meanings of Western history suggests that the dialectic of *Being and Time* aims not at total freedom from presuppositions, but rather at recovering the elemental pre-judgments that continue to flow beneath the level of our common sense. Fundamental ontology culminates not in a "new" way of understanding Being, but in the "oldest" way: "Its positive power must lie in its being *ancient* enough for us to learn to conceive the possibilities which the 'Ancients' have made ready for us" (19). Because the question of Being can be dealt with only in this sort of historical reduction, Heidegger says that "the question of Being does not achieve its true concreteness until we have carried through the process of destroying the ontological tradition" (26). [65]

Although the second part of *Being and Time* was never published, there are clues to what the destruction was supposed to retrieve. What has been forgotten in the misinterpretations of the tradition, Heidegger suggests, is the relation of Being to *time*. Ever since the Greeks, he claims, Being has been thought of as the "enduring presence" of a substance. The tendency to interpret Being as *presence* "has deteriorated into a tradition which gets reduced to something obvious—merely material for reworking, as it was for Hegel" (22). The historical reduction or "destruction" is designed to recover a deeper, more primordial sense of the temporality of Being which underlies our common-sense misunderstanding of Being as

---

65. In section 16 we will find that the historical reduction was supposed to have been guided by a "clue" which is "the problematic of Temporality" (39; cf. 19).

mere presence. What must be noted here is that Heidegger's goal is to disclose *trans*historical truth without reverting to *supra*historical meanings constituted by a transcendental subjectivity or consciousness in general. In his view, the same historical tradition that maintains and opens up the possibilities of life in our culture also tends to cover up and distort the transhistorical possibilities of understanding from which it springs. In gaining the world we have lost contact with our roots. But, since we are historical entities, we always have a vague and tacit grasp of these deeper sources and are therefore assured of the possibility of retrieving them.

It is obvious that there are a number of difficulties built into the central position Heidegger gives to history, some of which will be discussed in detail in Chapter V. For instance, how do we know when we have reached the deepest ontological concepts "by an investigation in which their 'birth certificate' is displayed" (22)? Heidegger seems to think that we can be assured of the primordiality of our account so long as we are moving in a direction opposite to that of everyday fallenness: Dasein's primordial Being is "*wrested* from Dasein by following the *opposite course* from that taken by the falling ontico-ontological tendency of interpretation" (311). Yet what reason do we have to think there is only one such course? We might also ask whether the springs and origins of Western history are to be regarded as transcultural or culture-specific. If the latter, how can fundamental ontology lay a foundation for ontology in the widest sense? Is historicity itself to be conceived of as absolute, or is it also historical? What are the relations among historicity, world-history, and historiography? Is it impossible for there to be two equally authentic but nonetheless incommensurable interpretations of the "origins" of history? Obviously the success of Heidegger's attempt to overcome historical relativism with the concept of historicity will depend on our ability to answer questions like these.

Heidegger's use of the dialectical method may be seen most clearly in the ways he starts with what one ordinarily says about things and then attempts to supersede the untruth of everydayness by showing us the deep underlying meaning in our ordinary language. In this way he leads us past the "surface" meaning of our language to light up the forgotten deep meaning. He recommends that we start with "what the everyday interpretation 'says' " (281) about death, guilt, or conscience, in order to recover what is implicit in our normal misinterpretations of these concepts. For instance, speaking of conscience, Heidegger says that we must show how the phenomena familiar to the ordinary interpretation of conscience point back to the primordial meaning of the call of conscience when they are understood in a way that is ontologically appropriate; [and] we must then show that the ordinary interpretation springs from the limitations of the way Dasein interprets itself in falling (294).

We can reach a deeper understanding by this method because "whenever we see something wrongly, some injunction as to the primordial 'idea' of the phenomenon is revealed along with it" (281). The everyday idea is not just a "mistake"; it is rather a masking or disguising of the phenomena and therefore contains the seeds of the deeper meaning.

Heidegger's method is also dialectical in its actual use of language. In order to recover our "rootedness" and "autochthony" (Bodenständigkeit), we must rework our language in such a way that it can once again bring to light the primordial significations it embodies. Since the tradition "blocks our access to the primordial 'sources' from which the categories and concepts handed down to us have been in part quite genuinely drawn" (21), we can retrieve these deeper sources only by "remembering" what our language really says. This attempt to recover the deep meanings of words is the source of the bizarre language in *Being and Time* which has so often been the target for Heidegger's critics. It has been referred to as a jargon, as word-mysticism, or most often as a pernicious attempt to conceal basically confused thinking under the cloak of hopelessly obscure verbiage. What must be realized, however, is that Heidegger sees his peculiar use of language as unavoidable if we are to escape the conceptual confusions of common sense and recover a deeper sense of the meaning of Being from the prevailing oblivion. Throughout *Being and Time* he relies on neologisms, erudite puns, and somewhat dubious etymologies in order to recapture

> the force of the most elemental words in which Dasein expresses itself, and to keep the common understanding from levelling them off to that unintelligibility which functions in turn as a source of pseudo-problems [Scheinprobleme] (220).

Heidegger's goal is to avoid the pseudo-problems built into the framework of our ordinary language by recasting language in a mold that will free it from such pointless puzzles. The consequence of this overhaul of language is that the style of *Being and Time* becomes "awkward" and "inelegant" (39), as Heidegger admits. Even the grammar of the languages handed down to us must be revised, he suggests, since the subject-predicate structure of the sentence contributes to the idea that the world at a basic level must consist of objects with properties. In order to talk about Being rather than entities "we lack not only most of the words but, above all, the 'grammar' " (38/9).

The method of *Being and Time* is also dialectical, then, in the way it shifts the meanings of ordinary terms as fundamental analysis proceeds. This awkward use of language is often necessitated by the priority of relations over objects which unfolds in the analyses. In Erasmus Schöfer's words, the language of *Being and Time* is determined by the need "to grasp . . . the expression of relations that determine human Dasein, and, unnoticed, govern its understanding of its self and its world."[66] Familiar words like 'truth', 'understanding', 'existence', 'conscience', 'death', and 'guilt' should no longer be expected to correspond exactly to our ordinary ways of using them. But this process should not be conceived of as a total break with our ordinary ways of speaking. As noted above, Heidegger's goal is to recapture the most original meanings of words embedded in our ordinary usage, not to invent a new language.[67]

Finally, throughout *Being and Time* Heidegger attempts to overcome the complacent self-evidence of common sense with "diagnoses" that reveal the roots of our seemingly "natural" ways of interpreting things. In his hermeneutic of Descartes and modern science his concern is to help us distance ourselves from the frameworks in which we normally perceive the world and to expose the presuppositions of these models to the light of day. Even if one is led to reject the idea that what we need is a "correct model" of our plain epistemic situations — as Heidegger himself did in his later philosophy — these critical examinations of the tradition remain forceful and persuasive. Heidegger's relevance for epistemology lies not so much in any attempt to *prove* the existence of the external world as in the endeavor "to point out why Dasein, as Being-in-the-world, has a tendency to bury the 'external world' in nullity 'epistemologically' before going on to prove it" (206). In Wittgenstein's language, Heidegger is interested not in *solving* the problem of skepticism but in making it *dissolve*.

---

66. *Die S̶p̶r̶a̶c̶h̶e̶ Heideggers* (Pfullingen: Neske, 1962), pp. 167/8.

67. It therefore seems misleading to say that Heidegger's ontology is like a " 'conceptual analysis' of a *revisionary* variety," as Richard Schmitt says in *Martin Heidegger on Being Human* (New York: Random House, 1969), page 258, note. For Heidegger, it is post-Cartesian "common sense" that is revisionary, not the primordial language of *Being and Time*.

III
Being-in-the-World

In the first chapter I suggested that a particular metaphysical picture of ourselves and the world is already presupposed in the stage I common-sense description of our ordinary epistemic situations. According to this picture, we are at a basic level subjects, distinct from a range of objects that are outside us. It also appeared there that, once this subject/object model is accepted as a faithful portrayal of our actual epistemic situation, skepticism will be unavoidable. The isolated subject, trapped within its veil of ideas, simply lacks the resources to determine with certainty whether or not objects exist in the external world. The counterintuitive result that we do not really know — cannot really be certain — about states of affairs in the world, seems to be inescapable.

It is Heidegger's view that the problem of skepticism that arises inexorably from the Cartesian model cannot be resolved from within the framework of that model. If we are to avoid the counterintuitive results that follow from the skeptical inquiry, Heidegger claims, then we must overcome the ontological presuppositions that structure the Cartesian model: "Descartes can be overcome only through the overcoming of that which he himself founded, through the overcoming of modern metaphysics — and that is at the same time the metaphysics of the West."[1] The Cartesian metaphysical picture that must be overcome arises with the reduction to subjectivity and its correlative tendency toward objectifying entities within the world. In Heidegger's view, the "pure 'I' " that results from this reduction cannot provide us with an appropriate understanding of our everyday situations.

> The ideas of a "pure 'I' " ['*reinen Ich*'] and of a "consciousness in general" are so far from including the *a priori* character of "actual" subjectivity that the ontological characters of Dasein's facticity and its composition of Being are either passed over or not seen at all (229).

Heidegger attempts to circumvent the ontological presuppositions

1. QCT 140, HW 92.

of the Cartesian model by offering us an alternative description of our plain lives. This description focuses not on the situations in which we are passive spectators, but rather on the contexts in which we are active and engaged in the world. As a result of the redescription, the common-sense account of our epistemic predicament presented in stage I of the skeptical inquiry comes to be seen as a philosophical construct which gives us only a distorted understanding of ourselves.

For Descartes, the self is to be understood as a *res cogitans*, a thinking substance which is more or less accidentally located in a body and surrounded by extended things. Heidegger rejects this objectified picture of the self. Instead of regarding the self as a substance, he first works out what he calls the "formal meaning of Dasein's existential composition" (43) in which being human is treated as a *relation*. Here the influence of Kierkegaard's definition of the "self" in *The Sickness unto Death* is apparent: "The *'substance'* of man is not spirit as the synthesis of soul and body," Heidegger says, "rather, it is *existence*" (117). We will see that the technical term 'existence' is designed to capture the way that man, as a "happening" or "event," takes a stand on his Being in his everyday activities. To be human just is to *care* about what it is to be human, and this is characterized in terms of a relation of the self to its own Being.

Since Dasein is always involved in a world, the "formal" definition of Dasein as a relation becomes concrete only as "Being-in-the-world." In the picture that takes shape in Heidegger's description of Being-in-the-world, there is no longer any way to draw a distinction between a subject and a set of objects that are to be known. The discovery of *res extensae* by a *res cogitans* comes to be seen as a feat that is possible only with the *breakdown* of our ordinary engagement in the world. Even more important, as the description progresses, we are led to see the self as embedded in a cultural and historical context. Far from being an autonomous and isolated subject, the self is pictured as the "Anyone" (*das Man*), a "crossing point" of cultural systems unfolding through history. To be human, in Heidegger's view, is to be a place-holder in a network of internal relations, constituted by a public language, of the communal world into which Dasein is thrown.

The first section of this chapter will work out both the formal characterization of Dasein as a happening and the concrete description of everyday Being-in-the-world. In section 8, I will examine Heidegger's claim that Dasein in everydayness is essentially the "Anyone" or the "They." Dasein is found to be caught up in and dependent on a cultural context from which it draws the meaningful possibilities for its concrete ways of being engaged in the world. In section 9, I will argue that, although Heidegger was uncertain about the status of language in *Being and Time,* we can find the seeds for what I will call a *constitutive* view of language in this early work. According to this view, which is explicitly developed in the writings following *Being and Time,* since language is the medium in which both self and world can first be discovered, the "meaning of Being" must be understood as embedded in the resources of language. Finally, section 10 will take up the question of authenticity and develop its relation to historicity. It should become clear that history is the source of all our possibilities, including those possibilities which make up the content of fundamental ontology. I hope also to show there that becoming authentic is not a matter of "transcending" the "herd," but on the contrary implies that one becomes more deeply and intensely implicated in one's historical culture.

It will often be useful, in working out Heidegger's notion of Being-in-the-world, to refer back to Dilthey's insights into the nature of "life." But a word of caution is in order here. Dilthey's epistemological starting point, his interest in the British empiricists, and the centrality of psychology in his early doctrines combined to make it impossible for him fully to overcome the Cartesian distinctions of "inner" and "outer." He was always inclined to hold to the idea of a private mental life that is to be distinguished from its "expressions" and "objectivations." Even in his most mature writings he is struggling with the Humean problem of identifying the self in the bundle of "impressions" (Impressionen) given in experience: "Basically I only have such impressions and not a self separated from them, nor something of which it is the impression."[2] It should become clear that Heidegger attempts to do away with such subjectivistic presuppositions. In the final picture of Dasein that emerges in *Being and Time,* there is no distinction to be drawn between a private bundle of internal impressions and the public ways that Dasein manifests itself in the world.

§7. *Self and World*

In order to by-pass the objectifying view of the self as a substance, whether mental, physical, or personal, Heidegger characterizes Dasein as *agency* or *activity* in the course of Being-in-the-world. We have seen that, as early as the winter semester of 1919/20 he was trying to conceptualize "factical life" in terms of its

2. WD 233, *Aufbau* 284.

"tendentious" structure and its movement toward "completion" or "fulfillment."[3] In his lecture notes for 1925/26 Heidegger describes himself as concrete, coherent "dealings" and as "motion":

> I *live* in the understanding of writing, lighting things up, walking in and out and the like. More precisely, I am — as Dasein — speaking, walking, understanding, intelligible dealings [Umgang]. My Being in the world *is* nothing other than this being-in-motion [Sichbewegen] that already understands in these modes of Being (LFW 146).

In *Being and Time* the self is characterized as a "movement" or a "happening" in a "life-context" (Lebenszusammenhang) (374/5). Far from being conceived of as a thing or object in any sense, Dasein is understood as the *event* or *occurrence* of a life as a whole.

When the self is interpreted as an event, its "Being" must be determined in terms of its consummation or completion. What it is to be an event — i.e., "what happened" — is defined by its outcome. In the same way, according to Heidegger, what it is to be a person — "who I am" — is defined by the achievement of my life as a whole. I can *be* a confirmed bachelor all my life only if I successfully avoid marriage right up until the very end. If I lose my resolve and let myself fall prey to deathbed nuptials, I will no longer *be* a confirmed bachelor all my life. This last-minute act will totally transform the Being of the person I am.

Thus the Being of Dasein can be ascertained only when it has run its course between birth and death — when its life is concluded and there is no longer any room for last-minute reversions or conversions. But Heidegger notes that this way of characterizing Dasein seem to lead to a paradox, for it appears that I can *be* something only when I cease to exist. In order to conceptualize life as a happening, therefore, he interprets Dasein as an ongoing process pointing toward its realization and completion. Dasein's Being-a-whole is to be understood as Being-*toward*-the-end: its Being-toward-death.

The conception of Dasein as a dynamic temporal happening provides the basis for determining "the formal meaning of Dasein's existential constitution" (43). The formal definition of Dasein is supposed to capture the essential structure of human life understood as movement along a temporal axis. The goal is to characterize "the formal existential totality of Dasein's ontological structural whole" (192), and this totality is reached by interpreting Dasein's Being as a

---

3. See the beginning of section 5 above.

Being-relation (Seinsverhältnis). What is definitive of Dasein, Heidegger says, is that "in its Being, it has a Being-relation to this Being" (12). But where one speaks of a relation, it is natural to look for the relata of the relation. What is being related to what in this relation?

A first clue to interpreting this obscure definition might be found in a comparison with Dilthey's two principal categories of life: essence and development. We found that Dilthey uses these categories to characterize life as having both a passive and an active aspect. Regarded as essence, life is seen as finite and limited. We are burdened by the irretrievable choices we have made in the past, with the result that life is always constrained by its factuality and givenness. Regarded under the category of development, however, life is seen as free and creative. As long as we are alive we have the capacity to redefine the meaning of our lives through our free choices. Life is essentially goal-directed, moving toward a stable configuration of meaning as a whole. It is "carried away," Dilthey says, toward the future goals and aims that it projects as the realization and completion of itself.

Heidegger's characterization of Dasein also sees being human as having both a passive aspect, which he calls "essence," and an active aspect, which he calls "existence."[4] On the one hand, Dasein is passive: it has been delivered over to its own life as a *task* which it must take up and which it has already taken up in some determinate ways. The concept of essence embraces the fact that we find ourselves thrown (geworfen) into a world in which we are already involved. We encounter our lives as a burden to be taken over in some way, as what we have to be: Heidegger says that it belongs to Dasein's essence that "in each case it has its Being as its own to be" (12). As already located in a world, Dasein has a capacity for Being, or ability-to-be (Seinkönnen) which it must realize and bring to completion. The raw, undifferentiated givenness of the task of life is revealed in the moods that disclose our "situatedness" (Befindlichkeit) in the world. In its attunement to the world Dasein can discover its "naked 'that it is and has to be' " (134). At the same time we find ourselves as already "in play." We are engaged and involved in the task of living and have already made choices that provide a basis for our future actions. "As essentially situated, Dasein has always already gotten itself into definite possibilities" (144), and these choices shape our "facticity" and limit our freedom.

---

4. My interpretation of Heidegger's "formal" definition of Dasein draws on Ernst Tugendhat's *Der Wahrheitsbegriff bei Husserl und Heidegger,* as well as his Heidelberg lectures in the Winter Semester, 1974.

Dasein is passive, then, to the extent that it is "already-in" (192) a world and is already caught up in the task of living. The project of my life stands before me as an enterprise I must take up and as a quest that has already been undertaken. Since Dasein is a finite entity, it can and will be a whole at some point. But Heidegger says that "as long as Dasein exists, it must always *not yet be* something as ability-to-be" (233). The undertaking of a life into which Dasein is thrown is characterized by a "lack of totality": "there is always something still outstanding which, as an ability-to-be of Dasein itself, has not yet become 'actual' " (236).

On the other hand, however, Dasein also has an active aspect. Regarded as existence, it is already "ahead-of-itself" (191) in projecting itself toward the culmination and realization of its life as a totality. Since life is essentially goal-directed and purposive, to be human is to be projected toward some final, definitive configuration of meaning for one's life. The Being-a-whole that is the ultimate aim or goal of life is called "existence": Heidegger says that "the Being itself toward which Dasein can comport itself in one way or another, and always does comport itself somehow, we call *'existence'* " (12). Because we care about our lives — because who we are matters to us — we have taken some stand on the point of our lives as a whole. As a "projection" (Entwurf) onto its completion, Dasein is always "beyond itself" in relating itself toward its defining possibility of being something or other in the end. Dasein is defined as a "self-projective Being toward its ownmost ability-to-be" (191). The active side of Dasein's constitution embraces its freedom — Dasein is "Being-free *for* its ownmost ability-to-be" (144). In other words, we are always free to make something of our lives as a whole within the confines of the factical situation into which we are thrown.

Having distinguished the passive and active aspects of Dasein, we are in a position to interpret the formal definition of Dasein found in section 4 of *Being and Time*. Dasein is "ontically distinguished," Heidegger says, "by the fact that for this entity, in its Being, this Being itself is *at issue*" (12). By this Heidegger means that Dasein is an entity that, in living out its life, cares about what that life amounts to as a whole. The outcome of our lives is something that matters to us; it is *at stake* or *in question* for us. And because the point of our lives is at issue for us, we always take some concrete stand on our Being-a-whole. Because we care about our lives, we take up specific self-interpretations and roles that express our sense of what it is to be. In taking a stand as a teacher, as a family man, as lazy and cowardly, and so forth, I express my sense of what my life is all about. To be involved in life, then, is to take over the task of living to which we are "delivered over," and to try to make something of it by relating ourselves toward our Being-a-whole.

But this means that what is definitive of Dasein is the concrete *relation* it has, in living, to its life as a totality: Dasein is unique among entities in that, "in its Being, it has a Being-relation to this Being" (12). This Being-relation Heidegger calls "existing." In existing, Dasein *decides* its own Being by being involved in the project of living in a determinate way.

> Dasein always understands itself in terms of its existence—
> in terms of a possibility of itself. . . . Only the particular
> Dasein decides its existence, whether it does so by taking hold
> or neglecting. The question of existence never gets straightened
> out except through existing itself (12).

Who we are, what we are, is determined by the concrete possibilities we take over in taking a stand on the project of our lives. I am what I do insofar as the actual possibilities I express in my actions define my Being. There is no human nature, no "proper function of man" or human essence beneath the masks we wear and the parts we play. Since the task of living is given a meaning and content only in the concrete ways we interpret our lives as a whole, Heidegger says that *"the 'essence' of Dasein lies in its existence"*(42).

The Being-relation of taking a stand should not be thought of as rooted in some inner plotting and calculating about one's life. Heidegger would say that our self-interpretations are for the most part unreflective and unthinking. They take shape not so much in introspection as in *action*. Every action involves certain commitments to the future—even if these implications have never been thought out. Everything I do expresses some long-range goals and aims for my life as a whole. Letting the baby cry, for instance, manifests my understanding of being a father just as much as my sudden show of concern when I am brought up short and made to reflect on my obligations. My understanding of my own Being is not a product of inward self-reflection; it is rather something that expresses itself in all my actions.

It follows, then, that, when Heidegger characterizes Dasein as the entity that "understands itself in its Being in some way and with some degree of explicitness" (12), this does not mean that Dasein has some unique mental faculty. Instead it means that we have a certain *know-how* in coping with our lives and with the world in which we find ourselves. In Wittgenstein's language, we are "masters of the technique" of living—we have an over-all competence in handling ourselves and our world that is expressed in our actions.

Through our competence in coping with life, our Being as a whole is disclosed to us. Heidegger says that "what is unique to this entity is that with and through its Being, this Being itself is disclosed to it" (12). As goal-directed, Dasein is a "disclosive Being toward its ability-to-be" (221) and therefore always has some sense of what life amounts to. By virtue of the fact that I am already under way in living, I have a grip on who I am and what I can be. And through this grasp of my own Being, I also have some grasp of the Being of the entities I encounter around me. I find myself contextualized in a world that is *already intelligible* to me because I know my way around in it.

> Thus Dasein's understanding of [its own] Being pertains with equal primordiality both to an understanding of something like a "world," and to the understanding of the Being of those entities which become accessible within the world (13).

The Being of Dasein just is its self-interpretations in the stand it takes on its life as a whole. Seen from the passive aspect, Dasein is *not yet* what it can and will be. As long as I am alive, there are still open possibilities before me, and my life is outstanding and incomplete. Seen from the active aspect of being-ahead-of-itself, however, Dasein is already what it is not yet in its factical Being. My plans and goals always point beyond what I have been so far, so I *am* as Being-toward-the-end. It should not seem unduly paradoxical, then, if Heidegger says that Dasein "*is* existentially that which, in its ability-to-be, it is *not yet*" (145).

The formal characterization of Dasein reveals what I have called the "temporal axis" of Dasein's Being. Regarded as a temporal happening, Dasein has a *teleological* structure: its Being is determined by the fact that it is beyond itself in its directedness toward the final realization of its possibilities of existence. Goal-directedness generates the tripartite "care" structure that is definitive of Dasein's formal constitution. As Dasein "comes toward" itself (Zu-kunft), it appropriates the possibilities of the world it is "already-in" and is thereby "among" or "at home with" (bei) the entities it encounters around it. Consequently, the definition of the "formal existential totality of Dasein's ontological structural whole" is found in the complicated expression, "ahead-of-itself-Being-already-in-(the-world) as Being-among (entities encountered within-the-world)" (192). The temporal axis of Dasein's Being plays a role similar to Dilthey's "structure": it provides the formal scaffolding in which any concrete life in particular is lived. But it must be kept in mind that, unlike Dilthey, Heidegger does not conceive of the temporality of Dasein as psychic or mental in any sense. For Heidegger, what he calls the "temporalizing of temporality" of Dasein is prior to and definitive of any of the traditional distinctions between inner and outer or mental and physical.

We have seen that Dasein's "happening" also has a *hermeneutic* structure: the events that make up a life gain their sense only from the projected point of the life as a whole, and the possibilities of projection are always determined by the events of that life. The hermeneutic structure of life may be made clearer by an analogy with the writing of an autobiography. If I were to write my autobiography, I would cast back over the events of my life in order to try to find the meaning of the whole. Past events and actions would stand out or recede in terms of my understanding of the point of the totality. Autobiography may be thought of as an explicit form of what we all do all the time: in a sense, we are all composing our autobiographies as we live. Whether consciously or not, we are constantly interpreting and reinterpreting the events of our lives in terms of our grasp of what they mean as a totality. Although the actual stances we take and the contexts we live in are shared and public, the final configuration of meaning we give to our lives—what we make of ourselves—depends on us alone. Because each of us has this unique responsibility for making something of his or her existence as Being-a-whole, Heidegger says that Dasein "is in each case mine" (42). The task of realizing my life as a totality is mine alone: it cannot be delegated.

In presenting the formal definition of Dasein in terms of a teleological and hermeneutical self-relation, Heidegger has quashed the tendency to see the self as an object or thing of any sort. The Being of Dasein is defined in terms of the way it relates to itself in undertaking the task of fulfilling itself and being someone. Since Dasein is fully circumscribed by the stands it takes on what is still outstanding for it, it makes no sense to look for an ego or bundle of impressions given first and then afterwards related to possibilities. The possibilities Dasein takes up in projecting onto its ownmost possibility *define* the Being of Dasein without remainder. There is no way to get past Dasein's interpretations to find a thing that is doing the interpreting. Heidegger says that "in each case Dasein *is* its possibility, and it 'has' this possibility, but not just as a property as of some mere thing" (42). We are left with no vocabulary with which to pick out a substantial subject that is related to interpretations as though they were properties.

The temporal axis of Dasein's Being is intersected at every point by an axis of involvement in the world. Dasein's temporal movement is coupled with a movement which Heidegger calls the "downward plunge" (178) into everyday preoccupations and concerns. Since Dasein is always involved in the world, the formal characterization of Dasein attains its full concretion only as Being-in-the-world. Only by taking a stand in the world can one either have a life to be or *be* that life in existing. The concept of Being-in-the-world embraces our involvements in everyday situations and is thus a correlate of the "plain" epistemic situations we hoped to describe in contrast to the Cartesian "philosophical" situations that have been taken as paradigmatic in traditional epistemology. As we shall see, in Heidegger's account of Being-in-the-world, the self no longer appears as a worldless subject which then has to get hooked up with a world. On the contrary, the self *becomes a self only through the total context of the world.*

Heidegger's goal in describing Being-in-the-world is to recapture a "natural conception of the world" prior to scientific abstraction or philosophical reflection. He tries to lead us away from the concept of the world as a totality of objects or as "everything that is the case." For him, the world is to be understood as "that *'wherein'* a factical Dasein as such can be said to 'live' " (65). In this deeper understanding of 'world' Heidegger is drawing on the ways we speak in ordinary language of being in "the world of theater," "the world of finance," "one's own world," or "le beau monde." Being-at-home (Sein-bei) in the world of one's prereflective everyday concerns carries with it the sense of "being absorbed in the world" (54), whether it be in "the 'public' we-world, or one's 'own' closest (domestic) environment" (65). Heidegger focuses on particular worlds, but his aim is to uncover an "ontologico-existential concept of *worldhood* " (65) that embraces the structure of every particular world.

Since his goal is to circumvent the objectifying tendencies of our common-sense interpretations, Heidegger describes the world in a language designed to express the wholeness of contexts of everyday activities. The paradigmatic situation he starts from is that of ordinary involvement in a workshop. What we encounter in our dealings in a workshop, Heidegger says, is "a totality of equipment" (Zeugganze) (68). The gear or equipment with which we are engaged is "constituted by various ways of the 'in-order-to' ['Um-zu'], such as serviceability, conduciveness, usability, manipulability" (68). By employing a term ordinarily used in giving reasons for actions (um. . . zu. . .), Heidegger emphasizes the way that equipment is generally encountered in terms of our practical needs and interests. In our prereflective engagement in the workshop, we are involved with an equipmental context that is functional in bringing about the achievement of our goals.

The relations of the "in-order-to" that make up a context of equipment are called "assignments" (Verweisungen) (68) or, later, "significance" (Bedeutsamkeit) (87). The hammer is encountered in hammering, which is *in order to* drive in a nail, which is *in order to* fasten two boards together, which is *in order to* support something. The in-order-to relations of the equipmental context are ordered around the "what-for" (Wozu) which is the work to be produced as the outcome of the activity. The referential-totality of the workshop is caught up in my activity as being "for" making a bookcase. The kind of Being of the equipmental totality Heidegger calls "readiness-to-hand" (Zuhandenheit). In the workshop the boards, hammers, and nails, the workbench, and even the windows, doors, and lights, are all "handy" for me as a skilled home repairman for whom everything is running smoothly. The ready-to-hand is thus in a sense "transparent": in my ordinary dealings in the workshop, I "see through it" to the work that is to be completed.

The intuitive account of equipment in terms of references or assignments is repeated and deepened in a terminology that practically defies translation. The key terms Heidegger uses are 'Bewenden' and 'Bewandtnis'. Both words lack a meaning in isolation, but can be used in idioms such as "Damit hat es sein Bewenden" (So the matter rested), or "Es hat folgende Bewandtnis" (The matter is as follows). These terms are related to the verb 'bewendenlassen', which means "to let (something) be as it is." The root of each of these words is the verb 'wenden' which means "to turn," and it is therefore related to the very 'anwenden', to "use," "employ," or "apply." In English we speak of "turning to a task" and "turning things over" in the sense of handling and manipulating them. I propose to use the suggestion of "how things have turned out" in translating the passages in which 'Bewenden' occurs. Heidegger also uses the prepositions 'mit' and 'bei' in these contexts. Here again the notion of use or employment seems to be what he is trying to capture. He focuses on the relative adverbs 'Womit' (by what means), and 'Wobei' (in doing which). The connotations of these terms imply a primary interest in the relations of means and ends in the ways things turn up in our activities.

Heidegger tells us that to say that an entity ready to hand has an assignment is to say that "*by means* of that entity there is a way it has turned out *in doing* something" (84).[5] My encounter with a hammer in the workshop is in terms of its being by-means-of (Womit) that hammer that I am hammering. That the hammer "turns out"to be used in hammering and not in stirring paint is

5. "Es hat *mit* ihm *bei* etwas sein Bewenden."

determined by my interests and goals in the workshop. Heidegger calls this way of making the functions of entities in the workshop explicit (ausdrücklich) by "taking them" in certain ways, "interpretation" (Auslegung). Interpretation is the "appropriation" (Zueignung) (148) of equipment in which one makes the totality one's own. This interpretation always involves taking "something as something" (149); the hammer is encountered *as* a hammer, the nails are encountered *as* nails. When Heidegger says that something is encountered "*as* something," he does not mean that we have consciously identified a thing and predicated some property to it. The 'as' of interpretation is "prepredicative" (149). "In interpreting," Heidegger says, "we do not, so to speak, throw a 'signification' over some naked thing which is present-at-hand, we do not stick a value on it" (150). Rather, it is the *totality* of the equipmental context as an interconnected field — a totality understood in advance — that is articulated into an as-structure in interpretation.

What is crucial about the description of the ready-to-hand in terms of the ways things have turned out to be is that the as-structure that determines how equipment is to count for us is always determined in advance by a hierarchy of goals and purposes. The what-it-is-for of hammering is to fasten nails, which in turn is to build a bookcase, which is itself subordinate to the goal of holding books. Heidegger says that this hierarchy of goals and purposes terminates in a "what-for" which is not itself *for* anything (84). What structures the entire framework of means/ends relations is an end that is not itself a means to anything else. This final "for-the-sake-of-which" (Worumwillen) of the workshop is the self-understanding of the agent in the context. That for-the-sake-of-which I am building the bookcase is ultimately my understanding of myself as, say, a good provider for my family. The pyramid of proximate and long-term goals implicit in my activity reaches its pinnacle in a conception of myself in terms of some role that makes up my own self-evaluations and self-understanding.

At this point we can see the connection between Dasein's formal determination and its concrete instantiation as Being-in-the-world. Dasein has been formally characterized as an entity that cares about its life and projects some plan for its life as a whole. As such a projection, it exists for the sake of certain goals. These goals determine particular aims and purposes that we undertake in the course of our lives. For instance, my interpretation of myself as a family man generates a set of tasks I take up, such as building a bookcase. The tasks I undertake in turn structure equipmental contexts into means/ends relations. My project of building a bookcase allows the boards, nails, hammer, and saw to count as equipment for fulfilling my aims. In Heidegger's language, my self-understanding is the source of a "foregoing letting 'be' " (vorgängig "sein" lassen) which "frees entities for their readiness-to-hand within the environment" (85). Only because Dasein is essentially goal-directed, projecting some point for its life as a whole, can the world be encountered as a context of the ready-to-hand.

In Heidegger's description of worldhood, our goal-directedness and the practical contexts in which we are engaged are welded together into a unified totality. Our purposive agency is always directed and under way. This goal-directedness lays out conditions of relevance for the equipment we encounter.[6] In other words, our self-understanding determines how entities will punctuate the environment: an office in a Federal building, for instance, is lit up in different ways for clerks, supervisors, janitors, and terrorists. It is the "whereunto" (Woraufhin) of our purposiveness that determines whether things will stand out as significant or recede into insignificance. But this means that Dasein's self-understanding and the context of means/ends relations in which it operates are indissolubly bound up with each other. The world "wherein" Dasein lives is inseparable from the self-interpretations that make up Dasein's "whereunto": "*That Wherein* Dasein understands itself beforehand in the mode of assigning itself is *that Whereunto* it has let entities be encountered beforehand" (86). The unified structure of the "wherein" and "whereunto" is "the phenomenon of the world" (86). Worldhood therefore turns out to be inseparable from Dasein's self-understanding in the stands it takes as existing.

Dasein's goal-directedness, in being for-the-sake-of-itself, therefore opens a "clearing," or "Spielraum" in which entities can count in some determinate way or other. Just as the passages in a text are always understood in terms of some pre-understanding of the meaning of the text as a whole, entities in the world are always encountered in terms of what Heidegger calls a "fore-structure" of understanding which is determined by our goals, interests, and needs. This kind of pre-understanding is always present. Even a scientific laboratory that is "outside of my scope" as a layman is articulated for me in advance to some extent: I encounter it as a laboratory and not as a place of worship or a stock exchange. As in the case of textual interpretation, then, there is never a "presuppositionless apprehending of something presented to us" in our encounters with the world. The Being of equipment is always sketched out in advance by our understanding.

6. I am indebted to Tom Bridges for the phrase, 'conditions of relevance'. Thomas W. Bridges, *The Concept of Meaning in Heidegger's 'Sein und Zeit,'* unpublished Columbia University doctoral dissertation (1972).

The model of Being-in-the-world that emerges in Heidegger's description of everydayness has important consequences for both the conceptions of the subject and of objectivity which are the metaphysical underpinnings of Cartesianism. First, the idea of a "worldless subject" encountering a world of objects is overcome. According to Heidegger, not only is the Being of entities determined by the relevance conditions originating in the self-understanding of Dasein, but the *Being of Dasein itself* is circumscribed by the world in which it is involved. When Heidegger says that "Dasein always assigns itself from a 'for-the-sake-of-which' to the 'by-means-of-which' of the ways things have turned out" (86), he does not mean that there is at first a subject with intentions, needs, and goals, which later comes to realize its aims in the world. On the contrary, the total context of a world that has been "freed" in advance is that *wherein* intentions and goals *first become possible*. Heidegger says that, in Being-in-the-world, *"Dasein 'signifies' ['bedeutet'] to itself:* in a primordial manner *it gives itself both its Being and its ability-to-be* as something which it is to understand with regard to its Being-in-the-world" (87; my emphasis). What Dasein can be and what it is become concrete only *in the world*.

There is thus a reciprocal relation between self-understanding and the totality of equipment. Through my understanding of myself as a home repairman, the context of the workshop is lit up in such a way that the equipment will have specific relevance conditions. The tools suitable for the job punctuate this world while the rest recede. At the same time, however, it is only through this context that *I can interpret myself* as a home repairman. In the workshop I can understand myself as an amateur or as a skilled artisan, but not, without further elaboration, as a bandit or mutineer.

In saying that "Dasein 'signifies' [bedeutet] to itself," Heidegger separates the intensifying prefix in the verb 'bedeuten' to emphasize its root meaning, "to interpret": I take over a possibility for my life in a context by *interpreting* myself in a certain way. Since Dasein just *is* the possibilities it takes up in interpreting itself, its self-interpretation in the workshop circumscribes the Being of Dasein without residue. In everydayness, according to Heidegger, "one *is* that with which one concerns oneself" (322). There is no way to drive a wedge between an "I" and the world to which it is related. "Self and world are not two entities, like 'subject' and 'object,' or 'I' and 'Thou'; rather self and world are the basic determination of Dasein itself in the unity of the structure of Being-in-the-world."[7]

7. GP 422.

"Worldhood" is an "existentiale" or essential structure of Dasein, not a categorial determination of things. This is why Heidegger says that "Dasein *is* its world in existing" (364).

The role in which Dasein understands itself and becomes what it is is defined by the interlocking network of significance which is the world. The world mediates my self-understanding and makes me the agent that I am. I can come to discover myself as an agent with beliefs and intentions only derivatively from the more primordial situations in which there is no clear distinction between agency and context of action. The Cartesian picture of a worldless subject with a reservoir of intentions who then somehow manages to effect behavior can arise only when everyday practical dealings in the environment have broken down. And, similarly, the picture of the knowing subject faced with the impossible task of transcending its veil of ideas to gain knowledge of objects outside it has no role to play in the description of everydayness. The epistemological subject can be discovered only in the rubble of shattered Being-in-the-world.

The second point that emerges from the description of Being-in-the-world has to do with the picture of the world as a collection of objects set over against the knowing subject. Seen from the model of Being-in-the-world, what it is to be an entity is bound up with Dasein's goals and interests in handling equipment in its everyday situations. Dasein's for-the-sake-of-which is tied up into a holistic context in which the particular relevance that an entity has in a situation is "ontologically definitive" for that entity (84). The *Being* of any entity is fully determined by the relations of "in-order-to," "what-for," "by-means-of-which," and "in-doing-which" which *place* it within the totality. Heidegger considers the objection that, in this conception of significance, "the 'substantial being' of entities within-the-world has been volatized into a system of relations" (87). If substance were identified with the primary substances of individuals and if equipment were understood as a mere aggregate of tools, then the objection would have to be taken to heart. But Heidegger rejects this objectifying concept of substance. The teleologically structured context of significance provides the horizon in which anything whatsoever can be discovered. For this reason Heidegger says that "the worldhood of the world provides the basis on which [entities that are ready-to-hand] can for the first time be discovered as they are 'substantially' 'in themselves' " (88).

It should be clear that Heidegger's conception of the "ontological definition" of entities in terms of their relations is closer to the model of internal relations found in Hegel and Dilthey than it is to that of the objectifying tradition. For Heidegger, the *essence* of any entity—its being what it is—is nothing other than its *actual place within a total context*—its "that it is." Far from its being the case that the world consists of the kinds of interchangeable particulars presupposed by the Cartesian model, "worldhood" is defined as a meaningful whole tied to the goals and ends of Dasein. Hence, as we shall see, there is no way to construct worldhood out of bare particulars to which accidental properties of usefulness and functionality have been tacked on. The attempt to rationally reconstruct the world out of a collocation of "bits" contingently related to one another is as futile as the attempt to appreciate a symphony by sounding each note in isolation and then imagining a relation among them.

The model of Being-in-the-world portrays our everyday situations in terms of a holistic context of internal relations woven into the plans and purposes of Dasein. The question now arises: If encountering the world as readiness-to-hand is our most primordial way of discovering the world, why does the Cartesian model strike us as so plausible and seemingly self-evident? Answering this question will be one of the primary concerns of Chapter IV, but we might sketch out a first approximation of Heidegger's answer here.

In our ordinary dealings in the world, our activities can run smoothly and efficiently only if the equipment we are using does not obtrude in any way. In everydayness, Heidegger says, "the being of what is most closely ready-to-hand within-the-world possesses the character of holding itself in and not emerging" (80). A skilled pianist would be unable to play if he were constantly compelled to notice the individual keys, the lighting and ventilation in the room, the relation of hammers and strings, the paper on which the music is printed, and so forth. Ordinary practical activities can be carried out only if what we are involved with is, in a sense, transparent. We see *through* the equipment to the work that is to be the outcome of the activity. For this reason, Heidegger calls the mode of "sight" in everydayness "knowing one's way around" (Umsicht) in contrast to the "mere seeing" of the contemplative attitude. This know-how is a generally tacit "feel" for the equipment at hand rather than an explicit knowing-that. The tools we deal with "are encountered as 'in themselves' in the concern which makes use of them without noticing them explicitly" (74).

The context of relations that makes up the world can come explicitly into view only when there is a disruption in the smooth flow of activities. Such a breakdown occurs when a tool is damaged and becomes unusable, when something is missing, or when something stands in the way of our work. When this happens,

Heidegger says, the equipment becomes "*un*-ready-to-hand" in the modes of "conspicuousness," "obtrusiveness," or "obstinacy" (73/4). The totality of significance is momentarily lit up when such a breakdown occurs, and we are compelled to deliberate explicitly about how to proceed. We must find a way to replace the missing or broken tool or to overcome the obstacle, and this requires an explicit consideration of the relations of in-order-to and the what-for of the work itself.

When we become circumspect and explicit in our deliberations, the mode of concern is still practical reflection. But we are no longer involved with the world as a coherent and smoothly functioning context. Heidegger says that the world can be sighted only in a process of its "*dis*worlding" (Entweltlichung) (65). As we deliberate about the un-ready-to-hand, we begin to see it explicitly as constituted by the as-structure of interpretation. We see the broken tool as a thing that had fallen under a particular interpretation but is no longer doing its job. The unusable tool

> just lies there; it shows itself as an equipmental *thing* which *looks* so and so, and which, in its readiness-to-hand as looking that way, has constantly been present-at-hand too (73; my emphasis).

When equipment obtrudes as mere items that can be brought under a variety of interpretations, we are on the way to regarding the world as a collection of objects—the present-at-hand (Vorhandene)—which can be made functional in different ways. This path, as we shall see, leads to grasping the world as a collection of substances with accidents.

When the context of significance is functioning smoothly, we are nonreflectively *absorbed* in the familiar world in which we find ourselves. The worldhood of that world is invisible. When the totality breaks down, however, worldhood can become momentarily visible—but only momentarily, since it is no longer a totality in the same sense. Only when the breakdown is complete does the possibility arise of seeing the world as "nature," that is, as an aggregate of externally related things. With the loss of practical reflection, the environment of our concern

> gets neutralized to pure dimensions. Places—and indeed the whole totality of places of ready-to-hand equipment oriented by our "know-how"—get reduced to a multiplicity of positions

for random *things*. . . . The world loses its specific around-ness; the environment becomes the world of *nature* (112; my emphasis).

From Heidegger's standpoint, the kind of wonder or awe that is supposed to be the origin of philosophy actually results from a collapse of everyday intelligibility, a breakdown that operates as a distorting lens on our ordinary sense of the world.

The account of the breakdown of a context provides us with a way of diagnosing the aura of obviousness and self-evidence which surrounds the objectifying conception of reality. Our ordinary prereflective understanding of the world is inexplicit to the extent that we see *through* the equipment to our goals and aims. The reflective contemplation of the collection of present-at-hand objects left by the disworlding of the world, on the other hand, is more explicit. Since entities are first explicitly *noticed* only after the collapse of the world, it seems self-evident that the world must have really consisted of brute objects all along. It is precisely this self-evidence that needs to be diagnosed and challenged if we are to overcome the distortions imposed on our thinking by the Cartesian model.

There are two serious objections which may be raised at this point to the description of Being-in-the-world as an alternative model of our plain situations. The first objection may be formulated as follows. Suppose we grant that the self should be regarded as bound up with a "world" in Heidegger's technical sense of the term. It may still be asked: Is this really so different from the Cartesian model? Indeed, we have done away with the *res cogitans* as a substance distinct from *res extensa*. But is there any reason why we can't regard this conception of Dasein as similar to the private world of a monad? If the relevance conditions that are ontologically definitive for entities are generated out of the self-understanding of a *particular* Dasein, what reason do we have to think that such private monadic worlds correspond to the real world? The holistic picture of self and world seems only to push the problem back a step. It is now no longer a question of whether the ideas of a thinking subject map onto the world; it becomes a question of whether the holistic structure revealed in the description of everydayness in fact represents the way things are in themselves, independent of the individual's articulation of the world in his practical affairs.

The second objection, which is closely related to the first, was clearly formulated by Husserl. In a manuscript entitled "das ist gegen Heidegger," Husserl writes,

The universal practical structure of the life-world [Leben-swelt], in its universality, is not primary for the theoretical man. His practical interests vary, and therewith what is significant; and significances also vary relative to the person. . . . Theoretical interest is concerned with what is; and that, everywhere, is what is identical through variation of subjects and their practical interests, i.e., the same things, the same relations, the same changes, etc., which are there in themselves, i.e., there for "everybody." [It is concerned] with the significances themselves only insofar as they are taken in their correlations; then anybody can verify (if he takes a theoretical attitude) that this thing here, counts for subject A as such and such a piece of equipment [Zeug], for B as quite a different one, that anything can be woven into equipmental contexts of many kinds, both for the same and for different subjects.[8]

The objection is a familiar one, raised against any position giving priority to internal relations:[9] it asks how we can account for the identification and re-identification of the relata of relations through changes of subject and interests. It seems that the possibility of re-identifying particulars must be dealt with in any description of our everyday practices; if this hiatus in Heidegger's account cannot be filled, then, we have good reasons for rejecting his description.

These objections lead to serious problems for Heidegger's model of Being-in-the-world only if his account is seen as portraying Being-in-the-world as the Being of isolated *individuals* with their own private worlds. In order to see how Heidegger's description of Dasein overcomes these objections, we must, first, expand the analysis to embrace his treatment of the "Anyone" (das Man) as the true "subject" of everydayness, and, second, discuss his conception of language as articulating a realm of shared intelligibility.

§8. Dasein as the "Anyone"

At the end of the discussion of worldhood in *Being and Time* it might appear that we are left with a picture of so many isolated

---

8. The transcription of this passage is found in the Louvain Archives, B. I 32 II, pp. 21ff. It is quoted in H. L. Dreyfus and John Haugeland, "Husserl and Heidegger: Philosophy's Last Stand," in M. Murray, ed., *Heidegger and Modern Philosophy* (New Haven: Yale, 1978), p. 233.

9. Cf. Ollman, pp. 256-262.

individuals constituting worlds out of their own self-understanding. Within the framework of such a picture, we would have no reason to think that these worlds are "public" in any sense. If *this* is Heidegger's achievement, one might say, then it does not seem to represent much of an advance over Cartesianism. But Heidegger does not leave the description of Being-in-the-world at this point. In the chapters of *Being and Time* that follow, we are led to see that the contexts of significance that mediate our self-interpretations are themselves embedded in a shared "we-world." The workshop in which I find myself can be disclosed as such only within an intelligible world that is essentially public.

Heidegger continues his description of everydayness by asking "*who* it is that Dasein is in its everydayness" (114). What emerges in the discussion that follows is not a portrayal of Dasein as an "individual" in any sense. Heidegger wants to develop a neutral conception of Dasein which, he says, is "*not* the egotistical particular, *not* the ontically isolated individual."[10] In the description of everyday Being-in-the-world, what emerges is a picture of Dasein which is closer to Dilthey's conception of "objective mind" than it is to the Cartesian subject or a monad. From this standpoint we see that the technical term 'Dasein' cannot be taken as shorthand for 'human being' as this term is generally used. There is no plural for 'Dasein', and Heidegger seldom speaks of "*a* Dasein." 'Dasein' is not a "count noun" that ranges over particular individuals, but is more like a "mass noun." It captures the idea of a "clearing" of intelligibility which can more properly be understood as a cultural totality than as a collection of individuals. On this view, instances of Dasein — which Heidegger refers to as "das jeweilige Dasein"[11] — are grasped as "crossing points" of cultural systems, as exemplifications of the "structural types" (in Dilthey's words) of the cultural world. Only when the objectifying tendency of individualism is circumvented can the Cartesian ontology be fully overcome.

Heidegger prepares the way for determining the "who" of Dasein's everydayness by noting that equipment not only is bound up in means/ends relations, but also points to users in a public world:

---

10. LL 172 (my emphasis).

11. 'Das jeweilige Dasein' is modeled on the German bureaucratic expression, 'der jeweilige Beamter' meaning "whoever happens to be holding the office at the time." This way of referring to a particular Dasein strengthens the conception of Dasein in everydayness as a mere office-holder and not a unique individual.

Any work with which one concerns oneself is ready-to-hand not only in the domestic world of the workshop but also in the *public world*. Along with the public world, the *environing nature* is discovered and is accessible to everyone. In roads, streets, bridges, buildings, our concern discovers nature as having some definite direction (71).

The natural world is already bound up into a totality directed toward shared interests and goals. The ready-to-hand equipment "speaks to us" of communal objectives in an intelligible world. What we find in this world points to others in the social context. The boat anchored at the shore is encountered as the possession of a friend. And even if it is a boat that is strange to us, Heidegger says, "it still points to others" (118).

What "essential structures" of Dasein make this shared intelligibility possible? Heidegger interprets the publicness of Dasein's understanding in terms of the existentialia of Being-with (Mitsein) and Dasein-with (Mitdasein).[12] These expressions point to the fact that Dasein can be "at home with" entities in the world only because at the deepest level it is in a "with-world" (Mitwelt) (118). To see why this is so, we must reflect on the fact that everyday Dasein is to be understood as factical agency and not as a contemplative subject ruminating over the contents of its own mind. Dasein, as concrete Being-in-the-world, always exists as a specific role "for the sake of which it is." The expression of Dasein's raw thrownness — "that it is and has [something] to be" — has always been given a concrete instantiation: to grasp Dasein as it is is to understand it *as* such-and-such — as a banker, dentist, waitress, truck driver. Since Dasein's essence lies in its existence and since existence is always worked out in the business of existing in the world, the *content* of Dasein's Being is fully contained in the concrete roles it takes over in being alive.

The discussion of Being-with is designed to lead us to see that the roles that define Dasein are essentially public, drawn from a set of pre-given possibilities made accessible in the social world. The fact that Dasein just is the roles it takes over in existing carries with it certain implications. Roles do not exist in isolation; they gain their definition and meaning from their relations to other roles. Just as I would not say that my child had understood a color word like 'red' unless she understood the relation of this word to other color

---

12. These technical terms are devised on the basis of an analogy with words like 'Mitarbeiter' (co-worker) in German. They could be translated 'co-Being' and 'co-Dasein'.

words, so we would not say of someone that he was truly a "liberal" unless he understood the relation of this interpretation to other possibilities such as being radical, moderate, conservative, or simply apolitical. Or, to refer back to an example used earlier, I can understand myself as "irreligious" only if I understand this possibility in relation to the possibilities of being pious, devout, and atheistic in the society in which I live.

It appears, then, that the possible roles Dasein can take over gain their meaning from a *field of contrasts* in which each role is seen as related to other roles within the social systems in which they are available as possibilities. To be Dasein in taking a stand involves a certain *competence* in getting along within the interrelated systems of one's culture. I take Heidegger's conception of Being-with or co-Being as referring to this kind of social competence. Being-with characterizes the Being of Dasein as essentially related to others in the field of meanings of the social world. Of course, the actual concrete systems determining these relations will depend on the type and level of the society at any time. In my society I can be a factory worker related to capitalists, but I cannot be a vassal at the service of a feudal lord or a slave owned by landed gentry. But Being-with is an *existentiale* to the extent that taking over a role always presupposes a mastery of *some* articulated structure of social systems that contain standards and norms for social interaction.

The social competence of Being-with also makes it possible to deal with equipment in the everyday world. We have seen that a context of equipment is always organized in terms of some goals and aims that articulate its relevance conditions. These goals and aims are in turn generated by the self-understanding of Dasein in some role or other. Therefore, our mastery of the social scale of possibilities of self-interpretation also makes possible our ability to handle equipment in standardized ways. To have social competence is to grasp the norms and conventions regulating the "correct" and "incorrect" use of equipment. We are attuned to one another in our dealings in the world because we are participants in the shared forms of life of our culture. We handle instruments as "anyone" does and we behave as "anyone" does because of our competence in social systems.

Heidegger says that Being-with is also the condition for the possibility of encountering what he calls the "Dasein-with" of others.

> Since the worldhood of that world, in which Dasein essentially is already, is thus constituted, it accordingly lets us encounter what is environmentally ready-to-hand as some-

thing with which we can be concerned in our know-how, and it does so in such a way that together with it we encounter the Dasein-with of others (123).

If Being-with is the mastery of shared norms and conventions for acting, 'Dasein-with' seems to refer to the way that Dasein manifests this competence in its actions. In taking over roles in its everyday activities, Dasein always *expresses itself* in publicly intelligible ways. Being-with embodies an immediate understanding of this expressiveness of others: "Being-with is such that the Dasein-with of others belongs to it" (123). When Heidegger says that "only so far as one's own Dasein has the essential structure of Being-with, is it Dasein-with as encounterable for others" (121), he seems to mean that our social competence displays itself in public expressions that are immediately intelligible to others through our shared participation in the common cultural world.

Dasein's essential expressiveness as Dasein-with manifests itself throughout the intelligible world. In its coherent activities and practices, Dasein manifests its social competence and grasp of common goals and interests. Through these expressions of human goal-directedness the world of everydayness is always already intelligible to us. The individual worlds of our personal involvements are therefore always interwoven into a shared we-world which is already more or less coherent and articulate. In this way Heidegger leads us to see that, in everydayness, we do not first encounter a realm of brute objects that are then miraculously endowed with functions. What we encounter is a world of expressions that are immediately grasped by us through our social competence.

To understand Being-in-the-world as essentially characterized by Being-with and Dasein-with has two important consequences. First, it seems that the traditional "problems of other minds" cannot get off the ground within the framework of this description. The problem gains its force from a picture of our relations to others as grounded in the identification of bits of behavior that can be made intelligible only if one can posit a private mental activity that is the source of the behavior. But for Heidegger this distinction between brute behavior and private meanings has no role to play. Dasein just *is* its meaningful expressions in the world. Heidegger says that "in that with which we concern ourselves environmentally the others are encountered as what they are; they *are* what they do" (126). In the context of everyday activities, there is no place for an elusive subjective domain distinct from Dasein's meaningful agency. When the distinction between inner and outer drops out, skepticism about other minds cannot find a foothold for insinuating its doubts. Dasein just is the roles it takes over in being for the sake of itself, and these roles just are what is manifested in Dasein's expressiveness.

Secondly, if others are their meaningful expressions in the world, it follows that, in everydayness, I also am nothing but my meaningful expressions. The question of who we are in everydayness is fully answered in terms of the public possibilities exemplified in our agency. In Dilthey's language, the self is a representative of social systems and a crossing point of the structural types built into the cultural world. This is why our lives can be thought of as commentaries on the public text of the shared social world: our actions become meaningful and human to the extent that they instantiate common interpretations of what it is to be human. By conceptualizing the self in this way, Heidegger carries through to its conclusion what was implicit in Dilthey's insight into the nature of life. When Dilthey's preoccupation with epistemology and psychology is abandoned, we find that being human cannot be thought of as being an individual or isolated monad *distinct from* the roles our agency exemplifies. On the contrary, the Being of Dasein is circumscribed by its *place* in a nexus of cultural interpretations—the "real me" shorn of its social bonds has no role to play. For this reason Heidegger says that the "who" of everydayness "is not this one, not that one, not oneself, not some people, and not the sum of them all. The 'who' is the neuter, *the Anyone* [das Man]" (126).

The conception of the everyday self which unfolds in *Being and Time* may be seen as closer to that found among the ancient Greeks than it is to our own modern picture. For the Greeks, to be human was to be a place-holder in the natural structure of the *oikos,* or, later, the *polis*. The most unhappy of all men in the times Homer describes was not the slave, but the free man (*thes*) who had no place in the world. Even for medieval Christianity, with its concerns about salvation, being human is most often conceived in terms of having a place in the hierarchical structure laid out in the divine plan. It was not until the cataclysmic events associated with the rise of modern science that the sharp modern distinction was drawn between the "persona" and the "true self" lying behind it.

What Heidegger is suggesting is that, although the modern objectifying concept of the self was an important cultural achievement, it does not provide us with a primordial portrayal of our everyday understanding of ourselves. The inward-turning tendency of introspection and self-reflection, which plays such an important role in modern thought, does not bring about the discovery of the real self so much as it tends to distort and conceal our most primordial everyday self-understanding. The dictum "Know thyself!" should not call for the stripping away of social masks to find a pure "I." True self-knowledge, on the contrary, is to be attained by looking away from the self-objectifying inwardness of modern thinking in order to recognize the self as a crossing point of cultural systems in the intelligible world.

> One's *own* Dasein becomes something that it can itself prox-imally "come across" only when it *looks away* from its "ex-periences" and the "center of its actions," or does not as yet "see" them at all. Dasein finds "itself" proximally in *what* it does, uses, expects, avoids — in those things environmentally ready-to-hand with which it is proximally *concerned* (119).

When Dasein's Being is understood as fully delineated by its social competence and expressions, then it is clear that "*knowing oneself* is grounded in Being-with which understands primordially" (124; my emphasis).

For this reason Heidegger says that "the 'subject' of every-dayness" is "the Anyone" (114). In the expressions of our social competence in dealing with the world, we handle tools and deal with others as "anyone" does. Since the structuring of roles and the criteria for operating in the world are applicable to anyone what-soever, I am not in any sense unique in my ordinary ways of Being.

> Proximally, it is not "I," in the sense of my own self, that "am," but rather the others, whose way is that of the Anyone. In terms of the Anyone and as the Anyone, I am "given" proximally to "myself" (129).

It follows, then, that my Being in everydayness is "representable" or "delegatable" (vertretbar) (126); because the self is nothing other than an exemplification of forms of life that are essentially public, *anyone* can fill in for me and take my place.

The source of the structures of significance that make up the world is therefore not the *res cogitans* or transcendental ego, but the public-in-general.

> The Anyone itself prescribes that way of interpreting the world and Being-in-the-world which lies closest. Dasein is for-the-sake-of the Anyone in an everyday manner, and *the Anyone itself articulates the referential context of significance* (129; my emphasis).

The Anyone is also the source of our pre-ontological understand-ing: "From the kind of Being of the Anyone," Heidegger writes, "everyday Dasein draws its pre-ontological way of interpreting its Being" (130). As we shall see, even the possibility of "authenticity," as Heidegger uses this term, is not to be equated with the traditional conception of transcending the social world to be true to a "real" self underlying one's masks and disguises. On the contrary, authenticity is a "mode" of being the Anyone:

> *Authentic Being-one's-Self* does not rest upon an exceptional condition of the subject, a condition that has been detached from the Anyone; *it is rather an existentiell modification of the Anyone—of the Anyone as an essential existentiale* (130).

The Anyone is an "existentiale," or essential structure of Dasein, not a condition that can be overcome. To be Dasein is essentially to be a nexus of the socially constituted relations of a culture. Since the Anyone defines Dasein as everyday Being-in-the-world, the structures that make up the formal characterization of Dasein become concrete and have a content only in Dasein's *being* the Anyone.

By interpreting Dasein as the Anyone, Heidegger's phenomenology of everydayness works to counteract the tendency toward the displacement of *meaning* into subjectivity which began with the rise of modern science. Dilthey had already taken the first steps toward relocating meaning into the world in his attempt to grasp the human life-world as "objective mind." For Dilthey, the world studied by the human sciences is a world that is already intelligible because it is shot through with meaning. But, to the extent that he still conceives of meaning as a product of something inner which is expressed in the outer world, Dilthey remains ensnared in Cartesian dualism. By regarding the self as nothing other than its meaningful expressions, Heidegger is able to fully break away from the Cartesian tradition. His conception of the intelligible world as a holistic field of meaningfulness undermines both the inclination to see reality as consisting solely of spatiotemporal particulars and the temptation to think of meanings and values as solely subjective. The world is seen as a *liber naturae* expressing the aims and interests of a culture.

If we are to understand the full import of Heidegger's conception of "meaning" (Sinn), then, we must avoid seeing it as referring to something inner in any sense. The concept of meaning is worked out in the analysis of the "existential structures of the disclosedness of Being-in-the-world" (166). Heidegger identifies three existentialia of what is called "Being-in as such": situatedness, understanding, and discursiveness (Rede). Situatedness and understanding correspond to the passive and active aspects of Dasein's formal determination. On the one hand, as situated, Dasein is disclosed as thrown into a definite range of pre-given, shared possibilities which determine how entities can matter to it. Dasein's situatedness is revealed by its "attunement" or "mood" (Stimmung) in everyday situations. As understanding, on the other hand, Dasein takes up the possibilities it discovers in its situatedness and projects itself onto some range of goals for its life as a whole. Since the possibilities we project are made possible by the social systems laid out in the public world, our stands are always attuned to one another in terms of a common background of intelligibility. The interpretations in which we appropriate and make explicit equipmental contexts always operate within a fore-structure of understanding that is essentially public.

Our understanding of equipmental contexts is itself grounded in the mastery of a more or less inchoate background of intelligibility which Heidegger calls "meaning." Meaning, he tells us, is that which makes possible that projection of possibilities in understanding (324). "Meaning is that wherein the understandability [Verständlichkeit] of something maintains itself" (151). It is clear, then, that with the concept of "meaning" Heidegger is trying to identify a source of intelligibility that lies at a level even deeper than that of the totalities of significance we appropriate in our interpretations. Whereas 'significance' refers to what as a matter of fact *has been* articulated in explicit interpretations, "meaning" embraces what "*can be* articulated in a disclosure by which we understand" (151; my emphasis).

What is the source of this most primordial level of intelligibility? Heidegger says that it is "discursiveness" or "talk" (Rede).

> What can be understood [Verständlichkeit] has always been articulated [gegliedert], even before there is any appropriate interpretation of it. Discursiveness or talk is the articulation [Artikulation] of what can be understood. Therefore it underlies both interpretation and assertion. That which can be articulated in interpretation, and thus even more primordially in discursiveness, is what we have called "meaning" (161).

The concepts of "discursiveness" and "meaning" are closely related, so to clarify one is at the same time to illuminate the other. I will concentrate first on Heidegger's use of the technical term 'Rede'.

The German word 'Rede' is quite properly translated as 'talk' or 'discourse', or even as 'speech' in constructions such as 'eine Rede halten' (to give a speech). Yet Heidegger seems to have something much deeper in mind in his use of this word. *"Rede,"* he says, is the "addressing and discussing of 'world' " (das Ansprechen und Besprechen von "Welt") (59), but this activity does not seem to consist solely in speech acts as these are ordinarily understood. The examples that Heidegger gives of "addressing and discussing" do not even seem to require any linguistic utterances: he mentions "concernfully reckoning up, planning, preventing or taking precautions" (406). Language *might* figure into such activities, but what is conveyed here is the notion of whole situations of involvement in the world rather than illocutionary acts. In fact, Heidegger tells us that "we must not overlook the fact that vocal utterance [stimmliche Verlautbarung] is not essential for *Rede"* (217).

A clue to what Heidegger intends with the use of the word 'Rede' is provided by his claim that 'Rede' is the "literal translation" of the Greek word 'logos' (32), which, he says, means "to make manifest" or "to let-something-be-seen" (offenbar machen, Sehenlassen) (32). In order to avoid begging questions, therefore, I propose in what follows to translate the term of art 'Rede' with the word 'logos'. This translation is justified in part by the fact that 'Rede' is etymologically derived from the Latin 'ratio' which, as Heidegger often points out, is the Latin interpretation of the Greek 'logos'.

The question is now relocated: we must determine how Heidegger understands the word 'logos'. This term is often discussed in the works that follow *Being and Time.* In the *Introduction to Metaphysics* (1935), 'logos' is defined as "collecting collectedness, the primal gathering principle."[13] The verb 'legein' connotes an ordering and ranking of things, a process of bringing the world into a coherent pattern. According to the late essay "*Logos* (Heraclitus, Fragment B 50)" (1951), 'legein' is "the letting-lie-before — which is gathered into itself — of that which comes together into presence."[14] A key idea in these works is that of the ordering and organization of entities into a cohering whole. In the *"Logos"* essay Heidegger says that the *logos* occurs as the *"hen panta,"* as "the essence of unification, which assembles everything in the totality of simple presencing."[15]

In the context of *Being and Time,* 'logos' seems to refer to the deepest level of articulation of a background of meaning which makes possible both our coordinated modes of projecting

13. IM 108, EM 98.

14. EGT 63, VA III 7.

15. EGT 70, VA III 16.

possibilities in understanding and our common ways of appropriating entities in interpretation. Insofar as Dasein is the Anyone, the Anyone must be understood as the source of *logos*. Heidegger's concept of *logos* might be compared to Dilthey's notion of the "objectivations of life" which organize a culture's understanding of Being into an articulated order of types in the public world. In the expressiveness of Dasein-with, Dasein lays out a field of meanings that manifest the shared aims, interests, and ideals of a culture. *Logos* appears in enduring texts, monuments, and natural settings, as well as in common practices, habitual responses, and fleeting gestures. To be acculturated into an intelligible life-world is to come to master the tacit understanding of Being embodied in these expressions.

Heidegger's conception of *legein* and *logos* might also be compared to Wittgenstein's notion of the "forms of life" that ground our shared understanding of one another. It includes the bedrock of regular practices, customs, and institutions that serve to organize the world into a comprehensible structure. The background of meaning articulated by *logos* guides and shapes our grasp of equipmental contexts and our projection of relevance conditions for the entities we encounter. Through *logos,* the world is focused and oriented in advance: in the shrines and memorials that surround us, in treasured documents and artifacts, and in the accepted, regular standards of conduct manifested in our culture's expressions—in all these the world speaks to us of appropriate ways of acting and dealing with things. In this cultural milieu, our expressions contribute to the focusing and orienting of the world. Through our activities in collecting, gathering, grouping, separating, and distinguishing, entities are released within a common scaffolding so that they can punctuate our lives in certain ways. In being acculturated into the framework of practices of the Anyone, we first find ourselves and *become human* as this is interpreted in our culture.

On the interpretation I am proposing, the concept of "meaning" would refer to the background of intelligibility that is articulated by *logos*. Like Dilthey's "objective mind," meaning seems to embrace the intelligible world which is "articulated into a structural order of types" through which others and human creations are immediately accessible as having some *point* for us. Meaning, Heidegger says, is that which *"can be* articulated" in our interpretations. Before any particular interpretation by an instance of Dasein, the world is already organized into constellations of meaning by *logos*. As commentaries on the text of the Anyone, we take over this background of meaning and work out our understanding of it in our interpretations of significance relations. To say that our lives are like commentaries on a text, then, is to say that all our actions are interpretations of the range of possibilities laid out by the Anyone. To the extent that our actions are always exemplifications or instantiations of common social structures, we differ from one another, as Dilthey says, only "quantitatively" and never "qualitatively."

If meaning is understood as something directly accessible in the intelligible life-world, then there is no longer any reason to think of it as inhering in an ontologically unclarified realm of Platonic forms or in the mental lives of people. Heidegger says that meaning is "not a property attaching to entities, lying 'behind' them, or floating somewhere as an 'intermediate domain' " (152). Instead, the background of meaning is something that is manifested everywhere in Dasein's expressions. This field of intelligibility sets up the guide rails along which Dasein's expressiveness as Dasein-with can make sense. A polite bow or a salute, for example, has a meaning because of its place against this public backdrop of meaning. In Heidegger's conception of the locus of meaning, there is no need to posit the existence of a mysterious realm of "intentional acts" that give meaning to our activities. Our meaningful expressions gain their significance not from a correlative inner state, but from the web of social systems and structures in which they appear. Anything — or nothing — can be going through a lieutenant's mind as he salutes a colonel while crossing a military base, yet this salute clearly has a meaning. The meaning of our expressions is determined not so much by our mental condition as it is by the way those expressions figure into the articulated framework of social structures generated by our everyday, customary ways of doing things.

It seems, then, that although we are individually responsible for the *configuration* of meanings our lives have as Being-toward-death, the *content* of our lives — the pre-given range of possibilities we take up — is always something essentially public and shared. My ability to take over a role and deal with equipment is always made possible by the norms and conventions embodied in the objectivations of life laid out by *logos*. To be human is to have mastered the range of possibilities embodied in the background meaning of one's culture and to have taken some stand on those possibilities.

We may now see how Heidegger can reply to the second objection raised at the end of the last section. We saw that Husserl criticized Heidegger's account of the ontological determination of an entity as its place in a practical context on the grounds that the functions of entities may vary relative to the interests of an agent. From a theoretical standpoint, what concerns us is what is "identical through variation of subjects and their practical interests." The problem Husserl raises is that of accounting for the identification and re-identification of entities through shifts of subjects and interests.

It is now apparent how Heidegger's conception of the shared meaning laid out by *logos* can explain the possibility of uniformity and continuity in our interpretations without recourse to uninterpreted objects. It is the background articulation of the world into coherent structures that guides our interpretations and grounds our harmonious ways of encountering entities in equipmental contexts. On this view, the fact that I can turn a screw with a chisel but not with a mallet, or the fact that I can use a hammer as a paperweight but not as a paint brush, is not grounded in some objective properties of the chisel or hammer as things-in-themselves outside all interpretations. It is based rather on the fact that my interpretations are always *in terms of* a mastery of public ways of interpreting things. The shared world of intelligibility — a world which, as we shall see, is ultimately found to be maintained in language — "controls and distributes the possibilities of average understanding and of the situatedness belonging to it" (167/8).

What should be kept in mind in considering Husserl's objection is not that changes or differences in practical interests are impossible, but that they take place only against the broad background of agreement in judgments growing out of our socialization into the shared forms of life of our culture. The meaning articulated by *logos* and grasped tacitly in the fore-structure of understanding makes possible our orderly ways of taking the public world. The attunement in our common identifications and re-identifications is possible not because we have access to the Being-in-itself of objects discovered in pure intuition, but because we participate in forms of life that are essentially public. In Heidegger's description of everydayness there is no need for a collection of brute, placeless, uninterpreted things to lay the foundation for the objectivity of our ways of taking the world. Since what an entity is is determined by its place in the practices of the Anyone, even the "brute objects" discovered by Husserl's "theoretical man" are contextualized in a framework of interests and goals of the public world and can therefore have no absolute existence independent of those interests.

§9. *Two Views of Language*

When the concept "Dasein" is understood as embracing not individuals but the Anyone, the existentialia of Being-in must be given an appropriate reading as structures of the social context itself. For this reason I have interpreted *logos* as the cultural articulation of norms and standards by Dasein as the Anyone, and "meaning" as the background of intelligibility that determines how things are to count or matter for a culture. The background of shared meaning makes it possible for exemplifications of Dasein to exist as commentaries on the public text of the world. There is continuity in our interpretive appropriations of equipmental contexts because we are participants in the shared forms of life of our culture. Since *logos* is the publicly accessible realm of expressions of the intelligible world, Heidegger says that "Dasein in general" *is logos* (349).

For Heidegger, the public world of expressions articulated in *logos* receives its fullest concretion in language.

> If *logos*, as the articulation of the understandability of the "there," is a primordial existentiale of disclosedness, and if disclosedness is primarily constituted by Being-in-the-world, then *logos* too must essentially have a kind of Being which is specifically *worldly*. The situated understandability of Being-in-the-world *speaks itself out as logos.* . . . The way in which *logos* is spoken out is language (161).

Heidegger says that the background of meaning is articulated into a field of "significations" (Bedeutungen) and that this totality-of-significations finds its most intelligible expression in words: "To significations, words [Worte] accrue" (161). In using the German word 'Worte', he emphasizes the fact that he is referring not to separate lexical items or vocables (Wörter), but to phrases and expressions as *used* in language. The totality-of-words that is language has a " 'worldly' Being" that can be encountered as equipment: "as an entity within-the-world, this totality thus becomes something which we may come across as ready-to-hand" (161). Only when our everyday encounter with words in use has broken down can we come to encounter language as a mere set of lexical entries and rules: "Language can be broken up into word-things [Wörterdinge] which are present-at-hand" (161). Heidegger therefore gives priority to the role of language taken not as "ergon," but as "energeia"[16] — that is, language in use in speech acts such as "assenting or refusing, as demanding or warning, as pronouncing, consulting or interceding, as 'making assertions,' and as talking in the way of 'giving a talk' [Redenhalten]" (161). That Heidegger recognizes the importance of language as a medium of shared intelligibility is clear in *Being and Time*. What is

---

16. This distinction comes from Wilhelm von Humboldt.

not clear in this early work is how he conceives of the *nature* of language. He concludes his brief discussion of *logos* and language with a question about "the kind of Being [that] goes with language in general": "Is it a kind of equipment ready-to-hand within-the-world, or has it Dasein's kind of Being, or is it neither of these?" (166). Unable to answer this question, he concludes that

> philosophical research will have to dispense with the "philosophy of language" if it is to inquire into the "things themselves" and attain the status of a problematic which has been cleared up conceptually (166).

But this attempt to sweep the problem under the rug seems disingenuous given the over-all point of view in *Being and Time*. For a key part of Heidegger's break with Husserl consists in the fact that, unlike his teacher, he leaves no room for anything like an unmediated encounter with things themselves. Our access to things, for Heidegger, is always mediated through a world that is shaped in advance by a mesh of cultural and historical interpretations, and these interpretations may very well turn out to be linguistically articulated.

At the time of the composition of *Being and Time,* it seems that Heidegger was torn between two incompatible views of the nature of language. In order to identify this uncertainty about language, we may draw a rough distinction between two conceptions of the nature of language which have appeared in history. The first may be called an *instrumentalist* view. On this kind of model, language is regarded as a sort of *tool* — one type of equipment among others which contributes toward making up the intelligible world. An instrumentalist view of this sort seems to be found in Dilthey. In his mature writings, Dilthey recognized the importance of language but still saw it only as an instrument for maximizing intelligibility. Although he says that in language alone life finds "its complete, exhaustive and, therefore, objectively comprehensible expression,"[17] he nevertheless seems to hold that the expressions of objective mind are intelligible in themselves, so that language is only an accessory in enhancing this intelligibility.[18]

From the instrumentalist's standpoint, our ability to use language is grounded in some prior grasp of the *nonsemantic significance* of the contexts in which we find ourselves. It is only because we have first understood the nature of reality that we can then come to comprehend the meanings of words. Language is seen

17. WD 228, *Aufbau* 267.

18. See the quote above, section 4, p. 51.

as a tool for communicating and ordering this prior grasp of reality. Although language may play a very important role in making the world intelligible, it is itself possible only against the background of an understanding that is *non*linguistic.

There is clear evidence in *Being and Time* that Heidegger was inclined to adopt such an instrumentalist view of language. The picture of words "accruing" to "significations" suggests that there is a prior grasp of the nonsemantic field of significance of the world which becomes the basis for gaining mastery over a language. Heidegger says that "*logos* for the most part speaks itself out as language" (349), but there is no reason to think that the realm of significations that comes to expression in language is necessarily bound up with language in any way. There is clearly the intimation that there could be a fully articulated sense of the world derived from our ordinary participation in contexts of significance prior to or independent of the mastery of a language.

The second conception of language might be called a *constitutive* view, a type of position which can be found in Wittgenstein's *Philosophical Investigations*. It pictures language not so much as a tool on hand for our use as a *medium* in which man dwells. On the constitutive view, language generates and first makes possible our full-blown sense of the world. The constitutivist maintains that the mastery of the field of significance of a *world* (as opposed to, say, an animal's dexterity in its natural environment) presupposes some prior mastery of the articulate structure of a language. The idea that one can first have a coherent and fully worked-out grasp of a totality-of-significations onto which a totality-of-words is later mapped is on this view incoherent. Instead, words and world are seen as interwoven in such a way that to enter into one is simultaneously to master the other. In Wittgenstein's metaphor, "Light dawns gradually over the whole."[19] Here there is no way to identify a nonsemantic field of meaning which can be grasped independently of the language that serves to constitute it.

There are also suggestions in *Being and Time* that Heidegger was moving toward this kind of constitutive view of language — a view clearly found in his later writings. The passages that support the contention that there is a constitutive view to be found in *Being and Time* occur for the most part not in the section dealing with language, but in the discussion of "idle talk" or "chatter" (Gerede). In these passages Heidegger suggests that language is more than one kind of equipment at our disposal for dealing with the world. Whereas the ready-to-hand is ontologically defined by its place in a

---

19. *On Certainty* (New York: Harper, 1972), p. 21.

total context, language plays the role of *generating* those contexts of activity and making possible the fact that there are such contexts at all. Heidegger says that language constitutes both the understanding and situatedness of everydayness, and lays out the possibilities of grasping the world and others:

> Proximally, and within certain limits, Dasein is constantly delivered over to this interpretedness [of the public language] which controls and distributes the possibilities of average understanding and the situatedness belonging to it. [Language], within its organized and articulated contexts of signification, preserves an understanding of the disclosed world, an understanding of the Dasein-with of others and of one's own Being-in (167/8).

Language on this view inhabits our lives and shapes the situations in which we find ourselves. Far from seeing language as something that Dasein as the Anyone merely has on hand, Heidegger says that the Anyone is *constituted* by language: "The Anyone is constituted by the way things have been publicly interpreted, which speaks itself out as idle talk" (252).

Heidegger also suggests that the articulation of intelligibility embedded in our public language extends across all dimensions of Dasein's Being: it prescribes the way our situatedness is to be taken, it organizes the world of our current concerns, and it dictates the ways that our possibilities can be projected in understanding. The linguistic structuring of our world, he says,

> pertains just as much to any traditional discoveredness of entities which may have been reached, as it does to one's current understanding of Being, and to whatever possibilities and horizons for fresh interpretation and conceptual articulation may be available (168).

Our ability to cope with the world is founded on our mastery of the schematizations that are "deposited" (168) in language: as Heidegger says, "language already hides in itself a developed way of conceiving" (157).

The prior articulation of the world in language is so all-encompassing that there is no exit from the maze of language. We can never encounter a world as it is in itself, untouched by the constituting activity of linguistic schematizations.

This everyday way in which things have been interpreted [in idle talk] is one into which Dasein has grown up in the first instance, *with never a possibility of extricating itself.* In it, from it, and against it, all genuine understanding, interpreting and communicating, all re-discovering and appropriating anew, are performed. *In no case is a Dasein, untouched and unseduced by this way in which things have been interpreted, set before the open country of a "world-in-itself" so that it just beholds what it encounters* (169; my emphasis).

On this constitutive view, then, the language in which we find ourselves generates the template through which we come to understand ourselves and the world. What is given most primordially is a "we-consciousness" of attunement and agreement in judgments which is made accessible in the public language.

The plausibility of the constitutive view of language may be brought to light by considering the weaknesses of the instrumentalist view. If the instrumentalist were maintaining only that a necessary condition for learning a language is that one develop certain skills and capacities in the process of one's acculturation, then there would be nothing wrong with the view. It seems clear that language learning is possible only for entities that are capable of orderly activity in the world. But, in fact, it seems that instrumentalists — and particularly proponents of the kind of view suggested by Heidegger's notion of a totality-of-significations to which "words accrue" — want to say more than this. The idea they put forward is that the individual *first* masters a wide range of nonsemantic meanings and *then* learns to associate words with these significations. The mastery of an intelligible world is taken to be prior to the learning of a language.

As Wittgenstein and the later Heidegger have shown us, however, this kind of position seems to be untenable. For although it is true that language can be learned only by an entity that is brought up within the social world, it does not seem to be possible to develop a fully articulated sense of the meanings embodied in that social world without *first* having mastered, to some extent at least, the *linguistic* structuring of that world. The ability to grasp the fields of contrast between different meanings and to engage in evaluations of these meanings requires that one first have acquired an understanding of the kind of "multiplicity" (to use Wittgenstein's term) that is contained in the grammatical structure of the world. The articulated background of meaning can fully enter into our lives as a source of intelligibility only if it does so in a form that is stamped by the articulations made accessible in language.

To express the same point in different terms, there is an *internal* connection between the forms of life articulated in *logos* and the linguistic articulations that these forms of life are supposed to ground. The connection is internal because there is no way to discover or encounter *significations* in the social world (in Heidegger's technical sense of this term) without making use of the grammar of the language that is supposed to be explained by these significations. Social "facts" about what a culture takes as important can serve as a basis for language only if they are encountered by us *as* facts of such and such a type. But the ability to pick out and identify the *relevant* facts about the world presupposes some prior mastery of the grammatical multiplicity of a language. Without this capacity for articulation there would be no capacity for evaluating the role the facts are supposed to play and, hence, no foundation for articulating the facts *as relevant*.

Wittgenstein makes a similar point about the foundations of mathematics. On the one hand, he wants to say that mathematics is based on certain very common and generally unnoticed facts of our human natural history. But at the same time Wittgenstein notes that in order for us to encounter these facts as mathematical facts (as opposed to, say, religious facts), there must already be some prior mastery of the system of mathematics. "But what things are facts?" Wittgenstein asks:

> Do you believe you can show what fact is meant by, e.g., pointing to it with your finger? Does that of itself clarify the part played by "establishing" a fact? — Suppose it takes mathematics [or, one could add, grammar, or our public understanding of what is to be] to define the *character* of what you are calling a "fact!"[20]

Similarly, human expressions in the intelligible world can "speak to us" of goals, interests, and needs only if we have mastered some part of the language in which we can articulate the expressions *as* expressions of a certain sort. If the background of meanings were utterly ineffable, we would never be able even to gain a foothold for discerning and discovering the shared human interests they embody.

The instrumentalist view also seems to assume that one can become an *agent* in the world, in the full-blown sense that characterizes Dasein in everydayness, solely on the basis of one's

20. *Remarks on the Foundations of Mathematics* (Cambridge, Mass.: M.I.T., 1967), p. 173.

grasp of the nonlinguistic background of meaning. But if Dasein as agency is characterized in terms of self-interpretations and self-evaluations drawn from the public pool of meanings, then it is not at all clear that it can engage in actions of the highly structured sort that Heidegger describes without having first mastered the public vocabularies of interpretation and evaluation. What makes us *agents* (in the full human sense of this word) is the ability not only to opt for whatever alternative seems to offer the most full and immediate gratification, but also to weigh and evaluate possible courses of action against an enduring sense of what it is to be human. This seems to be implied in Heidegger's definition of Dasein as the entity for which, "in its very Being, its Being is *at issue* for it" (12).[21] The capacity for deep evaluations seems to presuppose a mastery of the vocabulary in which we judge our acts as "courageous" or "cowardly," as "trustworthy" or "irresponsible," or as "humane" or "cruel."

Even our unreflective acts, to the extent that they are human actions, seem to presuppose some linguistic skills. For it seems to be part of our concept of "human action" that behavior counts for us as an action (as opposed to nervous tics, accidental slips, and habitual reactions) only insofar as we can, in principle at least, attribute to the agent a privileged description of a state of affairs the action was intended to bring about. For a large range of specifically human actions, we must understand the agent's behavior as displaying a degree of complexity or "multiplicity" that can be accounted for only in terms of the ability to make explicit his goals, beliefs, and general grasp of the situation in which he finds himself. And this in turn requires that we understand the agent as having mastered a language in which such a description can be made, a language that is essentially public. We are attuned to one another in the world—we are "traveling in the same circles"—only because we participate in a common linguistic background of understanding which shapes our actions.

It is true of course that ordinary activities like riding a bicycle or playing a musical instrument do not require a step-by-step internal monologue. Indeed, such activities would probably be impossible if one attempted a *sotto voce* commentary of this sort. But these activities are shot through with a linguistic component to this extent: actually undertaking to act, as opposed to mere skillful performance, can take place only against the background of a capacity to

21. This interpretation of Heidegger's conception of action has been developed by Charles Taylor in "The Self in Question," published in part as "Responsibility for Self" in Amélie O. Rorty, ed., *The Identities of Persons* (Berkeley: Univ. of California, 1976).

distinguish right and wrong, to reflect on alternatives, and to make explicit to oneself what one is doing and how one is doing. I ride a bicycle because I want to save energy, and I want this because I interpret myself as someone who is concerned about the future resources of the earth. I am riding instead of walking because I am in a hurry, and I interpret myself as someone who is punctual. Even if none of this has ever been explicitly in my thoughts, the *capacity* for this degree of articulation in my activities is a condition for my behavior being "action" in the sense of the word that characterizes everydayness. The difference between an infant's random bobbing and nodding and an adult's polite bow is that the bow presupposes some grasp of the rank and status relations holding between people. And such a comprehension of rank and status presupposes some minimal ability to articulate those relations in language.

Although animals and prelinguistic infants can busy themselves with tools, the complexity of the full human capacity for undertaking to act is impossible for them. Their activities do not participate in *our* "world"—where this term is used in a Heideggerian sense that implies a weave of contrasts among more or less explicitly formulated self-interpretations and evaluations. Animals and infants have not mastered the articulate structure of roles and goals—of norms, standards, and conventions—that make up our involvement in the human world. If this is the case, however, then we should also recognize that there are limits to the degree to which we can ascribe our peculiarly human mental language to nonlinguistic and prelinguistic creatures. If a concept gains its meaning from contexts of use in which it can be employed with a certain degree of grammatical multiplicity and if the concept is then extended to cases where there could be no such multiplicity, then it might be less misleading to understand this extended use as secondary, privative, or derivative. [22]

It would be foolish to deny that infants and animals feel fear or anger. But when I say of an ordinary adult that he is angry, I mean to imply that he could ascribe this term to himself, that he could correct me by saying, "It is not so much anger as frustration," that he could contrast his feelings with his former good mood, and that he could bring about changes in his feelings by attempting to characterize them. He can also articulate to himself in detail what

---

22. Wittgenstein suggests that if children of a primitive tribe played with toy trains, the game would "not make the same *sense*" (Sinn) to them as it does to children who have some knowledge of trains (*Philosophical Investigations* 282). Similarly, our language-games of the mental might not have the same *sense* when ascribed to animals or to inanimate things.

he is angry *about:* he can be angry *that* someone who could have come did not come, and so forth. In speaking of language users, we can ascribe to them the uses of terms like 'afraid' or 'angry' with grammatical objects that are propositional clauses ('afraid that . . .', 'angry that . . .') and there is no reason in principle why we cannot allow for unlimited iteration within these "that" clauses. When we speak of nonlinguistic creatures, our concepts do not obviously have this kind of grammatical multiplicity. The ascription is privative in the way that saying, "This tight screw does not *want* to come out," is privative. If we allow that a term like 'want' can vary in sense in this way, then we can say that an animal can no more "want" things in the ways we want them than a screw can "want" things.

It is perhaps for this reason that Heidegger says that biological creatures other than humans must be understood by way of a "privative interpretation" (50) and that the question of " 'living' . . . can be tackled only reductively and privatively in terms of the ontology of Dasein" (194). We have to acknowledge the sentience and capacity for activity of animals and infants. But this does not imply that they are capable of participating in our human "world." Animals can interact with the natural environment, but they cannot take over human roles and experience things with a capacity for self-evaluation as humans do. Their natural environments are interpreted through *our* world, and it is part of the grammar shaping our world that the same predicates we use in describing ourselves are also used for them. But their interactions with the environment cannot be understood as Being-in-the-world in Heidegger's sense of this term, since this is possible only where there is mastery of language.

The constitutive view of language avoids the puzzles in the instrumentalist view by working from the assumption that language is *necessarily* connected to "understanding" in the full human sense of this word. The centers of meaningfulness in the social world are grasped in the process of learning a language — not before. Only when a child has gained some mastery of the vocabulary that relates entities to human purposes — words that function like 'in order to', 'for which', 'for the sake of', 'by means of', and 'in doing which' — only then are we in a position to ascribe the agency of Being-in-the-world to the child. And only to the extent that we can grasp behavior as agency in this human sense can we say that the child is *in* a world. For this reason, Hans-Georg Gadamer, who starts from Heidegger's later thoughts about language, says that

language is not just part of the equipment with which men

who are in a world are outfitted; rather, it depends on language and is brought forth in language that humans have a world at all.[23]

We do not first disclose a totality-of-significations in the world and then go on to map language onto it. But neither is it the case that we first discover "names" and then find appropriate objects for them. Language and world are disclosed together. There is no way to separate the understanding of social significance and the language in which it is embedded.

If language constitutes the equipment we encounter in our ordinary dealings in the world, it is also the source of the possible *self*-interpretations that agents can have in the world. To understand the context of a workshop, for instance, is to understand what this network of equipment is *for* within the customs and practices of one's society as these have been laid out in the public language. But to understand what the context is for is also to understand the range of goals and purposes that structure the equipment. These goals and purposes are as much a part of what is articulated in the public language as the equipment itself is. However, since as everyday agency I *am* nothing other than my self-interpretations within the contexts in which I find myself, my Being in everydayness is constituted by the public language. The field of contrasting roles in which I find myself and become what I am is rooted in the semantic contrasts of my language. I discover myself as an "amateur" or "craftsman," as a "liberal" or a "conservative," as "frugal" or "generous," precisely because in my social competence as Being-with I understand the way that these and similar vocabularies of self-interpretation and self-evaluation serve to order fields of significance in terms of common ideals, values, and interests. To say that the "who" of everydayness is the Anyone, on the constitutive view of language, is therefore to say that the self is discovered in the public ways of interpreting laid out in language.

For Heidegger, Dasein's everyday pre-ontological understanding and its thrownness are constituted by language. Since the text-analogue of the social world is essentially linguistic and since our lives as commentaries on this text are guided by the linguistic structuring of the text, human existence is possible only within language. In the constitutive view, language is seen as inhabiting and shaping our lives—as a medium in which we can first *become* Dasein. For this reason Heidegger in his last works often says that we do not speak language, but rather that "language speaks us." "Language is

---

23. *Wahrheit und Methode* (Tübingen: Mohr, 1965), p. 419 (my translation).

not a work of human beings: language speaks. Humans speak only insofar as they co-respond to language."[24] We first *find ourselves* as humans within the field of meanings articulated by the public language. The picture of the isolated subject wielding words to convey information or gathering data to subsume under concepts has no role to play except in the limited, derivative cases in which our ordinary participation in language breaks down.

Although the constitutive view of language is not worked out in detail in *Being and Time,* we can find clues that Heidegger was struggling with these ideas at an early date. As early as the winter semester of 1925/6 Heidegger told his students that language is that "in which the understanding of Dasein, so to speak, grows up and is existentially."[25] But it is also clear that Heidegger had not yet developed a full constitutive view. In his own handwritten notes in the margins of his copy of *Being and Time,* next to a discussion of the relation between "significations" and "significance" (on page 87), Heidegger later wrote: "Language is not built up, but rather *is* the primordial essence of truth as there."[26]

The constitutive view of language first comes to play a central role in the later writings. In the *Introduction to Metaphysics* of 1935, for instance, Heidegger says,

> Words and language are not wrappers in which things are packed for the intercourse of talking and writing. It is in words and language that things first come into being and are (IM 11, EM 11).

In "The Origin of the Work of Art," also of 1935, the priority of language in determining our sense of what it is to be is expressed as follows:

> Language is not only and not primarily an audible and written expression of what is to be communicated. . . . Language alone brings entities as entities into the Open for the first time. . . . Language, by naming entities for the first time, brings them to word and to appearance (PLT 73, HW 60/1).

---

24. PT 25, PuT 41.

25. LFW 151.

26. Heidegger's marginal notes are found in the *Gesamtausgabe* edition of *Sein und Zeit,* vol. II, (Frankfurt a.m.: Klostermann, 1977), p. 117.

And in Heidegger's later essay, "On the Nature of Language" (1957/8), the constitutive view receives its sharpest formulation:

> Only where the word for the thing has been found is the thing a thing.Only thus *is* it. . . . The word alone gives Being to the thing. . . . The Being of anything that is resides in the word.[27]

To summarize the discussion in the last two sections: we started by noting that Dasein as Being-in-the-world is not an objectified subject, but is instead essentially the Anyone as a positive existentiale of Dasein's Being. Seen as Being-with and Dasein-with, Dasein interprets the world in terms of the public background of meaning which has been laid out in advance by the *logos* of customs and practices of the culture. This has the consequence that the Being of Dasein must be understood as essentially contextualized: there is no way to pick out a substantial subject distinct from its place in the system of relations of a culture. Finally, we traced the way that this background of intelligibility is embodied in the language use of a culture. Consequently the Being of Dasein is seen to be contextualized in the additional sense of being structured by a public language.

Although Heidegger, in *Being and Time,* seems uncertain whether to adopt a constitutive or instrumentalist view of language, I believe that the constitutive view is more consistent with his overall thought, and I will therefore emphasize that view in the interpretations that follow. Regarding the linguistic ordering of the world as primary in Heidegger's thought has three important consequences. First, in the constitutive view we can see language as the medium in which shared intelligibility is maintained. The objectivations of life in the public world "speak to us" in an intelligible way because we *hear* them through our shared mastery of linguistic structures which are essentially public. There is no need to speak of an ontologically unclarified realm of significations which is to be grasped prelinguistically. In fact, the constitutive view seems to dissolve the distinctions between *logos* and language and between significations and the words that "accrue" to them.

Secondly, the constitutive view of language might help to clarify why the world of everydayness must be regarded as a network of internal relations. Heidegger's phenomenological description of

27. OWL 62, 63; US 164, 166. It should not be assumed that all these quotes represent a single theory about language. Heidegger's conception of language constantly evolved through his later writings, though the priority of the constitutive role remained in the center of his thoughts.

everydayness leads us to see that the most primordial description of the world is irreducibly intensional. To say that a proposition is "intensional" (with an "s") is to say that it is true only under specific descriptions of the entities it is about. One test of intensionality is to determine whether the proposition remains true when alternative descriptions of the same entity are substituted in the context. For instance, "John believes that Ronald Reagan is a liar" may be true, but "John believes that the President of the United States is a liar" may be false (e.g., if John has not seen a newspaper in the last five years). Thus, a description of a person's belief is true only relative to that person's way of identifying the entities he has beliefs about.[28]

In a similar way, Heidegger's description of the everyday world as a teleological whole is "intensional." Within the framework of this description, entities are identified as falling into the contexts of intentions, goals, and purposes of agents. The Being of entities — their "ontological definition" — can be specified only in a language that consists of terms like 'for the sake of', 'in order to', 'by means of', and 'for which'. The sentences of this "intentional" language (the language that expresses our goals and aims in acting) are "intensional" insofar as they are true only under specific descriptions of the entities they concern. If it is true of me that "I am picking mushrooms *in order to* feed my family" and if it is also true, unbeknownst to me, that "the mushrooms I am picking are poisonous," it does not follow that "I am picking poisonous mushrooms *in order to* feed my family." In general, the descriptions of our agency are true of us only relative to specific ways of identifying the entities we are dealing with.

If the most primordial description of the world is framed in an intentional language and if such a language is inescapably intensional, then this has important implications for the so-called "thesis of extensionality." This thesis claims, roughly, (1) that there is an ideal formal language, with a canonical form modeled on standard first-order predicate calculi, all of whose contexts are extensional, and (2) that all true knowledge about the world can be expressed in this formalized language. The purpose of such an ideal language is to provide us with a uniform conceptual net by means of which we can map all regions of reality. It assumes that there will be some sort of isomorphism or homeomorphism between the nonlogical

---

28. In Quine's language, belief contexts are "referentially opaque": there is no "substitution *salva veritate*" in these contexts. See *Word and Object* (Cambridge, Mass.: M.I.T., 1960), §35.

primitive terms in the theoretical matrix and the aggregate of *externally related* basic particulars that make up reality. In other words, it presupposes an objectifying ontology.

If the most fundamental description of reality is irreducibly intensional, however, then this ideal of formalization cannot be sustained. The world that is constituted by our everyday language of intentions and goals is one in which entities are *ontologically defined* by their internal relations to other entities within the context of interests and goals projected by agents. But, given a world constituted in this way, there is no longer any reason to think that the world must ultimately consist of externally related basic particulars or primary substances. Since the Being of any entity is fully defined by its actual place in a network of relations generated by our goals and practices, the practical world is most primordially to be regarded as a mesh of internal relations. As we shall see in the next chapter, Heidegger regards the "objective world" studied by the natural sciences as derivative from and parasitic on the more fundamental teleological world of everydayness. If this is the case, however, then it appears that an extensional language lacks the resources to fully characterize our practical life-world.

On the constitutive view of language, it is the "grammar" of our intentional language that determines the *essence* or *Being* of the entities found in that world. As Heidegger says, "Essence and Being express themselves in language."[29] The point Heidegger is making here seems similar to what Wittgenstein has in mind when he says, "*Essence* is expressed in grammar," and "Grammar tells us what kind of an object anything is."[30] What Wittgenstein is rebelling against is the uncritical assumption that wherever there is a noun — be it 'chair', 'mind', 'pain', or 'number' — there must be some sort of *object* to which it refers. To counteract this tendency, Wittgenstein suggests that we understand both the meaning of words and the essence of objects as inseparable from our ways of speaking in ordinary language-games. Similarly, Heidegger is trying to lead us away from the unwarranted assumption that all there really is in the world is a homogeneous collection of externally related objects. If the correlate of the traditional concept of essence is seen as lying in the grammatical structuring of our linguistic practices, then our intentional language of everydayness should reveal that the essence of equipment is to be understood in terms of internal relations.

29. IM 44, EM 41.

30. *Philosophical Investigations,* §§371, 373 (my translation).

The fact that the Being of an entity is determined by the grammatical multiplicity of our language leads us to the third consequence of the constitutive view of language. I noted in section 4 that the most common objection to a philosophy of internal relations is that relations are internal only under certain *descriptions* of that entity. It is argued that the thesis of internal relations involves a confusion of reading the properties of language into things in the world. But it is clear that on the constitutive view such an objection can no longer arise. For if the Being of entities is constituted by our intentional language and if that language is intensional in the sense that its sentences are true only under certain descriptions of entities, then there is no longer any way to make a clear distinction between our descriptions of things and the way those things are in themselves, independent of our ways of talking about them. Word and world interpenetrate. Our shared intentional language discloses a teleological and holistic intelligible world in which present-at-hand objects simply have no role to play.

In interpreting Heidegger in such a way as to bring the constitutive view of language to prominence, I have emphasized the passages in which Heidegger develops what he calls the "positive" functions of the Anyone and of language in idle talk. In doing so, however, I have left to one side Heidegger's more notorious treatment of the "negative" function of the Anyone. In fact, it seems that Heidegger has an extremely ambivalent attitude toward the Anyone and idle talk. On the one hand, these are "positive" structures that make possible Dasein's Being-in-the-world: the Anyone is said to be a positive existentiale of Dasein, for instance, and Heidegger says that to refer to everyday language as "idle talk" has no " 'disparaging' signification" since " 'idle talk' signifies a *positive* phenomenon" (167; my emphasis). On the other hand, however, Heidegger also speaks of the "dictatorship of the Anyone" (126) that "levels down" (einebnen) the possibilities of Dasein's Being (127). Although "the dominance of the public way in which things have been interpreted" in idle talk *opens* the possibilities of Dasein's Being, it also "cuts off" Dasein's "primary and primordially genuine relationships-of-Being toward the world, toward Dasein-with, and toward its very Being-in" (170).

This ambivalence leads to a deep and pervasive tension in *Being and Time*. Although Heidegger recognizes the constructive role of language and culture in opening possibilities, he also tends to see them as pernicious, closing off the possibilities of authentic Being. As a result, the *logos* of authenticity is defined in terms of its "essential possibilities" of "silence" (Schweigen) and "reticence" (Verschwiegenheit) (164/5), and idle talk is taken as a characteristic of inauthenticity. This tension is probably also at the root of Heidegger's uncertainty about the constitutive and instrumentalist views of language. For if language always "amounts to a perverting of the act of disclosing into a closing off" (169), then one will tend to see language as a kind of equipment that can be laid aside in order to gain primordial access to the "things themselves."

One way to resolve this conflict would be to distinguish between a direct, prelinguistic encounter with the world and an inauthentic encounter mediated by linguistic schematizations. The claim that Heidegger intended to resolve the tension in this way receives ample support from the text. Heidegger speaks of a "prepredicative understanding" of the ready-to-hand (359), and says that interpretation is most primordially achieved "without wasting words" (157). He also tells us that our relationship to a hammer is "more primordial" in hammering than in mere seeing: "the less we just stare at the hammer-thing, and the more we seize hold of it and use it, the *more primordial* does our relationship to it become" (69; my emphasis). Achieving phenomenological access, Heidegger says, is possible only by "thrusting aside our interpretive tendencies" (67). These tendencies, we may assume, lie in the schematizations and categories of our public language. Finally, Heidegger asserts that understanding cannot be achieved through "merely verbal significations" (94) or through "mere knowledge of words" (5). For this reason he strives to avoid all "uninhibited word-mysticism" (220) in seeking primordial sources.

It is clear in *Being and Time* that Heidegger is trying to capture a level of encountering the world which is deeper than the level of explicitly formulating beliefs about objects. He draws a distinction between an "apophantic 'as' " of mere statements in which entities are treated as present-at-hand objects, and a "hermeneutic 'as' " which is a prepredicative *taking* of something *as* something in the course of our activities. As we shall see in the next chapter, Heidegger regards the preoccupation with the explicit predication of attributes to objects in statements or assertions as leading to a distorted understanding of the Being of entities. But to say that the hermeneutic 'as' is prepredicative does not entail that it is *prelinguistic:* in fact, we will find that predication is a secondary and derivative mode of language. As I have tried to suggest, our interpretations in different contexts have a continuity which is best accounted for by the common interests and goals we share *by virtue of our mastery of a public language.* Without this background of language, it would be difficult to see how undertaking actions in different situations could contribute to a more or less unified public world.

There is a way of resolving the tension that arises in Heidegger's thought concerning the Anyone and language which does not have to abandon his insight into the constitutive role of language. If we can see the distinctions between primordial and derivative, and between authentic and inauthentic, in terms of a distinction between deep and surface levels of language, then there will be no need to posit the existence of a direct, prelinguistic access to any sorts of things themselves. Such a distinction can be made once we have incorporated Heidegger's treatment of historicity into our interpretation. In the next section we will find that Heidegger interprets the subject of everydayness not only as contextualized in the horizon of a culture, but also as essentially *historical.* From the standpoint of authentic historicity we can see that the Anyone tends to close off possibilities of Dasein's Being precisely because of its superficial preoccupation with the "tradition" and its forgetfulness of its deeper "heritage."

§10. *Authenticity, Forgetfulness, and Historicity*

Heidegger's concept of "authenticity" has not been explicitly brought into the discussion of Being-in-the-world so far because, at first glance, it appears to have little bearing on the problem of skepticism. But if authenticity is supposed to be a mode of existence in which one has access to the things themselves (Sachen selbst) and if, as we have seen above, both the closure and the criterion for the correctness of the hermeneutic of Dasein are determined by "truth which is primordial and authentic" (316), then some account of authenticity must be provided. Furthermore, the relation of the authentic mode of existence to the Anyone must also be discussed if Being-in-the-world is to be seen as a genuine alternative to the Cartesian model.

What is authenticity within the framework of *Being and Time?* We have already noted that authenticity is an "existentiell mode" of the Anyone: *"authentic* existence," Heidegger writes, "is not something which floats above falling everydayness; existentially it is only a modified way in which such everydayness is seized upon" (179). *"Authentic Being-one's-self* does not rest upon an exceptional condition of the subject; . . . *it is rather an existentiell modification of the Anyone — of the Anyone as an essential existentiale"* (130). The Anyone is here conceived of as an existentiale, and being authentic is merely a particular way of being the Anyone. At the same time, however, Heidegger tells us that "inauthenticity is based on the possibility of authenticity" (259), so that inauthenticity is also an existentiell mode of the Authentic Self:

> . . . proximally and for the most part Dasein is *not* itself but is lost in the Anyone-self [Man-selbst], which is an *existentiell modification of the Authentic Self* (317; my emphasis).

Has Heidegger contradicted himself here? A close reading of these passages suggests that they do not necessarily conflict. For Heidegger seems to be drawing a distinction between "authentic Being-one's-self" and the "Anyone-self" as *existentiell modes* on the one hand, and the "Authentic Self" and the "Anyone" as *existentialia* on the other. In order to clarify these distinctions, we must return to a consideration of what I have called the two "axes" of Dasein's Being: the temporal axis of its thrown projection revealed in the formal characterization of Dasein, and the axis of involvement revealed in the description of everyday Being-in-the-world.

Seen from the standpoint of its everyday involvements, Dasein is the Anyone. In what Heidegger calls its "downward plunge" into mundane tasks and preoccupations, Dasein takes up the cultural possibilities into which it is thrown and acts in conventional ways as anyone would act. As the Anyone, we are merely exemplifications of the roles, vocations, and offices laid out for us in the social world. Because our practical agency is always regulated by this pre-given social structuring, we are capable of acting in sensible, normal ways.

Heidegger says that in everydayness Dasein is "falling" (Verfallen): it is absorbed in the exigencies of the task of life with no overview of the significance of the project of living. The term 'falling', according to Heidegger, "does not express any negative evaluation, but is used to signify that Dasein is proximally and for the most part *at home in* the 'world' of its concerns" (175). It is a *positive* possibility, and not "a bad or deplorable ontical property of which, perhaps, more advanced stages of human culture might be able to rid themselves" (176). Since falling is our mode of openness to entities, it is an *existentiale* of Dasein.

Seen from the standpoint of the temporal axis of its formal structure of Being, on the other hand, Dasein is portrayed as a self-relation. It is the dynamic temporal movement in which, as "delivered over to itself," it is already "ahead-of-itself" in comporting itself toward its "ownmost possibility": its possibility of Being-a-whole. As a happening that will be consummated, Dasein is Being-toward-the-end or Being-toward-death. Here 'death' refers not to some future event but to the essential finitude of our Being. As contingent entities, we constantly stand before the possibility of having no more possibilities. Our Being has a teleological structure precisely because, as finite beings, our lives *will have* a final configuration of meaning, and we care about that final configuration.

The notion of "Being-toward-death" brings into Heidegger's description of Dasein the source of our sense of individuality and uniqueness — a sense of singularity that Christianity tries to account for in terms of the immortal soul, and the Cartesian tradition in terms of the mind as the unique center of experience. For Heidegger, what gives Dasein its "mineness" (Jemeinigkeit) is the fact that, in taking over public possibilities, it relates itself toward its own unique possibility of giving its life a meaning *as a whole*. Only because Dasein projects itself toward the Being that is at issue for it, can it be open to the world as falling: "Dasein *can* fall only *because* its understanding-situated Being-in-the-world is at issue" (179).

It is therefore because Dasein is an Authentic Self, as a unique, disclosive projection onto its Being-a-whole, that it can take any particular types of existentiell stands in its life. Each instance or exemplification of Dasein has its own unique life to live, whether it does so as integrated or as dispersed. For this reason Heidegger says that it is only because Dasein *can be* authentic — that is, because it is an Authentic Self that *can* take responsibility for its ownmost possibility — that it can be inauthentic in the sense of having failed to take over the task of its life:

> But only insofar as [Dasein] is essentially something that *can be authentic* — that is, something of its own — can it have lost itself. As *modes* of Being, *authenticity* and *inauthenticity* . . . are both grounded in the fact that Dasein in general is characterized by mineness (42/3; my emphasis on 'can be' and 'modes').

Dasein's ability to exist in the inauthentic mode of the Anyone-self is made possible by the fact that, as an Authentic Self, it has a unique task of Being-a-whole and it *can* take over responsibility for that task.

It remains the case, of course, that the actual possibilities for our concrete self-interpretations are those which have been laid out in advance by the Anyone. In taking a stand on my life as a whole, I understand myself as a teacher, spouse, father, cook, or whatever, and these are all possible roles I take over more or less as anyone would. In this sense my Being in everydayness is still delegatable or representable: *anyone* could come in and take my place because, as a place-holder in a shared nexus of roles, I *am* the Anyone. But there is one possibility each of us has which is *not* delegatable in this way. Although all the concrete roles I take over are public and not unique, there is one possibility that is mine alone: my Being-toward-death as the possibilty of appropriating these public meanings in an integrated and coherent way. My life is Being-toward-the-end in a double sense: (1) as finite, I face the culmination of my life as a whole; and (2) my life has an ultimate end, or goal — that of taking responsibility for my finite existence and making something of it. Only when Dasein is regarded as an Authentic Self can it be seen as having this privileged possibility of attaining the end of life. "The Anyone never dies because it *can*not die," Heidegger says, "for death is in each case mine" (425).

We can see, then, that the existentiell modes of authentic Being-one's-self and the inauthentic Anyone-self are both modifications of the biaxial structure of Dasein as both the Anyone and the Authentic Self. From this description of the possible modes of Dasein's life it seems that the distinction between authenticity and inauthenticity does not hinge on "what" one is in the sense of what kinds of concrete roles one takes over. Since all possibilities are derived from the Anyone, the range of possibilities on which one draws in taking a stand will be the same for both. Instead the distinction lies in "how" one takes a stand: it is, so to speak, a matter of style rather than content. What makes authentic Dasein exceptional is, in part, the way it takes up the possibilities of the Anyone and projects them as a coherent and unified configuration of meaning for its life as a whole. In contrast, when Dasein is inauthentic, it lives in such a way that it is blind to its own finitude and is dispersed in the possibilities of the Anyone with no sense of the point of its life as a totality.

In both cases we are still commentaries on the linguistically articulated text of our culture. The only difference lies in the *quality* of that commentary. To be authentic is to recognize the gravity of the task to which one is delivered over and to take full responsibility for one's life. Authentic Dasein lives resolutely, coherently, with "sober joy," expressing in each of its actions a sense of its Being-toward-the-end. The inauthentic Anyone-self, on the other hand, is dispersed, distracted, and fleeing in the face of its own death. It tends toward conformism, becomes preoccupied with social standing, and is insensible to the fact that its life as a whole is at issue for it.

Heidegger makes it clear that a necessary condition for grasping primordial and authentic truth is that one actually be in the authentic existentiell mode. This mode is characterized as "resoluteness" (Entschlossenheit). Resoluteness has nothing to do with transcending the Anyone to attain the position of an "Übermensch." On the contrary, Heidegger says that

> even resolutions remain dependent upon the Anyone and its world. The understanding of this is one of the things that a resolution discloses, inasmuch as resoluteness is what first gives authentic transparency [Durchsichtigkeit] to Dasein (299).

In resoluteness, "one's ability-to-be becomes authentic and *wholly transparent*" (307; my emphasis). Whereas the Cartesian tradition might take the concept of "transparency" as referring to the attainment of complete clarity through the grounding of our beliefs in the intrinsic intelligibility of the *lumen naturale,* Heidegger uses this term to indicate that authenticity brings with it a more sharply defined sense of what it is to be human. He defines 'transparency' as "seizing upon the full disclosedness of Being-in-the-world *throughout all* the constitutive aspects that are essential to it, and doing so with understanding" (146). Thus, transparency also reveals that our thrownness is something we can never get behind in order to make it fully intelligible.

As transparent, then, authentic Dasein understands its own structure, including its finitude and thrownness into the Anyone, and it is in a position to project itself onto its ownmost possibility with a sense of the uniqueness and wholeness of its life. Transparency does not add some new item of information to one's stock of understanding. Nor does it provide a "categorical imperative" that will guide all one's actions. In fact, transparency, as the mode of "sight" of authenticity, seems to have no content at all. But as the "art of existing"[31] it does point to a capacity for grasping life in a different way. When one sees one's life as a thrown projection, the alienating sense of the self as the enduring presence of a particular type of substance is undermined, and the way is paved for grasping human existence as temporal, as a "happening" (Geschehen). And with this transformation of self-understanding comes the potential for a new insight into the temporality of Being in general.

Although authentic transparency can light up the temporality of our own Being, it does not seem sufficient to provide a basis for a fully worked-out fundamental ontology. In order to see how

---

31. See above, section 6.

authenticity can provide a "content" for fundamental ontology, we must bring in the account of authentic historicity. At the beginning of the fifth chapter of Division II of *Being and Time,* Heidegger suggests that the account of Dasein in terms of its futurity as Being-toward-death may have been "one-sided" (373). There is the "possibility of a more radical approach to the existential analytic," he says, a way of understanding Dasein that is *"more primordial* than the projection of its authentic existence" (372; my emphasis). This deeper account must embrace not only Dasein's "Being-toward-the-end," he says, but also its "origins"—its "Being toward the beginning" (373). If we are to understand the *whole* happening of Dasein as it *"is stretched along and stretches itself along"* (375), then we must embrace the entire "temporalization-structure of temporality," a structure which Heidegger calls "historicity" (332).

The term 'historicity' is used by Heidegger in two distinct but related senses. First, it refers to the "temporalizing" (sich zeitigen: literally, "bringing to fruition") through which Dasein is open not only to entities in the world, but to the past and future as well. When Dasein is regarded as a happening, it is seen as flowing outward into the future and backward into the past in its character of "having-been" (Gewesenheit). As a dynamic temporal unity, it appropriates the possibilities of the past in projecting them toward future goals. Heidegger says that "Dasein 'is' its past in the way of *its* own Being, which, to put it roughly, 'happens' out of its future in each case" (20). The past "happens" out of the future because Dasein, as teleological, always takes up the past in directing itself toward what it will be. But since Dasein is always caught up in the concrete stream of events of world-history, its historicity also has the second sense of referring to Dasein's actual rootedness in a historical context.

In order to fill out the account of Dasein's Being, Heidegger inquires into the "authentic happening of Dasein" (382). Since this question now asks about the beginning and origin of Dasein, it leads to the question of the *source* of Dasein's possibilities. The idea that resoluteness in the face of one's own death could be the source of Dasein's "content" is explicitly ruled out:

> One's anticipatory projection of oneself onto that possibility of existence which is not to be outstripped—on death—guarantees only the totality and authenticity of one's resoluteness. But those possibilities of existence which have been factically disclosed are not to be gathered from death (383).

What then is the source of Dasein's possibilities? The answer remains the same as before: it is the Anyone. Heidegger says that Dasein "understands itself in terms of those possibilities of existence which 'circulate' in the average public way of interpreting Dasein today" (383). This "average public way of interpreting Dasein" makes up the "tradition" into which Dasein is constantly falling. But it now appears that authentic Dasein appropriates the traditional possibilities floating in the Today in a unique way. In resoluteness, Heidegger says, Dasein "discloses current factical possibilities of authentic existing *from the heritage*" (383). What distinguishes authentic Dasein from the inauthentic, therefore, is not that it has access to *new* possibilities, but that it can take up the tradition *as its heritage*.

The distinction between authenticity and inauthenticity seems to reveal two different ways of taking over the text of history. The inauthentic mode of relating to the past is forgetfulness. As we have seen, in our everyday concern with the world we must draw a horizon around ourselves in order to be able to focus on our daily affairs. This unavoidable preoccupation with the world blinds us both to our ownmost possibility and to our rootedness in and indebtedness to the past. Heidegger says that everydayness is characterized by "groundlessness" and "homelessness." We are "uprooted" in the "obviousness and self-assurance" of the public interpretations, and we "drift along toward an ever-increasing groundlessness [Bodenlosigkeit]" (170). As an inauthentic Anyoneself, we tend to drift into socially approved slots and accept everything at face value as "one" does, without any sense of the deeper origins of our possibilities. In everydayness we are "lost" in the tradition:

> In whatever current way it has to be [zu sein] and thus with whatever understanding of Being it may have, Dasein has grown both into and in a traditional way of interpreting itself. In terms of this it understands itself proximally and, within a certain circumference, constantly. By this understanding, the possibilities of its Being are disclosed and regulated (20).

In contrast to the forgetfulness of inauthenticity, authentic Dasein *remembers* its historical roots and can find the underlying meaning of what is passed down in the tradition. Authentic understanding still operates within the framework of understanding handed down to us by the past:

> The authentic existentiell understanding is so far from extricating itself from the way of interpreting Dasein which has

come down to us, that in each case it is in terms of this interpretation, against it, and yet again for it, that any possibility
one has chosen is seized upon in one's resolution (383).

Even authentic Dasein remains contextualized in the traditional
ways of understanding that are mediated by the Anyone. But
authenticity enables us to see that the possibilities handed down to
us by the Anyone are made accessible only in a corrupt and
distorted form. It therefore opens the possibility of working
through the Anyone's warped commentary on the "primal text" of
history to recover the hidden, deeper meanings that underlie the
tradition and make it possible.

Dasein's "authentic happening" is defined as "fate" (Schicksal).
Fate refers to the "simplicity" with which Dasein takes over its own
inherited resources and projects itself onto the point of its life as a
whole. As such, it characterizes the happening that binds together
Dasein's birth and death and gives its life a steadfastness (Selbst-
ständigkeit) and connectedness as a whole. But, as the happening
of fate, Dasein is also always contextualized in a social world; its
happening is always a "co-happening" of a community and a people. This co-happening Heidegger calls "destiny": "Our fates have
already been guided in advance in our Being with one another in the
same world and in our resoluteness for determinate possibilities"
(384). Authentic Dasein's resolute openness to future and past
makes it a participant in the "sending" and "heritage" of its culture
as a whole.

According to Heidegger, "it is not necessary that in resoluteness
one should explicitly know the origin [Herkunft] of the possibilities
upon which that resoluteness projects itself" (385). In resoluteness
"there is hidden a *handing down* to oneself of possibilities that have
come down to one, but not necessarily *as* having thus come down"
(383). It seems, then, that an explicit grasp of the heritage *as*
historical is not necessary to resoluteness: a peasant who has never
studied history can be resolute. But if authentic Dasein *does* have
an explicit knowledge of the source of its possibilities, then authenticity takes the form of "retrieval" or "repetition" (Wiederholung).
The possibilities are explicitly understood as those of the "Dasein
who has been there" (das dagewesene Dasein), with the result that
authentic Dasein "chooses its hero" (385); that is, it models its life
not on the Anyone, but on authentic possibilities that have existed
before.

Becoming authentic therefore brings about a new relationship to
the past and history. Whereas inauthentic Dasein is absorbed in the
possibilities of the present and sees no real significance in the past,

authentic Dasein understands its own Being as a commentary on the historical possibilities of its heritage. It thus sees its life as a dialogue with the past. Repetition involves a "reply" or "rejoinder" (Erwiderung) to the possibilities that are handed down (386). In this rejoinder, Dasein does not deny the past or treat it as something external to itself. On the contrary, authentic Dasein *appropriates* the past as the horizon in which it is and, thereby, explicitly rejects the preoccupation with the Today which characterizes the Anyone. Heidegger says that the dialogue with the past "is at the same time a disavowal [Widerruf] of that which is working itself out as the 'past' *in the Today*" (386).[32]

The difference between authenticity and inauthenticity lies not in *what* possibilities are available, then, but in *how* those possibilities are *heard* and taken up. In both cases the sources or origins of our understanding are historical, rooted in our heritage. But inauthentic Dasein *hears* these possibilities as "tradition" — that is, in terms of the fads and trends that dominate the Today and allow the past to be seen as something ultimately removed from us. Inauthentic Dasein experiences no sense of continuity with the deep historical roots and ground of its understanding. "Lost in the making present of the *Today,* it understands the 'past' in terms of the 'present' " (391; my emphasis). When Dasein is "authentically historical," however, it "deprives the Today of its character as present, and weans one from the conventionalities of the Anyone" (391).

The Anyone understands itself as alienated from the past; it sees what has been as a series of events that are now gone and are only of potential antiquarian interest. Authentic Dasein understands its relation to history quite differently: it sees itself as indebted to the heritage and implicated in the destiny of its people. Understanding itself as a happening which participates in a "world-historical happening" (19), it can no longer interpret itself as a self-defining object or substance that, as enduring presence, is alienated from the past. Instead, authentic Dasein recognizes that it is carrying forward the flow of the past by projecting itself ahead into the destiny of its community.

Authenticity therefore releases Dasein from its "self-entangle-

---

32. My emphasis on the last three words. As David Hoy has pointed out, the translators' gloss on this passage is precisely the *opposite* of what Heidegger means. In the footnote on page 438 of the English edition, they claim that "one makes a rejoinder to this proposal from the past by 'reciprocating' with the proposal of other possibilities as a sort of rebuke to the past, which one now disavows." What one "disavows," however, is the superficial reading of "the 'past'" in the Today. Cf. Hoy, "History, Historicity, and Historiography in *Being and Time*" in M. Murray, ed., *Heidegger and Modern Philosophy*.

ment" and preoccupation with monetary affairs to bring it fully into a wider context of the heritage and destiny to which it belongs. The project of my Being-toward-death is understood as deeply entrenched in the broader project of realizing a communal destiny that transcends my own limited existence. Whereas Dilthey was still inclined to describe the self as an objectified "monad" that reflects the historical universe but is nevertheless still a unique individual,[33] Heidegger's conception of our *belongingness* to history dissolves the boundaries of individuality and makes us participants in the over-all flow of history.[34] For this reason, authenticity is described as "loyalty" (Treue) and "reverence" (Ehrfurcht) "for the sole authority which a free existing can have — of revering the repeatable possibilities of existence" (391). The sole authority for Dasein is the heritage, because it is the sole source of what can be understood. It alone can provide the ultimate "content" for fundamental ontology.

As we have seen, then, the true springs and origins of the meaning on which "the understanding of Being nourishes itself" (324) are historical. The background of intelligibility articulated by a culture is, in its deepest level, a perpetuation of the heritage — although usually in a disguised form. The Anyone, lost in the present as "making-present," makes these springs and origins accessible only in a distorted way. The Anyone comes to take the Today as of the greatest consequence. In inauthentic historicity, history is seen as a progression toward the enlightened standpoint of the present. Since the Today alone represents the culmination of human dreams and aspirations, as well as the final attainment of clarity and understanding, the conventions, norms, and standards of the Today are the highest authority for the Anyone. The Anyone does not just provide us with the criteria for handling equipment and dealing with others. It also insists on the consummate *importance* of living precisely within the confines of these norms and standards as given today.

The tension in Heidegger's attitude toward the Anyone and

---

33. WD 214, *Aufbau* 246.

34. "The full authentic happening of Dasein," according to Heidegger, consists in its "fateful destiny in and with its 'generation' " (384/5). In a footnote on page 385 he points out that the concept of "generation" is drawn from Dilthey's GS V 36–44. In this 1875 work, Dilthey argues that the "generation" is the basic unit of history since it provides the context and framework in which individuals can first be identified and meaningfully examined. Since the generation is the smallest unit for historical study, the individual is only an abstraction from this wider context; it is not elementary in historiography.

language can be resolved, then, if we observe that the Anyone articulates possibilities in two different ways. On the one hand, it is the source of the fields of contrast that make possible our social competence and, hence, our encounters with equipmental contexts. In this respect, the Anyone's role is positive: it makes our agency in the world possible, and is thus a condition for the possibility of there being any Dasein whatsoever. The linguistically articulated background of intelligibility is the medium in which the primordial sources and roots of our pre-ontological understanding are maintained, even though they are generally made accessible in a form that tends more to conceal than to reveal.

On the other hand, however, the Anyone in its preoccupation with Today also gives us a misleading understanding of what it is to be. When we have fallen into the tradition, the Anyone imparts to us the idea that we are objectified substances alienated from the past and, ultimately, from our world and each other. It furthermore maintains that its present attitude is the only correct position, so it is immediately *important* that one fall into step with the Today. In imparting this misleading "information" the Anyone's role is negative, since it tends to close off our authentic possibilities of relating to the past and evaluating what is truly important. Only authentic historicity makes possible a critical detachment from the superficial aura of obviousness and self-evidence of the Today. By overcoming the forgetfulness of the Today, one overcomes one's sense of alienation from one's heritage and destiny and can then attain a deeper grasp of the deep and coherent possibilities for one's life. Seeing itself as participating in history and contributing to it, Dasein can be *"for* what is world-historical *in its current situation"* (391; my emphasis).

Heidegger's ambivalent attitude toward language arises from the fact that he concentrates primarily on the ways that the schematizations of language tend to contribute to the *mis*understandings of the tradition. As a result, in *Being and Time* he fails to recognize the possibilities of nonobjectifying language. Since he tends to think that language must always be pernicious, the only authentic modes of language are "silence" and "hearing." He calls on us to turn away from language in favor of the things themselves without realizing that these things may be themselves linguistically constituted. When this confusion is cleared away, however, Heidegger no longer has any reason to resist the constitutive view—as the writings soon after *Being and Time* attest. When Heidegger defines 'resoluteness' as "the undisguised letting-be-encountered by that which it seizes upon in taking action" (326), this need not be understood as a prelinguistic or nonlinguistic access to the "things themselves." If we assume that the primordial roots and sources of our heritage are also embedded in language, then the authentically historical encounter with the world may still be seen as constituted by language. Authentic dealings with equipment are undisguised not in the sense of being unmediated encounters with the things themselves, but as being liberated from the objectifying schematizations of the language of the Today.

On the reworking of *Being and Time* that I am proposing, the origins, roots, and grounds that history passes on to us will also be seen as flowing within the medium of language. We might therefore see Heidegger as drawing a distinction in *Being and Time* between different levels of language which is comparable to the distinction between "surface grammar" and "depth grammar" found in Wittgenstein.[35] On the one hand there is the "superficial" way that language articulates the world in idle talk and in the tradition. At this level, Heidegger later says, "the nature of language plays with us."[36] It misleads us into thinking that we and the world are to be understood as the enduring presence of substances and that the interpretation of Today is the only way of seeing things that carries any weight. On the other hand, language also contains a "deep" understanding which for the most part is covered over. In order to grasp this deeper level, we must "make an effort to live properly with language" and "hear what language really says to us."[37] The deep grammar articulates the roots and origins of our heritage and makes them accessible to us as such.

On this interpretation of Heidegger's conception of language, we may distinguish three kinds of linguistic articulation that serve to constitute our sense of what it is to be:

(1) At the deepest level, language is the medium in which the possibilities of understanding of the heritage are conveyed to us. It contains the sources and origins of our most primordial understanding of the world. As Heidegger says, "the essential is always handed over to the future as the authentic *heritage*."[38] We reach this deepest level of language by *"doing violence"* to common sense (311) and by actually working through world-history in order to remember its disguised message. Since authentic historicity is

---

35. *Philosophical Investigations* 664. Cf. *Remarks on the Foundations of Mathematics,* I 108.

36. WCT 118, WhD 83.

37. WCT 118/9, WhD 83/4.

38. LL 198 (my emphasis).

retrieval or repetition, the remembering of fundamental ontology itself must be a retrieval of the possibilities handed down in our heritage. In *Kant and the Problem of Metaphysics* Heidegger describes the project of fundamental ontology as follows:

> The philosophical "remembering" of the concealed projection of Being on time, as the deepest happening *(Geschehen)* in the understanding of Being of ancient metaphysics and beyond, assigns a task of *repetition* or *retrieval* to the basic question of metaphysics (KPMe 250, KPMg 234/5; my emphasis).

The unpublished "phenomenological destruction of the history of ontology" was to have achieved this retrieval. Since authentic and primordial truth is first arrived at in this process, the destructive side of *Being and Time* was crucial to unfolding the content of fundamental ontology. As we shall see below in Chapter V, the results of the published portions of *Being and Time* cannot be thought of as complete in any sense without the historical part.

(2) At an intermediate level, our language opens a world of equipment structured in terms of our goals, interests, and needs. In learning the intentional language of the 'in order to', 'for which', 'in doing which', 'by means of', and 'for the sake of', we simultaneously come to encounter equipment as interwoven into networks of internal relations. This is the language that lays out the possibilities of encountering the world in terms of what Heidegger calls the "hermeneutic 'as'." It is more primordial than the language of tradition, but it is not the most primordial level of encountering the world, since everydayness still tends to treat the world as "present" (Gegenwart) and fails to distinguish what is valuable in the Anyone from what is concealed.

(3) Finally, the level of language that is most remote from our primordial sources is also the level that common sense takes as most obviously primary. This is the superficial level of mere *assertions* or *statements* uttered from the disengaged, objective point of view of the contemplative or theoretical attitude. The "apophantic 'as'" of this kind of explicit predication encourages us to see the world as consisting of present-at-hand substances with accidents—the correlates of the subject and predicate of the statement. The self-evidence and obviousness of this way of understanding the world is conveyed to us in the language of tradition. Heidegger says that "the tradition passes down rigid propositions and meanings, rigid ways of asking and answering. . . . This external tradition is a failure of life."[39] Forgetfulness is already carried

---

39. LL 197.

in the second level of language, but in the language of tradition our loss of contact with our roots is "aggravated to complete groundlessness" (168). As we shall see in the next chapter, Heidegger's diagnosis of the conception of justification in the Cartesian model sets out from the kind of ontological picture we get from focusing on this surface grammar of explicit assertions or statements.

IV

Diagnosis of the Cartesian Model of Justification

In the last chapter we examined Heidegger's way of dealing with the first presupposition of the Cartesian model, the picture of our everyday or plain epistemic situations as structured by the subject/object ontology. The description of everydayness leads us to see that our ordinary situations are better understood in terms of the model of Being-in-the-world than in the schematism of the subject/object dichotomy. In the course of our active lives, we are *engaged* in the world in such a way that there is no distinction to be drawn between an isolated subject accumulating data on the one hand and the collection of items that are to be known on the other. Dasein, as Being-in-the-world, is always "contextualized." It is, from the outset, the Anyone as a community unfolding in history. The epistemological "subject" appears on the scene only when our everyday dealings in the world have broken down. From the standpoint of the model of Being-in-the-world, the "I" that Descartes discovers through his methodological doubt is by no means the most primordial self. On the contrary, it is seen to be part of the debris left by the collapse of our most primordial Being as Being-in-the-world.

The picture of everydayness that emerges is of a holistic system of internal relations in which the "ontological definition" of any entity is fully circumscribed by its actual place in an equipmental context. I have tried to suggest that these contexts themselves are constituted by the teleologically structured intentional language of a historical culture. Since we all live in this linguistic medium, we all participate in a common intelligible world of shared goals, purposes, and interests. Given Heidegger's description of everydayness, the objectifying ontology has no role to play. The Cartesian assumption that our ordinary lives are to be portrayed in terms of subjects holding a set of beliefs about objects comes to appear to be a "dogmatic" prejudice with no foundation in our actual lives.

It seems clear, however, that the attack on the subject/object ontology by itself will not satisfy the skeptic. For he might maintain that Heidegger has simply *ignored* the problem of justification, which is the aim of epistemology in the broad sense. Husserl expressed this feeling of dissatisfaction in the marginal notes to his copy of *Being and Time*. He suggests that Heidegger's reversion to

147

"anthropology" leaves the task of grounding our encounter with the world untouched. Although Husserl does not seem to grasp the import of the existential analytic for the traditional conception of the "ego," his objection to Heidegger's method might seem well taken when seen from the point of view of the traditional understanding of the aims of epistemology.

> Heidegger transposes or transverses the constitutive phenomenological clarification of all regions of entities and universals of the total region of world into *anthropology*. The whole problem is translation: Dasein corresponds to the ego, etc.; and thereby everything becomes deeply unclear and loses its philosophical value.[1]

For Husserl and for Cartesians in general, a philosophical anthropology cannot satisfy the concern with providing an ultimate clarification of our experience. On the assumption that we do in fact have beliefs about the world and that philosophy can and should provide clarifications for these beliefs, Heidegger's fundamental ontology seems simply to side-step the issue of justification instead of settling it.

The skeptic might try to establish the validity of his own mode of inquiry by an analogy with science. Suppose we grant that for a farmer the sun is ready-to-hand as a life-giving orb that rises each morning in the East, warms his fields during the day, and sets in the West in the evening. In the summer the sun is large and warm to nourish his crops; in the winter it is a smaller source of light near the southern horizon. Now the scientist understands the language in which this description is framed, but he knows that "in reality" the sun is a medium-sized star in which innumerable thermonuclear reactions are taking place. What appears as the rising and setting of the sun is actually the turning of the earth on its axis as it revolves around the sun. And what appear to be seasons on earth result, in fact, not from changes in the sun, but from the position of the earth and its angle of inclination as it orbits the sun.

The scientist's conception of the sun is based on established canons of evidence and objectively determined data. To deny the validity of such a view and the orderly methods by which it has been reached would seem to be irrationalism of the worst sort. Even if one were to insist on the validity of the farmer's view, one

---

1. Husserl's marginal notes in his copy of *Sein und Zeit,* preserved in the Louvain archives under the signature "K X Heidegger I," quoted by Terrence Malick in the "Translator's Introduction" to ER, p. xiin (my emphasis).

could maintain, as Dilthey at one time did,[2] that there are *two* equally valid ways of grasping the world — as the human intelligible world and as the natural order studied by the physical sciences. Whereas our attitude toward the former may be regarded as part of our poetical imagination and therefore beyond criticism, our beliefs about the latter, it might be argued, can and must be justified. The skeptic might then argue that *his* inquiry is to be understood as an extrapolation from scientific modes of thought. If we have beliefs about the physical objects around us, then we have a right to inquire into the justification for these beliefs. The skeptical inquiry differs from the scientific only in the global nature of its interests and in its search for intrinsic intelligibility as opposed to theory-relative explanations. If the skeptical challenge leads to unpalatable results, so much the worse for our web of beliefs. At least we have faced up to the rational enterprise of methodically examining what we uncritically hold to be true.

Heidegger would agree that the skeptical inquiry gains its significance through its analogy with science. In fact, he believes that the modern form of skepticism has its origins in the theoretical attitude that has opened the possibilities of modern science. But Heidegger also sees the skeptic's extrapolation from theory-relative explanations to a global, theory-free justification of our everyday attitude as illegitimate. As we shall see, Heidegger suggests that the skeptic makes use of scientific modes of inquiry that are legitimate within their own regions of the life-world, but then attempts to extend these modes beyond the boundaries in which they are applicable. As a result, in order to undertake his project, the skeptic must in effect abrogate the very conditions that would make his inquiry possible. When the skeptical inquiry is seen as illegitimate, the idea that there is a special activity of providing global epistemological justifications of our everyday practices is deflated. It follows, then, that Heidegger's approach to traditional epistemology is two-pronged: first, he offers us a new model of our everyday epistemic predicament; but, secondly, he also diagnoses the Cartesian conception of justification in order to undermine the apparent significance of its type of investigation.

Heidegger's examination of the Cartesian conception of justification may be divided into three parts, which will be worked out in the following three sections. First, he analyzes the structure of scientific activity as a mode of Dasein's comportment toward the world, in order to show that the contemplative attitude, which is

2. See for example WD 163-167; GS I 14-21.

derived from science, is a "founded mode of Being-in-the-world." Second, he leads us to see that *because* the Cartesian model is a founded mode, its enterprise of rationally reconstructing our everyday understanding from theory-neutral "units" is incoherent. The reconstruction seems to gain its sense from regional modes of producing intelligibility, yet it could be carried out only by simultaneously abrogating the conditions for the possibility of any inquiry whatsoever. And, third, Heidegger argues that fundamental ontology has access to possibilities of understanding which are in principle closed off to the sciences, and that consequently neither science nor a "naturalized epistemology" can ever replace philosophy. In the picture that emerges, the idea that there are *two* worlds — an informal everyday world in which we encounter entities as bound up with our practices, and a "real" world of objects studied by science — is found to be an illusion. There is only *one* world, and that is the world studied by fundamental ontology.

§11. *Epistemology as a Founded Mode of Being-in-the-World*

If both science and Cartesian skepticism are understood as human *activities,* then both the "theoretical attitude" of science and the purified "contemplative attitude" of the Cartesian model must be seen as specialized modes of Being-in-the-world. And to the extent that Being-in-the-world is characterized by certain essential structures, this means that science and Cartesian foundationalism are determined by some form of *situatedness* and *goal-directedness.* These types of inquiry must be interpreted as thrown into a range of pre-given possibilities and as projections of possibilities along the guidelines laid out in the fore-structure of a pre-ontological understanding of Being. But if this is the case, Heidegger suggests, then science and Cartesianism must be understood as derived from and parasitic on our everyday Being-in-the-world. To demonstrate that the Cartesian model is a "founded mode" of Being-in-the-world, Heidegger tries to show us, first, that the theoretical attitude of science is derived from the practical attitude of everydayness, and, second, that the contemplative attitude of the Cartesian model emerges naturally from the standpoint of pure theory.

Heidegger's critique of science begins from a conception of science which is quite different from that of the Cartesian tradition. For Descartes, science is to be understood as a *corpus* in which certain and indubitable truths are methodically bound together into a whole. All rational inquiry is interwoven within a single methodology and program of "unified science": "If someone wishes to make a serious investigation of the truths of nature," Descartes says, "he should not choose some particular science, for they are all interconnected and interdependent."[3] For this reason Descartes says that science is the collection of all "certain, evident knowledge" (*ibid.* 5). *Prima philosophia* establishes the methods for the sciences and lays out their first principles. But the overarching concern of philosophy and science is the ultimate construction of a final body of interconnected truths about the world.

In contrast, Heidegger maintains that this definition of science as "the totality of systematically grounded true propositions" is "not complete nor does it reach the meaning of science" (11). Instead of viewing science as a system of propositions, he suggests that we see it as a human activity. His interest is in "an *existential conception of science*" (357) in which the sciences are grasped as "ways in which man behaves [Verhaltungen]" (11). To grasp the "meaning" of science, we must work out an "*ontological genesis* of the theoretical attitude" (357). The account of the genesis of science is not a report on the actual series of events that led to the development of modern science. Instead, Heidegger is concerned with "those conditions implied in Dasein's composition of Being [that] are existentially necessary for the possibility of Dasein's existing in the way of scientific research" (357). Since "the existential conception [of science] understands science as a way of existence and thus as a mode of Being-in-the-world" (357), its aim is to show how this highly refined and specialized way of discovering entities arises out of our everyday modes of dealing with things.

Heidegger works out the derivation of the theoretical attitude through an analysis of the "change-over" that occurs in the transition from the "hermeneutic 'as' " of everyday involved dealings in the world to the "apophantic 'as' " of mere statements or assertions (Aussage) about things. The "apophantic 'as' " refers to our way of encountering the world by formulating explicit beliefs about objects. These beliefs are modeled on the simple predication in which a subject term picks out an object and a predicate term ascribes some property to it. In Chapter I we found that the Cartesian model assumes that our most fundamental situation in the world is one in which we are formulating beliefs about things in terms of this sort of subject-predicate model of the workings of language. Before I can begin hammering, it is claimed, I must believe that there is a hammer in my hand, that the hammer is hard, that the

---

3. Descartes, *Rules for the Direction of the Mind,* trans. L. J. Lafleur (Indianapolis: Bobbs-Merrill, 1961), p. 4.

nails are rigid, and so forth. We also saw in section 3 that this subject-predicate model of language leads naturally to a "substance/accident" ontology: the world must consist of substances with attributes correlated with the subject and predicate terms of our statements.

In contrast to this Cartesian picture of our basic encounter with entities in terms of the apophantic 'as' of statements, Heidegger's description of everydayness leads us to see that there is a more primordial way of discovering equipment. Whereas the Cartesian model starts from "mere seeing" and tries to build practical affairs up from this basis, Heidegger emphasizes the ways we *handle* and *manipulate* equipment with skillful know-how in our everyday dealings with the environment. The ways we seize on things and put them to use in our day-to-day activities is called the "hermeneutic 'as' " of everyday interpretation. What we come across in this articulation of the world into the hermeneutic 'as' is not discrete, interchangeable objects with properties, but rather ready-to-hand equipment tied up into a mesh of internal relations generated by our purposes, aims, and objectives in the context. Equipment manifests itself in terms of relations of the "in order to," "by means of which," "in doing which," and "for which" within a totality governed by a "for the sake of which." In this description of our practical affairs, the picture of a subject formulating beliefs about objects has no role to play.

The ontological genesis of science begins by showing how this hermeneutic 'as' of everydayness changes over into the kind of explicit thematizing of entities according to the apophantic 'as' of statement-making which characterizes the theoretical attitude. This transition parallels the account of the breakdown of equipmental contexts briefly discussed above in section 7. Heidegger's concern is with the "limiting cases" (Grenzfälle) of "pure, inexplicit, unthematic *having to do with* something, and the thematizing determination of a present-at-hand thing."[4] Between these limiting cases "there are many intermediate gradations" (158), and it is possible that neither "pure" involvement nor "pure" uninvolved thematizing is ever realized in practice.

Since Being-in-the-world has a hermeneutical structure, Dasein always operates in the world with a pre-understanding of what it is up to and how things can count. This fore-structure of understanding provides us with a "preview" or "overview" of the contexts in which we are engaged. Our self-understanding in a context, Heidegger says, carries with it "a more or less explicit *overview*

---

4. LFW 158 (my emphasis).

[Übersicht] of the equipmental totality of the current equipment-world" (359; my emphasis). We "know our way around" in the context, and our actions express a grasp of the *point* of the "totality of ways things have turned out" (Bewandtnisganzheit) (359). On the basis of this prior grasp of a totality, we go on to appropriate the context in interpretation. Heidegger says that this initial form of interpretation takes the form of "deliberating" (Überlegung). In deliberating, we "lay out" (auslegen) the 'as'-structure of the equipment by "laying over" it (überlegen) an interpretation in terms of our overview of the whole. Deliberation, Heidegger says, falls under the schema of the "if . . . then . . .". The end we seek (the "in doing which") is related to a "by means of which" in terms of what the work is *for*—e.g., "if this or that is to be produced, put to use, or averted, then some ways and means, circumstances, or opportunities will be needed" (359). This ordinary, skillful activity, in which the totality of an equipmental context is articulated into means to ends, is "taking something *as* something": it is the hermeneutic 'as' of practical activity.

There is no reason to think that the "if . . . then . . ." schema that structures our deliberations in the world requires any explicit linguistic formulation. I can express my deliberation in my actions without thinking or with my mind a million miles away. Being a master of cooking, for instance, I can reach for the spatula and turn the eggs while my mind is absorbed in my plans for the garden. Our most trivial daily activities can be conducted without any particular mental accompaniment. In contrast to this normal flow of purposive activity, Heidegger claims, our practices take an "explicit" form only when something is encountered as "*un*-ready-to-hand" (359). When equipment becomes unusable for some reason, our ordinary unthinking deliberation in the smooth flow of affairs changes over to what Heidegger calls "envisaging" (Vergegenwärtigung) (359). Envisaging is more explicit in its examination of the "if . . . then . . ." structure of interpretation, but it is still "prepredicative" to the extent that it is not a matter of predicating universal "properties" to isolated "objects." We should keep in mind, however, that to say that the hermeneutic 'as' is prepredicative is not to say that it is prelinguistic. Even our prereflective deliberations have a linguistic component insofar as they are guided by an understanding of what is involved in undertaking an action, an understanding that is articulated in advance through our mastery of the public language.

Heidegger says that "interpretation is carried out primordially not in a theoretical statement but in an action of our concernful know-how" (157). When there *are* linguistic utterances in such situations, they are part of the "expressions" of Dasein's self-understanding which make up the Being of Dasein as meaningful expression. If I say "The hammer is too heavy" or just "Too heavy! Hand me the other hammer!" such utterances are not statements designed to impart information about the objective features of things. They are expressions that serve to disclose the shared intelligibility of the network of internal relations. The utterance, Heidegger says, "gives expression [Ausdruck] to a concernful deliberation" (360). It speaks *into* the framework of human interests and goals, not *about* objects with properties.

When the equipmental context breaks down completely, however, the entities we are dealing with can first obtrude as mere present-at-hand objects. The complete collapse of a world of significance opens the possibility of encountering entities in terms of the "limiting cases of statements" that are taken as paradigmatic examples of language in logic and ideal science (157). The hammer, no longer of use, just stands there as a brute object that can fall under different interpretations but no longer has any *particular* role. In this case an utterance like "The hammer is heavy," whether audible or silent, may express the apophantic 'as' of mere assertion. Here the utterance indicates that an object—the hammer—has a weight; it has the "property" of heaviness; it exerts downward pressure; it falls if it is unsupported. In the predication of the mere statement, the hammer comes to be taken as a "corporeal thing subject to the law of gravity" (360/1).

Heidegger says that "in its function of appropriating what is understood, the 'as' no longer reaches out into a totality of ways things have turned out" (158). There is an "explicit *restriction* or *narrowing down* [Einschränkung] of our view" (155) that severs the hammer's ties to its field of relations and reveals it as a mere *thing* abstracted from the context. In the conscious predication of a property to an object, the entity "is leveled down to a mere thing and, as this present-at-hand thing, it is no different from other random things . . . insofar as I grasp them as mere things that are there."[5] If the *meaning* of our ordinary discourse about equipment is contained in the full grammatical multiplicity of its uses in expressing intelligibility in practical contexts, then what the assertion says about the hammer

> no longer has any "meaning"; that is to say, the entity in itself, as we now encounter it, gives us nothing with relation to which it could be "found" too heavy or too light (361).

5. LFW 158.

With the collapse of our ordinary involvement in the world, the name-and-object model of language obtrudes in its "self-evidence" while the constitutive role of language is concealed.

The change-over from the hermeneutic 'as' of everyday interpretation to the apophantic 'as' of mere statement-making has two components. First, there is a change-over in *our* mode of comportment to entities. When the hammer breaks and I step back from my involvements in order to formulate a proposition about it, I might at first focus on it within the framework of "common sense." I see the hammer as a plain, everyday "object" which can fall under various interpretations but is not defined by any particular use. Concerned with repairing or replacing it, I notice the juncture between the head and the handle in relation to the possible uses it might have. If this common-sense approach fails to resolve the obstruction, I might proceed to a more refined level of investigation by setting up experiments to test the physical properties of the parts of the hammer. In this movement to specialized ways of examining the present-at-hand object, the origins of the theoretical attitude may be seen. The object is now a "mere thing" to be examined from a theoretical standpoint.

Since this sort of transition evolves out of our ordinary ways of dealing with broken tools, it is clear that the skeptic is right in maintaining that the theoretical discovery of entities as objects for thematic scientific investigation is "continuous" with common sense. But it also appears that common sense itself arises only as the result of a *change-over* in our plain, everyday ways of taking things. As a specialized and derivative mode of relating to things, then, the standpoint of common sense cannot be taken as a faithful reflection of our most primordial ways of dealing with the world. Common sense and the theoretical attitude support each other's claims to being basic, but they do so at a level where the genuinely basic level of encountering the world has been left behind.

The second component of the change-over from everydayness to mere assertions concerns the way that entities themselves are encountered. In the transformation of ordinary dealings with equipment into the attitude in which we explicitly formulate statements about objects, entities are stripped of their internal relations in the context and are seen as mere things with accidents. The hammer, for instance, is no longer seen in its relation to the workshop as a whole.

In the "physical" statement that "the hammer is heavy" we *overlook* not only the tool-character of the entity we encounter, but also something that belongs to any ready-to-hand equipment: its place [Platz]. Its place becomes a matter of indifference. This does not mean that what is present-at-hand loses its "location" altogether. But its place becomes a spatio-temporal position, a "world-point," which is in no way distinguished from any other (361/2).

What Heidegger has called the "ontological definition" of an entity—its *place* within a context of internal relations—is transformed into a mere space-time position. From this account of the origins of mere "things" it appears that the conception of the world as consisting of corporeal objects, connected solely by the external relations of space and time, is not our most original way of encountering the world, but is rather a result of the *breakdown* of everydayness.

In Heidegger's view, the tendency to concentrate on the statement as the paradigm of language use, together with the conception of truth as correspondence, is the source of the objectifying ontology that sees the world as consisting of primary substances with accidents. The subject-predicate structure of the statement seems to give us "an unambiguous proof," he says, for the view that entities are "objects" with "properties."[6] It is because we read the "surface grammar" of the elementary proposition into the world that we are blind to the internal relations constituted by our intensional language of purposes and goals. If we were to make visible the innumerable uses of language which make up human expressiveness, Heidegger claims, we would see that there is no way to reduce all these different language-games to the form of the elementary proposition "without essentially perverting their meaning" (158). Our one-sided preoccupation with the subject-predicate grammar of the statement is revealed as the source of the narrow ontological interpretations of the tradition. Heidegger tries to lead us to see that this subject-predicate schema does not give us a useful clue to grasping the Being of entities. The pervasiveness of this ontological dogma in the West is a product of the fact that the hermeneutic 'as' of everydayness is generally tacit and unnoticed whereas theoretical discovery in terms of the apophantic 'as' is explicit. Because readiness-to-hand and the hermeneutic 'as' are "invisible," the priority of statements and objects is what is most striking to us.

Heidegger therefore leads us to see that the theoretical attitude of scientific inquiry arises from the *collapse* of our most primordial ways of being involved in the world. What does the theoretical at-

6. WT 38, FD 28.

titude consist in, according to Heidegger? Here it would be easy for him to say that it consists either in the complete loss of *praxis* or in the fact that the subject matter of science is the present-at-hand. But Heidegger is too sensitive to the complexity of science to make such simplistic claims. For, first of all, he sees that every mode of theoretical inquiry has its own kind of practice. Scientists are involved with laboratory equipment and technical devices that they have mastered in being indoctrinated into their worlds of activity. And "even in the 'most abstract' way of thinking out problems," Heidegger says, "one manipulates equipment for writing, for example" (358). But, secondly, it is also obvious that the subject matter of a science may be the ready-to-hand as such. The sciences of economics, cultural anthropology, and history, for instance, study the milieu in which equipment is ready-to-hand for the people involved: "The ready-to-hand can become the 'object' of a science without having to lose its character as ready-to-hand" (361).

What distinguishes the theoretical attitude from everydayness is not the loss of practice or the priority of the present-at-hand, then, but the fact that the entities studied by the scientist have been "decontextualized" or "released from their set" (entschränkt) in the *scientist's* environment (362). Although the scientist's apparatus is still functioning as ready-to-hand, the entities that are the theme of his research are "disworlded" in the sense of no longer having a place in *his* world. The metallurgist analyzing the chemical make-up of the hammer, for example, no longer discovers the hammer in its ontological definition of hammering. Similarly, the sociologist studying the sexual mores of his culture no longer encounters them as pertaining to him in any way. In the theoretical attitude, the scientist distances himself from the goal-directedness of the contexts of everydayness in order to focus on entities in terms of specific theoretical interests and goals. Entities are thus freed from their ordinary contexts and are projected in terms of more precisely delimited regional concerns.

The decontextualization of entities in the sciences gives rise to the idea that scientific inquiry is "objective" in the sense of being liberated from all interests and assumptions. But Heidegger suggests that this objectivity is relative: the entity is "disworlded" in its ordinary readiness-to-hand, but it can undergo this process of disworlding only by being placed into a *new* context of relevance conditions in the scientific framework. Heidegger says that the scientific community lays out a "ground plan" or "blueprint" (Grundriss) for how the entity is to count in their activities as scientists. In a Kuhnian language, we might say that the scientific attitude is achieved when a "paradigm" qua disciplinary matrix for the science has been laid out.[7] "The full existential determination of science," Heidegger says, is characterized by the totality of determinations of

> the basic concepts of the understanding of Being by which we are guided, . . . the guide-books on method, the structure of its conceptualizations, the appropriate possibilities of truth and certainty, the types of grounding and proof, the mode in which it is binding, and the way it is communicated (362/3).

Through its textbook adoptions, technical journals, research-grant awards, ideal models for experiments, and other expressions, the community of interpreters decides what is to count as "normal science" for a particular region of entities and determines how entities are to be encountered by that science.

The paradigm of scientific activity articulates the shared interests, goals, and ideals that govern the relevance conditions for encountering domains of entities in the sciences. Scientific research, Heidegger says,

> is accomplished through the projection of a definite ground plan [Grundriss] for the natural processes in the region of entities, for example, in nature. The projection sketches out how the procedures of knowing must adhere to the opened region. . . . Through the projection of the ground plan and the determination of exactitude and rigor, method secures for itself its proper area of objects (Gegenstandbezirk) within the region of Being (AWV 271, HW 71).

Events and entities can count as relevant for a science only if they are interpreted as falling into this ground plan or blueprint: "It is only within this blueprint that a natural event becomes visible as such" (*ibid.*).

Heidegger's "existential conception of science" makes it clear that there can be no context-free discovery of "objects" as they are in themselves, or of "bare facts" outside of any interpretation. What is discovered in the theoretical attitude has been constituted by the language-games of the sciences. Heidegger claims that it is to the

7. Thomas S. Kuhn, *The Structure of Scientific Revolutions* (Chicago: University Press, 1970) and "Second Thoughts on Paradigms" in *The Essential Tension* (Chicago: University Press, 1977).

credit of the earliest natural scientists at the dawn of the modern era that they understood that "there are no 'bare facts' " (362). For them, "a fact is only what it is in the light of a grounding conception and always depends upon how far that grounding reaches."[8] When science degenerates into "positivism," however, scientists forget that their conceptualizing determines what is to count as a fact, and they come to see their activities as a "pure discovery of entities in the world" (363). The loss of the insight of the original scientists then paves the way for the distorted picture of *pure reflection* as the unmediated ascertaining of context-free facts.

What is forgotten in the theoretical attitude of pure discovery is that science involves a "working over" (Bearbeitung) of entities to make them fit the blueprint of the scientific projection. Heidegger says that "science is a working over of the real", and that what counts as real is consequently *produced* by this working over.[9] The ground plan or blueprint of the science lays out in advance the ways that entities are to be worked over, and thereby determines the "objectiveness" (Gegenständigkeit) of the object domain of the science. Objectiveness "sketches out in advance the possibilities of posing questions" and lays out the standards for working over the data until "it fits into the standardized objective context of the theory."[10] Not until new data have been made to fit the context of the theory can they *count as data* for that particular science. Heidegger recognizes, of course, that data can bring about modifications in the theory as well. What he emphasizes, however, is that the determinations of objectiveness for a science generally remain unchanged in this process. The projection of objectiveness is like the riverbanks through which both theorizing and data-collecting flow.

The shared paradigm of scientific objectification for the sciences is embedded in the expressions of the scientific community. But there is also a constant interaction between the scientific community and the wider culture in which it operates. Out of this interaction there arises a prevailing "attunement" or "mood" (Gestimmtheit) for an age. The mood of the modern technological age is called "framing" (Ge-stell).[11] The technical term 'Ge-stell' refers to

8. WT 67, FD 51.

9. QCT 167, VA I 48.

10. QCT 169, VA I 49.

11. QCT 19, VA I 19. Cf. Edward G. Ballard, "Heidegger's View and Evaluation of Nature and Natural Science," in J. Sallis, ed., *Heidegger and the Path of Thinking* (Pittsburgh: Duquesne, 1970), pp. 46ff.

the "frame" or "framework" in which modern man is "disposed" (bestellt) to treat everything he encounters as a "fund" or "stock" (Bestand) of energy at his disposal. The world is seen as a nexus of forces at our disposal to be reckoned with and dominated in order to obtain energy for our needs. In framing, Heidegger says, "Nature becomes a gigantic filling station, an energy source for modern technology and industry."[12] Through the interaction of science and common sense, the capacity for objectification that was brought about with such effort and cost by the first scientists degenerates into something which appears to be self-evident and commonplace. It is transparent to *anyone* that the world consists of objects of certain types. The assumption that there are facts that can be discovered by anyone becomes part of the store of obvious truths of the Anyone.

It seems to follow, then, that the stage I common-sense description of what we know and how we know it is actually the offspring of a theoretical attitude which itself arises only when our everyday involved understanding of the world is shattered. When Heidegger says that the theoretical attitude of science is a "founded mode" of Being-in-the-world, he means that the whole constellation of ideas that make up the scientific viewpoint—language as statements, the world as consisting of objects, the priority of a disinterested attitude, the concern with technological domination—is possible only for a specialized mode of concern that characterizes the community of interpreters in the world of the theoretical attitude. As a mode of Being-in-the-world, however, scientific activity must be understood as *situated* in the attunement of a culture and as *projecting* entities in terms of relevance conditions laid out in advance by our communal interests and purposes. The situatedness and projection of science are therefore parasitic on the grasp of what it is to be which is articulated by the *logos* of our historical culture. For this reason, the sciences cannot claim to have a privileged access to the ultimate truth about the world which is denied to our pre-ontological understanding.

To sum up the account of the derivation of science from Being-in-the-world, we have found that the subject matter of scientific inquiry is decontextualized to the extent that it can be dealt with in a way that attains a level of generality not found in ordinary situations. For example, although the Being of a hammer for a carpenter in a workshop is ontologically defined by his activity of

---

12. *Discourse on Thinking,* trans. John M. Anderson and E. Hans Freund (New York: Harper Colophon, 1966), p. 50. *Gelassenheit* (Pfullingen: Neske, 1959), p. 18.

hammering, the scientist can see the hammer as an object with properties, stripped of its ties to any particular context of practical use and subject to various interpretations. But at the same time we have seen that the results of science are also *recontextualized* in a regional framework of interests. The understanding of the Being of entities in the theoretical attitude is governed in advance by a blueprint of objectiveness which is derived from our prescientific grasp of Being and is made accessible in the expressions of the community of scientists.

What science encounters is therefore shaped by the goals, ideals, and interests of that community. As long as the scientific community recognizes that the entities it deals with are shaped by its projections, scientific inquiry has a legitimate and valuable role to play. When scientists forget their own constituting role in projecting domains of entities, however, the misleading conception of the possibility of "pure reflection" can arise. Pure reflection understands itself as having unmediated access to a context-free and theory-neutral given that can serve as a foundation for rationally reconstructing the edifice of our common-sense beliefs. Heidegger's analysis of the ontological genesis of science diagnoses this conception of pure reflection by showing its roots in the breakdown that is the source of modern science.

The second step in Heidegger's attempt to show that epistemology is a founded mode of Being-in-the-world consists in tracing Descartes's discovery of the *cogito, sum* back to the initial achievements of the early scientists. Heidegger suggests that the conception of foundationalism implicit in stage I of the Cartesian model and explicit in stage III has its roots in the development of modern mathematical physics. The central role of the *ego cogito* as a self-grounding ground, he contends, is rooted in a certain conception of mathematics. Mathematical physics is the paradigm of the sciences, according to Heidegger, not because it applies mathematics to nature, nor because it attains greater exactitude, but rather because of *"the way in which nature itself is mathematically projected"* (362).

The significance of this notion of a "mathematical projection" is explained in terms of the etymology of the word 'mathematical'. To a Greek speaker, Heidegger says, 'ta mathēmata' originally meant "that which man knows prior to his observation of entities and his dealings with things."[13] Because the mathematical is always known in advance, "we do not first get it out of things but, in a certain

---

13. AWV 271, HW 72.

way, we bring it along with us."[14] For the Greeks, numbers were only especially important *examples* of this kind of knowledge. If there are four apples on a table and one is taken away, for instance, our knowledge of the "three" that remain is not something we learn from the apples. It is something we bring with us to the encounter. In Heidegger's view, then, the conception of mathematics as the pure study of quantities is *derived* from this more original understanding of the mathematical as what is known in advance.

What distinguishes the mathematical projection of physics from earlier ways of understanding the Being of entities is its concern with what I have called "unitizing" (in section 3). Mathematical physics works entities over in order to reduce them to one homogeneous type — the physical — for which the only "real" properties are those pertaining to mass, velocity, and spatiotemporal position. Heidegger characterizes this way of projecting the Being of entities by contrasting it with the understanding of Being implicit in the Aristotelian conception of motion. Aristotelian science understood motion in terms of the hidden "powers" and "natures" in things. On this view everything has a natural *place:* fire rises because its place is above; earth seeks the lowest level because that is its place. "Each body has *its* place *according to its kind,* and it strives toward that place."[15]

In contrast, the Galilean and Newtonian view regards all objects as alike and explains motion in terms of a few basic laws which hold with absolute generality for all objects. For modern science,

> all bodies are alike. No motion is spatial. Every place is like every other, each temporal point like any other. . . . All determinations of bodies are sketched out in one basic blueprint, according to which the natural process is nothing but the space-time determination of the motion of mass-points. This fundamental design of nature at the same time circumscribes its region as everywhere homogeneous (WT 91, FD 70/1).

The new way of understanding the real does not come about as the result of the discovery of new facts. To the extent that we can speak of "facts" here, the Galilean scientist deals with the same facts that were available to the Aristotelian. The difference lies in the way the Galilean projects these facts according to a new "blueprint." In the projection of mathematical physics, entities come to be seen as

14. WT 74, FD 57.

15. WT 83, FD 65.

interchangeable bits with no inner principles or internal relations to other components of nature. The totality of units is made intelligible not through grasping their concealed meanings, but by seeing them as collocated into a coherent arrangement by a system of laws. Heidegger contends that physics becomes mathematical in the quantitative sense because of the way it unitizes entities in its projection.

> Because the projection establishes a homogeneity of all bodies according to relations of space, time and motion, it also makes possible and requires a universal uniform measure as an essential determinant of things, i.e., numerical measurement. The mathematical projection of Newtonian bodies leads to the development of a certain "mathematics" in the narrow sense (WT 93, FD 72).

Mathematical physics becomes the prototype for all sciences, then, because it provides a way in which the unitized variables and constants within the theoretical framework can be systematically mapped onto the quantifiable units projected by the theory. Permutations within the world can be systematically modeled by the theory only if the quantitative aspects of nature are raised to prominence and the qualitative aspects are played down. As a result, the view arises that only that which is quantifiable can be counted as real. Heidegger quotes Max Planck, who says, "Wirklich ist, was sich messen lässt," "Reality is what can be measured."[16] Quantifiability also comes to be the criterion used to distinguish the "hard sciences" from such "soft sciences" as history, philology, and literary criticism.

So long as the intelligibility of natural processes is seen as lying in the interpretation of the "concealed qualitites, powers and capacities" in things,[17] it is natural to see nature as like a text that expresses a divine plan. Within this kind of picture, understanding is rooted in a correct interpretation of a structure of symbols according to the key made accessible in revelation and Scripture. When nature is projected as a homogeneous domain of units with no hidden powers or internal relations, however, intelligibility must reside not in the meaningful text of nature itself, but in the system of *laws* that make up the theoretical nexus. It is for this reason, Heidegger

16. QCT 169, VA I 50.

17. WT 93, FD 72.

says, that the projection of objectiveness of modern physics is "axiomatic": the foundation for our understanding becomes a network of basic *propositions:*

> The projection is axiomatic. Insofar as all cognition and knowledge expresses itself in propositions [Sätzen], the knowledge which is taken and proposed [gesetzte] in the mathematical projection is of such a kind as to propose things in advance on their foundation. The axioms are fundamental principles [Grundsätze].[18]

Through the axioms or laws, the mutability of the given is articulated into an intelligible form: "Only within the boundaries of rule and law [Gesetz] are facts revealed as the facts they are."[19]

Heidegger's claim is that the Cartesian reduction to the subjectivity of the *ego cogito* precipitates out of the grounding of intelligibility in propositions which is characteristic of mathematical physics. When intelligibility can no longer be grounded in the interpretation of revelation by Church tradition, there arises a will to the "self-grounding" of knowledge. Heidegger says that "where the project [Wurf] of the mathematical projection is ventured, the projector of this project places himself on the base that is first projected in the projection."[20] In other words, the mathematical projection of objectiveness has no foundation other than the projector himself. What is needed, therefore, is a proposition (Satz) that can serve as the fundamental principle (Grundsatz) on which all other principles are founded. If this principle is to provide us with genuine intelligibility, it must be intrinsically intelligible and certain, and it must establish from out of itself the meaning of Being for all entities. "It must be a basic principle—*the* absolute basic principle."[21]

What proposition can serve as such a self-grounding ground for the axiomatic system of physics? According to Heidegger, only the self-reflection of thinking itself can provide an ultimate foundation.

---

18. WT 92, FD 71. Heidegger is here relying on the etymological connection of 'setzen' (to set) and 'Satz' (proposition). I will try to capture this connection by translating 'setzen' with 'propose'.

19. AWV 272, HW 73-4.

20. WT 97, FD 75.

21. WT 80, FD 103.

If anything is given at all, it is only the *proposition* in general *as such,* i.e., the proposing, the position [Position], in the sense of a thinking that asserts. The proposing, the proposition, only has itself as what can be proposed. Only where thinking thinks itself, is it absolutely mathematical, i.e., a taking cognizance of that which we already have (WT 104, FD 80).

The proposing that proposes itself is the *ego cogito.* In thinking itself, the "I think" is self-fulfilling and self-verifying. Only the thinking that thinks itself can serve as an ultimate self-grounding principle of all principles. It is clear, then, that Heidegger does not regard the *cogito, sum* as an inference. He sees Descartes as finding the *sum* in the very performance of proposing the proposition. The *cogito, sum* is the highest certainty because its truth lies immediately in the performance of proposing.

On the basis of the highest principle of the *cogito,* the Being of all entities can be determined in advance. For the first time in history, Heidegger says, that which underlies all entities as their basis—the "sub-jectum" or "hypokeimenon"—becomes the "I" as self-positing and self-proposing. The "I" becomes the self-grounding ground of all grounds. As a result, the term 'ob-jectum' ("that which is thrown over against"), which in Descartes's *Meditations* is still used to characterize the mental, now comes to be taken in its modern sense as the objectively real. Things that are not the "I" are essentially such as stand as something else in relation to a 'subject', which lie over against it as *objectum.* The things themselves become 'objects'."[22] The Being of all entities is determined by their relation to the subject. In Heidegger's view, then, Kant's "Copernican Revolution" was already a *fait accompli* in the rise of modern science.

When the thinking of a subject is made the basic principle of all metaphysics, entities come to be grounded in the "re-presenting" ("Vor-stellen," "placing before") of the subject. Entities are encountered as "standing against" (gegen-ständige) the representing of the "I." Heidegger says that "re-presenting is a fore-going, dominating ob-ject-ification."[23] It is the "placing-before" of representing that grounds the Being of entities.

Objectifying in re-presenting delivers the object over to the

22. WT 105, FD 82.

23. QCT 150, HW 100. "Vor-stellen ist vor-gehende, meisternde ver-gegen-ständlichung."

ego cogito. In this delivering over, the *ego* proves itself to be the ground of its own activity (the delivering over that re-presents); i.e., proves itelf as *subjectum.* The subject is subject for itself. . . . All entities are therefore either objects of the subject or the subject of the subject (QCT 100, HW 236).

The capacity for encountering the world as a collection of "objects" in this sense of the term was first made possible by the cultural achievement of modern science. The Greeks, Heidegger says, could never have experienced the world as mere objects set over against subjects.[24]

The objects that can be represented with complete certainty are the *cogitationes* or "ideas" of the thinking subject. For only when objects are given with the certainty of the self-grounding ground of the "I think" can they serve as building blocks for certain and in-dubitable knowledge in the sciences. Thus, the epistemological reduction of the subject to its "veil of ideas" — to the incorrigible and indubitable mental contents that are immediately given — is seen as rooted in the requirements of the projection of mathe-matical physics.

Heidegger claims that the Cartesian conception of the essence of entities as *extensio* also has its roots in mathematical physics. Un-critically taking over a tradition that interprets the essence of Being as *substance,* Descartes seeks the Being of entities in that which is self-dependent and endures through changing accidents. Since mathematics deals with entities *"which always are what they are"* and *"constantly remain"* through change (96/7), Descartes assumes that only "that which is accessible in an entity *through mathematics* makes up its Being" (96). What is accessible through mathematics in modern physics is the measurable extension of bodies. Instead of trying to interpret the world as it is encountered in everydayness, then, Descartes

> prescribes for the world its "real" Being, as it were, on the basis of an idea of Being whose source has not been unveiled and which has not been demonstrated in its own right — an idea in which Being is equated with constant presence-at-hand (96).

In his understanding of Being as the enduring presence of the *res ex-tensa* represented by a subject, "Descartes explicitly switches over philosophically from the development of traditional ontology to mod-ern mathematical physics and its transcendental foundations" (96).

24. SvG 140/1.

In Heidegger's diagnoses of the Cartesian model, both dualism and monism are found to originate in the requirements built into the ideal of intelligibility of modern science. The Cartesian tradition has generated a set of unexamined, dogmatic ontological presuppositions which have continued to define the issues for debate up to the present. The conception of intelligibility as lying in an axiomatic system, the correlative demand for ontological homogeneity, the picture of the object as what stands over against a subject, the view that knowledge consists in correct representation—these are the common grounds from which modern controversies between materialists and dualists spring. As Heidegger says, "The whole of modern metaphysics, including Nietzsche, remains within the conception of entities and of truth initiated by Descartes."[25]

The ontological genesis of the theoretical attitude is designed to lead us to see the sciences as specialized modes of projection which are conducted within the framework of the intelligible world of everydayness. The sciences, of course, have a legitimate and valuable role to play as human forms of life. In decontextualizing entities from their ordinary situations, they provide us with a capacity for generalization not obtained in everydayness. But their greater generality in decontextualization is possible only by virtue of the fact that, at a deeper level, their objects are recontextualized within the projection of objectiveness laid out in advance by the blueprint of a theory. Consequently, the regional modes of scientific activity must be understood as parasitic on our everyday pre-ontological understanding of the world. Only for humans who have already mastered the shared intelligible world of equipment and Being-with can there be anything like the "pure discovery" of what is merely present-at-hand.

Heidegger seems to think that different modes of discourse have their own logic and criteria of legitimacy. Each regional activity lays out in advance a conception of the Being of the entities with which it deals, specific guides as to what questions and answers will count as significant, and different views as to what methods and techniques of investigation will be appropriate. Heidegger says that things "stand in different truths."[26] On this view, then, there can be no real conflict between the ways the sun is discovered by the farmer, the astrophysicist, the meteorologist, and the poet. The idea that there is a conflict appears only for the disengaged attitude

---

25. AWV 278, HW 80.

26. WT 26, FD 20.

of common sense which, warped by the forgetfulness of the tradition, sees all interpretations as structured by the apophantic 'as' of context-free statements and then insists that only one representation of states of affairs can be "correct." In its dogmatic assumptions, Heidegger says, "Common sense misunderstands understanding" (315); it is blind to the role of the fore-structure of understanding in articulating different regions of the life-world, and it tends to think that all areas of human thought and inquiry can be brought before a single impartial tribunal of pure reason. Common sense "fails to recognize that entities can be experienced 'factually' only when Being is already understood" (316) and that Being is understood in different ways in different regions of the life-world.

From Heidegger's standpoint, the language-games of poetry, humor, religious inspiration, aesthetic judgments, and legal decisions, to name only a few areas of the life-world, are all more or less autonomous regions of projection which are grasped by virtue of our participation in the intelligible world constituted by our historical language. The attempt to impose the paradigm of one mode of inquiry onto all these regions leads not so much to greater rationality as it does to an impoverishment of human possibilities of understanding. In order to break the spell of this Enlightenment dogmatism, Heidegger says "the fundamental question" must be that "of the justification and limits of the mathematical in general."[27]

§12. *Justification and Grounding*

Heidegger's goal in working out the "existential conception of science" is to show that both the theoretical attitude and the Cartesian contemplative attitude are derived from and dependent on Being-in-the-world. The Cartesian, fascinated with the possibility of the *relative* decontextualization of entities in the theoretical attitude, is blind to the fact that entities are still contextualized in a theoretical projection. The Cartesian's goal is to attain a totally prejudice-free position from which he can encounter "brute data" as the basis for rationally reconstructing our everyday beliefs and practices. But if all our modes of encountering entities are shaped in advance by our pre-ontological understanding of the world, there can be no such thing as a "pure discovery" of something immediately given. Because Descartes failed to appreciate the role

27. WT 95, FD 73.

of Dasein's understanding in encountering the world, Heidegger says, the road was blocked "to seeing the founded character of all sensory and intellective perception, and to understanding these as possibilities of Being-in-the-world" (98). If the discovery of the present-at-hand in the contemplative attitude is *derivative from* a prior discovery of the ready-to-hand in practical affairs, then it does not seem that the present-at-hand can provide a basis for accounting for everydayness.

Heidegger considers a natural objection the Cartesian could make to this critique of his enterprise. The Cartesian might admit, it seems, that the discovery of present-at-hand things is possible only for a being that has already discovered the world in everyday equipmental contexts. But he might also point out that his concern is not with the *actual* way we happen to discover entities. Such questions are in the domain of the *quaestio facti* and are irrelevant to the Cartesian. We saw in Chapter I that Descartes says his interest is not in the actual order of discovery, but in the *rational order* that justifies or grounds our beliefs and practices. The "rational reconstruction" is supposed to provide an answer to this kind of *quaestio juris*. Its goal is to provide a global philosophical clarification of everydayness by showing how our plain understanding of the world can built up from simple units by means of intrinsically intelligible principles.

The rational reconstruction provides us with a "stratographic" form of grounding for our beliefs and practices. According to this account, one first orders sensory data into a stratum of extended substances which serve as "the fundamental stratum upon which all other strata of actuality within-the-world are built up" (98). One then goes on to distinguish the primary and secondary qualities of things, and finally one tacks on such value-predicates as 'beautiful', 'ugly', 'useful', and 'useless'. This kind of account is supposed to make everydayness fully intelligible for the first time by showing how it is grounded in basic units.

It is surprising that, in the context of his critique of Cartesian foundationalism, Heidegger does not seem to have an adequate answer to this line of objection. He claims at one point that "our pre-phenomenological experience shows that in an entity which is supposedly a thing, there is something that will not become fully intelligible through thinghood alone" (99). But this seems to be nothing more than bald assertion where some kind of argument is needed. He also says that "if we are to reconstruct the thing of use, which supposedly comes to us in the first instance 'with its skin off'," we must *previously take a positive look at the phenomenon whose totality such a reconstruction is to restore*" (99). But no

Cartesian would take issue with this requirement, for it is the totality that the method of unitizing and generalizing is to reconstruct, and it is of course necessary to "take a look" at it in advance. Heidegger seems to be most candid when he simply says the we have no guarantee that the world of significance can be built up from present-at-hand things with values (101). But the fact that we have no assurance that something can be done hardly seems to be a sufficient reason to reject an enterprise at the outset. If there is a prospect of elucidating our everyday experience of the world through such a reconstruction, the Cartesian might say, it is simply obscurantism to deny the project before it begins.

Although Heidegger's reply to the Cartesian in the context of his discussion of Descartes in *Being and Time* is unsatisfactory, it seems that the description of Being-in-the-world does provide him with a way of dealing with the claims of the ideal of rational reconstruction. What is revealed by the Cartesian's objection is the fact that the legitimacy of the foundationalist project hinges on a specific but tacit conception of the conditions for achieving ultimate intelligibility. The *quid facti/quid juris* distinction presupposes a clear and sharp distinction between the ways we *actually* come to arrive to our beliefs and the *reasons and grounds* that make those beliefs intelligible. Once the goal of achieving understanding and the quest for certainty have been conflated, the factual story of how we come to hold our beliefs can no longer be thought of as making our beliefs and practices genuinely intelligible. What is required for true and ultimate intelligibility is a global justification of our lives as a whole. Only when we have demonstrated that our horizon of everyday activities has a firm foundation in intrinsically intelligible self-grounding grounds will we have achieved genuine understanding.

At the core of the Cartesian enterprise, then, lies the assumption that the foundationalist reconstruction of our beliefs and practices is a necessary condition for making our lives fully intelligible. We have seen that this assumption is built into the stage I commonsense description of our epistemic predicament and that it serves as the *pretext* for attempting the stage III reconstruction. Hence, if Heidegger can undermine this motivating pretext for Cartesian foundationalism, the basis for the traditional ideal of grounding will also be deflated. What Heidegger's account of everydayness reveals is that the Cartesian project is fundamentally incoherent: its assumption that there is something *un*intelligible about our daily practices which requires a special sort of philosophical clarification or elucidation is an illusion.

The imputed lack of clarity in our everyday situations first comes on the scene as a result of the stage I common-sense description of our ordinary prephilosophical lives. We are pictured as observers collecting information about the world and on this basis formulating the kinds of beliefs that are supposed to underlie our practices. We found in the last section, however, that this stage I common-sense account of our mundane situations is a philosophical construct extrapolated from modes of theoretical inquiry. It is the product of viewing ourselves through the distorting lens of contexts in which the structure of Being-in-the-world has collapsed, and therefore cannot be taken as a faithful portrayal of our plain epistemic situations.

In order to shake off the blinders imposed by this common-sense view of ourselves, Heidegger redescribes our plain contexts in an ontologically appropriate manner. From the standpoint of this redescription of everyday situations, the apparent *lack* of clarity about our practices and beliefs is seen to be rooted not in some deep, intrinsic puzzlement inhering in everydayness, but in the refracted light of the theoretical attitude that is already at work in common sense. In this respect Heidegger's method is similar to that of Wittgenstein, who says that for certain areas

> undertaking to give an explanation is from the outset mistaken for the simple reason that one only needs to correctly put together what one *knows,* and not add anything to it, and the satisfaction sought for by the explanation follows all by itself.[28]

The description of everydayness reveals that Being-in-the-world has a hermeneutical structure. In our daily encounters with the world, we have found, individual "items" of equipment can be discovered only within a whole or totality of significance which is grasped in advance through our *self*-understanding in the situation. It follows, then, that all intelligibility is rooted in a horizon of generally tacit understanding that arises from our concernful involvement in the world. Heidegger says that even the pure, objective, disinterested modes of the theoretical discovery of "nature" are only "limiting cases" (65) of our concernful pre-ontological understanding. Every encounter with a context of equipment is embedded in a horizon of prereflective understanding which lights up our activities but itself remains invisible as our practices proceed.

---

28. "Bemerkungen über Frazers *The Golden Bough,*" ed. Rush Rhees, *Synthese,* XVII (1967): 233–253, p. 235.

If all our practices take place within a horizon of vague and inexplicit everyday understanding, then even the possibility of something obtruding as *unintelligible* is determined in advance by this understanding. The mysterious article I find while digging in my garden, for instance, can be puzzling to me only because I already have a prior grasp of what should and should not be there. Given the fore-structure of my understanding, I can ask whether it is a human artifact or a natural formation. But even if the mystery remains unsolved, the questions I can ask and the kinds of answers that would make sense are always guided by my attuned understanding of "ordinary" interpretations and my rudimentary grasp of scientific vocabularies. Without this understanding, nothing could ever strike me either as familiar or as strange.

For this reason Heidegger says that all explanation presupposes understanding. "In all explanation," he says, "one discovers understandingly that which one cannot understand; and all explanation is thus rooted in Dasein's primary understanding" (336). The legitimate task of seeking explanations is always conducted within a horizon of understanding that guides our questioning and establishes procedures for attaining clarity and elucidation. Through our mastery of the shared language of the Anyone, we have developed specific habits and expectations that enable us to see things as obvious or puzzling. We are already attuned to one another in our attitudes as to what is to function as a normal form for making things intelligible. A prior understanding of the linguistically articulated world is a precondition, then, for requesting explanations or grounds as well as for discriminating the unintelligible present-at-hand from the background of what is already intelligible in the context.

We can imagine conditions under which *any* entity can come to be isolated as present-at-hand and treated as in need of explanation. A detective trying to make sense of how a crime was committed, for instance, might take even the most mundane item in a room and ask how it came to be there. And it is certainly true that great advances have come about in the sciences through the ability of individuals to step back and question what had been taken as obvious and self-evident. But such cases of departing from established habits and expectations make sense only against a *background of shared understanding* which remains constant through such shifts. In other words, we can make sense of unintelligibility and a demand for explanation only within a horizon of intelligibility which is not itself thrown in question. For this reason the regional inquiries of the sciences can accomplish their tasks only within the framework of pre-understanding common to the community of interpreters. "Any interpretation which is to contribute understanding," Heidegger says, "must already have understood what is to be interpreted" (152).

But these observations suggest that there is something fundamentally incoherent in the Cartesian's project of providing *global* intelligibility for our horizon of everydayness. The Cartesian goal is not to provide explanations or clarifications for particular regions within the familiar horizon of the life-world. The foundationalist enterprise is supposed to provide global and intrinsic intelligibility for the horizon of everydayness as a whole. For this to be possible, the Cartesian must set aside or bracket all the "prejudices" and "opinions" built into our everyday understanding in order to start afresh from a pure, disinterested, disengaged standpoint. But this ideal standpoint, if it could be achieved, would leave him without *any* horizon in which to conduct his inquiry. As the foregoing account of the conditions for the possibility of any inquiry suggests, however, this Cartesian undertaking would be impossible. There is no such thing as a pure, horizonless standpoint for providing intelligibility. Where there is no horizon for an inquiry, there is no inquiry.

The Cartesian enterprise is incoherent, then, because it must tacitly *presuppose* that we understand the horizon of everydayness while simultaneously pretending that its own justifications and grounding will first make that horizon intelligible. The Cartesian is thus forced into the position of trading on our pre-ontological understanding in order to undertake the task of explaining that same understanding. But he could undertake the project of making the horizon of everydayness intelligible only if he could establish a vantage point *outside of* the horizon of Being-in-the-world from which the grounding is conducted. What Heidegger wants us to see, however, is that there can be no such horizonless vantage point. If all inquiries are possible only within the framework of Being-in-the-world, then there is no way for the Cartesian to gain access to a standpoint, free of all "prejudices," from which to ground our understanding of the world.

The argument I am attributing to Heidegger here is similar to Wittgenstein's argument for the "autonomy of grammar."[29] Wittgenstein argues that if we wanted to explain or justify the grammar of our language over against another, the statements in which the

29. See his *Philosophical Grammar* (Oxford: Blackwell, 1974), pp. 40, 63, 97, and *Philosophical Remarks* (Oxford: Blackwell, 1975), pp. 53, 55. Also, G. E. Moore, "Wittgenstein's Lectures in 1930-33," in his *Philosophical Papers* (New York: Collier, 1966), pp. 272/3.

justification was framed would have to presuppose the very grammar they were supposed to justify. The purported justification, since it would rely on the correctness and intelligibility of what it was supposed to establish, would be "pointless." Similarly, the Cartesian rational reconstruction must presuppose the intelligibility of the very horizon that is supposed to make intelligible. The Cartesian is thus in a paradoxical position, for his foundationalist enterprise can play the role it was intended to play only if it in fact has *no* role to play. There is no "God's eye" point of view the Cartesian can attain to begin his grounding of everydayness.

The structure of this argument is transcendental. It is designed to show that a condition for the possibility of undertaking a rational reconstruction of our beliefs is that we *already* understand what the justification purports to make intelligible. It therefore undermines the *pretext* for stage III of the Cartesian inquiry—namely, the assumption that there is somethng unintelligible about our plain situations that demands a global form of grounding if it is to be made intelligible. The same argument might also be taken as showing that there is something incoherent about the stage II skeptical challenge to our everyday beliefs. For if our lives are regarded as commentaries on the text-analogue of the Anyone and if the skeptic is seen as casting very general doubts on the veracity of this text-analogue, then the skeptic's doubt, as a mode of Being-in-the-world, would be possible only if it in effect abrogated the conditions for its own possibility.[30] If meaningful activity is possible only within the linguistically constituted horizon of everydayness, then there is no way for the skeptic to undermine this horizon without making his own activity meaningless. His activity would make sense only if there were a horizon of understanding *outside* the horizon of Being-in-the-world. But, as I have suggested, there is no such external vantage point.

The skeptic's inquiry strikes us as meaningful because we tend to assimilate it to regional forms of inquiry which are perfectly in order as they are. But regional inquiries are concerned with the intelligibility of entities *within* a pre-given horizon of understanding. The Cartesian takes an illegitimate step in assuming that the methods for attaining intelligibility for entities discovered *within* a horizon are also applicable for attaining intelligibility *for that horizon itself.* In Heidegger's language, the skeptic has failed to appreciate the "ontological difference" between Being and entities: the methods of doubt and justification that are appropriate for examining entities have no legitimate application to the horizon of

---

30. This line of argument will be developed below in section 14.

understanding which makes it possible to encounter any entity whatsoever.

The main type of objection raised against transcendental arguments of this sort is that, although it may be the case that our meaningful behavior is possible only if certain beliefs are unchallenged, this does not imply that the beliefs are true. It may be that we *have to* hold all sorts of beliefs, and yet it might nevertheless be the case that states of affairs are really quite different from what we believe them to be.[31] The standard rejoinder to this objection is to ask the skeptic to make explicit in detail *how* states of affairs could be so radically different from the ways we now conceive them. If the skeptic's hypothesis makes sense, he should be able to give us some idea of how things could be so discordant. Since the grammar of our language constitutes what can be intelligible to us, however, there is no way for the skeptic to fill in the details of his account of how things might be different without making them less different than he wanted them to be. The skeptic replies in turn that we should try a process of extrapolation to make clear to ourselves how things could be different. As we see things differently from primitive men, he suggests, so intergalactic civilization of the year 10,000 will see things differently from us. The defender of the transcendental argument on his side declares that this extrapolation makes no sense to him and asks for more details.

Richard Rorty has argued convincingly that this quarrel must end in a stalemate.[32] In the formulation of the argument that I am attributing to Heidegger, however, there is no way for the skeptic even to attain the initial foothold he needs to raise his objection. For in order to draw a distinction between our beliefs, on the one hand, and what states of affairs are like independent of our beliefs, on the other, it must be possible for the skeptic to make sense of a clear division between our ways of talking about the world and the way the world is in itself, irrespective of our ways of talking and acting. But, as we have seen, this kind of distinction can no longer be drawn, given Heidegger's alternative model of Being-in-the-world. If language serves to *constitute* the world, then there is no way to make sense of a world as it is in itself, independent of our language. *The* world can only be *our* linguistically articulated world. On the constitutive view of language, then, there is no way

31. See Barry Stroud, "Transcendental Arguments," *Journal of Philosophy*, 65 (1968): 241–256.

32. "The World Well Lost," *Journal of Philosophy*, 19 (1972): 649–665.

we can step outside the maze of language to compare alternative conceptual schemes.

Heidegger's conception of the conditions for intelligibility leads us to see that the pretext that motivated the Cartesian rational reconstrucion is an illusion. The contemplative attitude only *seems to* provide us with the prospect of a special sort of context-free, horizonless grounding because it is parasitic on the ordinary regional modes of explanation that make up the theoretical attitude. When it is understood that these regional activities are possible only within the horizon of pre-ontological understanding, then the idea that there can be a special mode of global inquiry into the *quaestio juris* of the horizon of everydayness itself is deflated. All justification and explanation must be carried out *within* the actual frameworks laid out by the fore-structure of our understanding.

It is clear, then, that Heidegger's model of Being-in-the-world brings about a *reversal* in the Cartesian conception of grounding and grounds. The ultimate ground for our understanding of the world does not lie in access to theory-neutral facts or context-independent objects that can be used to reconstruct our experience of the world. Instead, the ground for our beliefs and practices lies in nothing other than the shared agreement in judgments which we attain in being acculturated into the publicly intelligible world. "Facts" and "objects" can be encountered as such only through the modes of projection that are made possible through our mastery of the public world of meanings embedded in language. Only when we have already come to participate in this shared world can we accomplish the specialized feat of discovering anything like "brute data" or "bare facts" decontextualized from all ordinary situations. It follows, then, that the units uncovered by Cartesian reductivism are no more privileged as building blocks for a rational reconstruction of everydayness than are the mundane things we deal with in our ordinary situations.

Although we can discover grounds and explanations *within* our regional projections, there is no way to reach a ground "outside of" the way we project the meaning of Being in our everyday lives. Being-in-the-world, like Dilthey's "life," is "that behind which we cannot go" to bring it "before the judgment seat of reason." The meaning of Being opened by *logos* and made accessible in our pre-ontological understanding is itself the ground of all grounds. But it is also, as Heidegger says, an "abyss" (Abgrund) which cannot in turn be grounded. In his words,

> the meaning of Being can never be contrasted with entities, or with Being as the "ground" which gives entities their

support; for a "ground" ["Grund"] becomes accessible only as meaning, even if it is itself the *abyss* [Ab-grund] of meaninglessness (152; my emphasis).

To treat the shared background of meaning that is grasped in our pre-ontological understanding of the world as something that could be grounded would be to treat the horizon that makes the discovery of entities possible as if it were just one entity among others. But the horizon is not an entity and it cannot be grounded. Heidegger says,

> Insofar as Being is as ground, it itself has no ground. This is the case not because it grounds itself, however, but because every grounding—and that includes precisely those grounds that ground themselves—remains inappropriate to Being as ground. Every grounding, and indeed every appearance that something could be grounded, must degrade Being to the level of entities. As Being, Being remains ground-less. . . . Being: the abyss [Ab-grund] (SvG 185).

Since philosophers have always sought grounds that are necessary, eternal, and universal, the conception of grounding that emerges in *Being and Time*—the ungrounded forms of life of finite, historical Dasein—must appear as the "abyss of meaninglessness" (152).

From the Heideggerian perspective, we neither *have* intrinsically intelligible grounds, nor do we *need* them. Our linguistically and historically shaped practices have no source of intelligibility outside of themselves. Heidegger would agree with Wittgenstein when he says, "you must bear in mind that the language-game . . . is not based on grounds. It is not reasonable (or unreasonable). It is there—like our life."[33] In a similar vein, as we shall see later, Heidegger says that the disclosing of a world by Dasein is ultimately inexplicable: " 'In itself' it is quite incomprehensible why entities are to be *discovered,* why *truth* and *Dasein* must be" (228).

Heidegger's reversal of the traditional conception of grounding has the consequence that we can never attain the kind of complete and absolute clarity about our lives that Descartes hoped to find in his unified science. We can strive to make our background of understanding more explicit by interpretation, but we can never achieve a complete and final explication. This is the case because the process of making our pre-understanding explicit constantly transforms that understanding. Fully working out what is implicit

---

33. *On Certainty,* 559.

in the institution of voting, for instance, modifies and enriches our understanding of the practices that make up that institution and thereby generates a wider background of understanding. Since our attempts to grasp our cultural reality constantly generate a new reality that itself remains largely tacit and unclarified, there can be no *final* formal theory of that reality. In other words, there can be no closure for the task of making explicit the open-ended structure of our pre-ontological understanding.[34]

That this is so should be clear from the fact that Being-in-the-world has a hermeneutic structure. All our interpretations take place within a hermeneutic circle in which things are discovered only in terms of a pre-understanding of the whole. We can constantly strive to move toward deeper and fuller clarity about this background of pre-understanding, but we can never reach a point where all assumptions have been made explicit. For this reason the Cartesian ideal of finding a horizonless vantage point is an illusion. All inquiry, justification, and grounding are contextualized within the framework of our unfolding horizon of pre-understanding.

The open-endedness and hermeneutic structure of our everyday lives may be seen by examining a particular situation. If I find myself in a humiliating situation, for example, I have a prior grasp of what is at stake in that context through my mastery of the norms and conventions of my society. But I also have the power to change the meaning of that situation (within certain limits) by my actions. I can relieve its awkwardness by making a joke of it, or I can turn it into a tragic situation by some extreme action. Since situations are always subject to reinterpretation, there is no such thing as an absolute, fixed meaning that a situation has. And because a situation is characterized by a meaning, there is no way to discover "facts" in a situation which can be the basis for a final account of that context. Our cultural reality forms a holistic, evolving web of meanings that defies all attempts to make it fully explicit by atomistic and reductivistic methods.

Each situation is "unique" in the sense that it is shaped by a particular defeasible meaning. But at the same time the meaning of each situation is also "general": a situation is always already intelligible to us as agents in the world by virtue of our common mastery of a vocabulary for identifying and evaluating the contexts in which we find ourselves. Only a limited range of actions will make sense in an awkward or humiliating situation, for instance. We grasp the situations in which we find ourselves through our

---

34. The problems this raises for Heidegger's project of fundamental ontology will be discussed in Chapter V.

social competence in the shared understanding of the community of interpreters to which we belong. This factical "thrownness" into the public world lays out in advance the paths along which the meaning of a situation can be reinterpreted. But the background of intelligibility that articulates situations can be neither grounded in a self-grounding ground nor systemized into a closed conceptual net. It is simply there – inexplicable in itself, yet the all-encompassing source of our everyday intelligibility.

Heidegger's picture of Being-in-the-world therefore appears as a seamless whole whose meaning is rooted in a generally tacit background of understanding constituted by our historically unfolding language. On this view, " 'nature', as the categorical aggregate of those structures of Being which a definite entity encountered within-the-world may possess, can never make *worldhood* intelligible" (65). The networks of internal relations which make up equipmental contexts and are constituted by our intentional language can never be reduced to systems of relations between *relata* that are what they are independent of the contexts in which they are found. Heidegger says that the internal relations generated by our language of purposes and goals – the "in-order-to," "for-the-sake-of," "for-which," and so forth – are such that "they resist any sort of mathematical functionalization" (88). The unitizing projection of the mathematical cannot account for the totalities of equipment in which we find ourselves, because the units in these totalities are what they are only in their internal relations as projected in terms of our evolving self-understanding.

Once we understand that there can be no context-free units for rationally reconstructing our horizon of understanding and that there is no *motive* for such a reconstruction, we can see that Cartesian unitizing and generalizing has no role to play in clarifying our Being-in-the-world. There is no *prima philosophia* that can find ultimate building blocks that ensure intrinsic, final intelligibility. Cartesian foundationalism, far from finding the true units out of which the mosaic of understanding is composed, should be seen as "inventing" a highly specialized realm of objects which offer us no prospect of a more genuine understanding than we had at the outset.

We have seen that, when the world of significance is understood as made up of contexts of internal relations, there is no way to distinguish the "essence" of an entity – what it is in itself – from its actual "existence" within the totality. But if the essence/existence distinction is collapsed, then this seems to carry with it the downfall of the *quid juris/quid facti* distinction that motivates Cartesian foundationalism. For if our knowledge of what an entity is in itself is nothing other than our grasp of its actual place in a context, then the *justification* for our grasp of that entity must lie in the way we *actually* come to encounter the entity as holding that place. Our understanding is justified by our actual modes of dealing with entities in the course of our meaningful expressions in the world. Understanding originates not in the discovery of "building blocks," but in the fact that, to return to a metaphor used earlier, "light dawns gradually over a whole": a background of understanding arises in the course of our practices, and our practices are guided by that encompassing background. In the course of this clearing and disclosing, entities are discovered in their places in the whole.

If the *quid juris/quid facti* distinction is obliterated, then the distinction between *a priori* and *a posteriori,* which has been used to demarcate the legitimate realm of philosophical activity, seems to fall as well. What is given "a priori" is a background of understanding which is rooted in the ways an ongoing culture interprets itself and its world in a language which is unfolding through history. At the deepest level, according to *Being and Time,* there are enduring historical meanings that serve as the origins and springs of our understanding. But even these deep meanings are not timeless, immutable truths transparent to pure reason. The deep necessity we find in our pre-ontological understanding is anchored not in access to a Platonic realm of meanings or in a *lumen naturale,* but in our deep attunement in language and in history.

In rejecting these traditional distinctions, however, Heidegger is not led to embrace naturalism. For he sees naturalistic points of view as always projected within the confines of particular forms of objectiveness, so that they can never give us more than regional pictures of the human situation. He therefore explicitly repudiates all attempts to assimilate his philosophy to sociology or anthropology.

> Anthropology is that interpretation of man that in principle already knows *what* man is and therefore can never ask *who* he is. Because with this question, it would have to recognize itself as shattered and surmounted. How could this be exacted from anthropology when it has only been able to achieve the express and subsequent securing of the self-certainty of the subject? (QCT 153, HW 103; my emphasis).

As long as the sciences uncritically project their subject matter along the objectifying lines of their blueprints, a "naturalized epistemology" can never fulfill the goals of fundamental ontology.

Heidegger's conception of grounding should also be distinguished from those of pragmatism and conventionalism. Some forms of pragmatism assume that our practices and beliefs are grounded in the fact that they have greater "cash value" or usefulness in our lives than other beliefs and practices. This seems to suggest a picture of grounding in which we are brought before an array of systems of understanding so that we might pick and choose among them to find the most practical. From Heidegger's standpoint, however, this picture is incoherent. There is no vantage point from which we could "step outside" our own horizon in order to survey *alternative* conceptual schemes. Pragmatism, like Cartesian foundationalism, starts from a model that is legitimate for dealing with *entities* — e.g., ordinary instances of stepping back and deciding about the usefulness of different tools — and then illegitimately tries to extend that model to the horizon that makes possible the discovery of any entities whatsoever. But the horizon of understanding as a whole can never be given such a pragmatic grounding.

Similarly, conventionalism pictures the ground of our pre-ontological understanding as lying in a more or less explicit choice made at some time between competing frameworks. But this image is also incoherent, according to Heidegger, for it suggests (even if only for the purposes of elucidation) that there might have been a time when there was Dasein, without any particular horizon, who then selected one horizon from a stock on hand for its consideration. Since to be Dasein just *is* to be in a historical horizon of possibilities, however, there could be nothing like a "social contract" in which *our* horizon originates. Again, such a picture of grounding starts from a model of choice applicable to *entities* — e.g., particular political systems — and then illegitimately attempts to apply the picture to the horizon that makes possible any choices whatsoever.

In the conception of the grounds for our beliefs and practices which emerges in *Being and Time,* we are left with a historical and linguistic background of understanding which appears "arbitrary" to the extent that it lies over an "abyss of meaninglessness." But in embracing such a view Heidegger is not committed to irrationalism or anti-rationalism. The techniques and procedures for grounding and justifying *within* the regional sciences are left in order as they are. What Heidegger rejects is the way that a single conception of reason as "an all-inclusive ideal of culture" is imposed throughout the world without criticism or evaluation.[35] Such an ideal is "grounded in a faith in the unopposable power of an *immutable* reason and its principles" (*ibid.*). Evaluating our thinking

35. QCT 180, VA I 61.

in terms of such an ideal, however, is "like the procedure of trying to evaluate the nature and capability of a fish by how long it is able to live on dry land."[36] What is called for, then, is not a turn to irrationality, but a critical reflection on the historical origin of our modern concept of "rationality":

> Again and again a call rings out for reason to be the standard for actions and omissions. Yet what can reason do when, together with the "irrational" and the "antirational" all persistently neglected as being on the same level, it forgets to meditate on the essential origin of reason and let itself into its advent? (EGT 60, VA III 4).

§13. *Science and Fundamental Ontology*

In Heidegger's diagnosis of the Cartesian conception of justification and grounding we come to see the ideal of absolutely global, intrinsic intelligibility as fundamentally incoherent. The Cartesian draws his picture of the methods for attaining intelligibility from regional modes of inquiry which are in order as they are and then attempts to extend those methods beyond the boundaries of their legitimate application. In saying that our regional modes of inquiry are in some sense "in order as they are," however, we expose Heidegger's notion of "fundamental ontology" to a line of criticism which has not yet been adequately dealt with. Heidegger seems to see the regional sciences as capable of proceeding without the aid of philosophy. He says that "the positive sciences neither 'can' nor should wait for the ontological labors of philosophy to be done" (51). If the sciences can conduct their business independent of philosophy, however, it is no longer clear what role fundamental ontology has to play with respect to the sciences. More precisely, since the methods and assumptions of physics are granted as legitimate, what prohibits us from following Dilthey[37] in saying that there are two distinct but equally valid "worlds"—the intelligible human world and the natural causal world—both of which are of interest for different areas of our lives, but neither of which has any absolute priority? In what sense is the picture of the world presented to us by Heidegger's account of Being-in-the-world "superior" to that of natural science?

36. LH 272, WM 147.

37. See above, opening of Chapter IV.

To answer these questions, it will be necessary to round out Heidegger's diagnosis of the theoretical attitude with an account of his ways of trying to demarcate the boundaries and limits of science as a human form of life. Throughout his writings, Heidegger is concerned to show that the "scientific-technological" mode of activity is severely limited in its possibilities, and that philosophy is consequently neither an "underlaborer" nor a self-contained discipline, but is rather a crucial enterprise that can open a level of understanding that is in principle closed to the sciences. In Heidegger's view, the modes of projection of the sciences must close off certain types of understanding which can be disclosed only by philosophy. If this is the case, however, then what has been referred to as Heidegger's "existentialism" can no longer be thought of as arising from bourgeois egocentrism or from a fascination with "life" in its dynamic structures. It is rooted instead in the pressing need for uncovering possibilities of understanding which are essentially closed off by the predominance of theoretical and scientific modes of thought.

When Heidegger tries to establish the priority of philosophical understanding over the regional sciences, he does not intend to disparage or demean the sciences. He says that, in criticizing science,

> . . . *we want neither to replace the sciences nor to reform them.* Nevertheless, we want to participate in the preparation of a decision; the decision: Is science the measure of knowledge or is there a knowledge in which *the ground and limit of science* and thus its genuine effectiveness are determined? (WT 10, FD 8; my emphasis in the second sentence).

During the period when *Being and Time* was composed, Heidegger regarded philosophy as the source of the "knowledge" that enables us to evaluate the sciences and open possibilities they leave closed. For this reason Heidegger says, "All sciences are grounded in philosophy, but not *vice versa.*"[38] Although the sciences are distinct from philosophy in the sense that philosophy does not have on hand some new "information" that the sciences have so far neglected to incorporate into their theories, they are nevertheless dependent on philosophy to the extent that they are possible only within a framework of understanding which is closed off to them but is open to philosophy.

We may consider three respects in which Heidegger claims that fundamental ontology is prior to or superior to the sciences. First,

38. WCT 131, WhD 90.

the sciences cannot grasp their own essence as modes of human activity because they cannot comprehend the theoretical frameworks in which they operate. Secondly, the sciences are governed by a "nonappearing content" which is their essential subject matter but which they cannot fully deal with; thus, something may be concealed by the sciences without their ever being able to determine whether or not this is so. And, thirdly, man is "uprooted" and "homeless" in the sciences. The sciences tend to conceal our "thrownness" into the world, and consequently they lead us to a conception of the self as a "subject" that grounds a world-view. As a result, relativism seems to be a necessary concomitant of science. In each of these respects, Heidegger believes that philosophy has an important role to play, since it is not itself subject to the same limitations.

The first respect in which Heidegger sees philosophy as prior to science lies in the ability of philosophy to step back and grasp the essence of the sciences. "When we speak of the sciences," he writes, "we shall be speaking not against them but for them, for clarity concerning their *essence* [Wesen]."[39] It is the task of philosophy to try to comprehend the "essence" of science because, in Heidegger's view, the sciences themselves cannot grasp their own essence. Heidegger supports this claim with an argument designed to show that any attempt on the part of a science to grasp its own essence must be incoherent. Sciences, as we have seen, are constituted by the ways that entities are worked over to make them fit a blueprint of objectiveness which is presupposed by the science. Since a science is always conducted within a pre-established framework of projection, however, Heidegger claims that there is no way for a science to grasp its own framework. For in order to do so, it would have to treat its framework as an entity that could be worked over into an "object" and examined within the framework of that science. But the framework of inquiry of a science could be treated as an object for scientific research only if the scientist had at his disposal a wider framework from within which he could conduct his inquiry. If the framework of projection constitutes that science, however, then there is no way to assume that one has a different framework without also assuming that one is no longer involved in the same science.

This obscure line of reasoning becomes clearer in the examples Heidegger provides. He says, for instance, that

physics, as physics, can make no statements about physics. All the statements of physics speak in terms of physics. Physics itself is not a possible object of a physical experiment (QCT 176, VA I 57).

Needless to say, physicists can and do make statements about physics. But in doing so, Heidegger suggests, they are taking off their scientist hats, so to speak, and putting on philosopher hats: "the present leaders of atomic physics, Niels Bohr and Heisenberg, think in a thoroughly philosophical way."[40] The logic and criteria of validity of their discourse is therefore philosophical and not scientific.

Heidegger also says that mathematics cannot represent the essence of mathematics:

> If one wants to assert something about mathematics as a theory, then one must leave behind the region of objects and the method of representing of mathematics. One can never make out what mathematics itself is through a mathematical calculation (QCT 177, VA I 57).

For mathematical activity, the background attunement that shapes the projections of mathematics is something that can never be described through a mathematical calculation. It is conceivable, for instance, that there could be a method of projection according to which "11 + 111" were to add up to "11,111" and not be "122." But as a matter of fact mathematicians do not calculate in this way. *That* they do not or *why* they do not, one might say, is not itself part of mathematics. Deciding the base of arithmetical calculations is no more part of calculating than setting the calibrations on a ruler is part of measuring.

Heidegger considers the case of a science that might be said to grasp itself, namely, history. A historian, it appears, can write a history of historiography. Of this science, however, Heidegger seems only to *assert* that it cannot grasp its own essence as science: "the study of history [Historie]," he says, "never grasps its essence as historiography, i.e., as science" (*ibid.*). The point here seems to be that the human sciences must also work over their object domains according to a specified blueprint of objectiveness, and therefore can never fully grasp themselves as sciences as long as their subject matter is fit into a mold in advance. But this argument, designed to show that all sciences are in principle prohibited from grasping their essence, seems less plausible in the case of the

40. WT 67, FD 51.

human sciences. It is not at all clear why sociologists, for instance, could not work out a sociological study of the modes of projection of the community of sociologists without abdicating their roles as sociologists. As long as Heidegger regards a scientific framework as an existential phenomenon, there is no reason why the human sciences cannot describe and illuminate these frameworks.

Although the stronger claim that *no* science can grasp its own essence seems unjustified, however, it does seem that Heidegger is entitled to the weaker claim that the sciences are generally committed to a kind of "forgetfulness" in their modes of activity. It belongs to the essence of the sciences, he says, that they are a "business" or "industry" (Betrieb)[41]: science, by virtue of its shared attunement, is always institutionalized. This institutionalized business of science is, as we have seen, defined by the activities of the community of interpreters who make up the scientific community. The interactions among the members of the scientific comunity—its congresses, research awards, peer evaluations, etc.—are part of what defines a science according to the "existential conception of science." These practices lay out the paths for consistency in method and objectification in the individual regions of inquiry. The business of science, Heidegger says, brings about "regulated mobility of transference and integration of activities with respect to whatever tasks happen to be of paramount importance."[42]

The active role of the community of scientists that articulates a background of shared attunement must remain for the most part concealed if scientific work is to proceed smoothly. As a result, scientists are generally blind to the predetermined guidelines along which their activities move. Heidegger says that the course of their research is generally "accomplished by *recapitulating* what has already been ontically discovered" (51). Scientists are therefore inclined to interpret Being as objective presence without being able to distance themselves from the traditional understanding. In contrast, Heidegger holds that the authentic thinking of philosophy overcomes the forgetfulness of the institutionalized business of science and "remembers" the "wellsprings" and "origins" of our understanding of Being. As the study of frameworks, ideally it should not operate within the confines of a pre-established framework of objectiveness, but should instead be open to possibilities in "thinking." It is Heidegger's view, then, that only the

41. AWV 275, HW 77.

42. AWV 277, HW 79.

nonobjectifying and noncalculative thinking of philosophy can distance itself from the forgetfulness of science and the tradition in order to reflect on the essence of the sciences. The case that Heidegger makes for the second respect in which he thinks the sciences are limited is considerably stronger than the first. He claims that, because the sciences can gain access to a realm of entities only by *working them over* in their projections, there must be a "nonappearing content" (unscheinbare Sachverhalt) that holds sway in the sciences and can never be fully grasped by those sciences.[43] The scientist, who must always see the world through a template of objectiveness given to him in advance, can never evaluate his worked over "objects" in comparison with the region of entities with which he is involved. For this reason Heidegger says that the domain of interest of a science is "that which cannot be dealt with" (das Unumgängliche)[44] by the science. Physics, for example, is directed toward "nature." But since it deals with nature only to the extent that the natural can be worked over to fit the ground plan of the mathematical, there is no assurance that the physicist has gained access to the natural in an appropriate way.

Scientific representing can never embrace the essence of nature, since the objectiveness of nature is only *one* way in which nature can antecedently come to appearance. For the science of physics, nature remains that which cannot be dealt with (QCT 174, VA I 54).

Viewed from within the perspective of *Being and Time,* what physics cannot deal with would be something that is embedded in our deep, pre-ontological understanding of our historical springs and roots.[45]

Because the sciences always encounter entities within the framework of their own methods of objectification, the regions to which they are referred remain inaccessible to them.

The essence of their regions—history, art, poetry, language,

---

43. QCT 171, VA I 51.

44. QCT 174, VA I 54.

45. Within the context of the 1953 essay, "Science and Reflection," what Heidegger has in mind with the notion of "das Unumgängliche" seems to be closer to the later concepts of "Erde" and "Geheimnis" than it is to anything in *Being and Time.* For our purposes, however, it does not appear that anything hangs on the difference between Heidegger's early and late writings.

nature, man, God — remains inaccessible to the sciences. At the same time, however, the sciences would constantly fall into the void if they did not operate within these regions. The essence of the regions I have named is the concern of thinking. As the sciences *qua* sciences have no access to this concern, it must be said that they are not thinking (WCT 33, WhD 57).

The price the sciences pay for their higher level of generality in following the mathematical paradigm of unitizing is the inability to obtain access to the regions they are supposed to make intelligible.

It remains possible, then, that something is left out in scientific modes of representation. Heidegger says that

> scientific representation can, on its side, never decide whether nature does not sooner withdraw itself through objectiveness than bring its concealed essential richness [Wesensfülle] to appearance. Science never allows this question to be asked; because, as theory, it has already deposited itself in the region bounded in by its objectiveness (QCT 174, VA I 55).

If something has been left out by a science, there is no way for the science itself ever to discover this fact.

Heidegger suggests different possible examples of what might be left out in the sciences. In the natural sciences, for instance, he says there is an "essential richness" which cannot be grasped "through the modes of representing and ascertaining that correspond to objectiveness."[46] "The botanist's plants are not the flowers of the hedgerow; the 'source' which the geographer establishes for a river is not the 'springhead in the dale' " (70). Furthermore, psychology, which represents man as an objectified psychophysical unit, cannot deal with man's "ek-sistence" as "Da-sein." Historical studies (Historie) cannot deal with history (Geschichte) as a "calling" or "sending" (Geschick). Many of Heidegger's later essays may be thought of as attempts to capture the "essential richness" of entities while avoiding the objectifying tendencies of the tradition. In the essay, "The Thing," for instance, Heidegger portrays an everyday jug as a "fourfold" (Geviert) of "earth, sky, divinities, and mortals."[47]

The most powerful case Heidegger makes for the claim that there

46. QCT 174, VA I 54.

47. PLT 179, VA II 53.

is a "nonappearing content" that the sciences cannot deal with is found in his treatment of linguistic theory. In the technological mode of cultural attunement, "framing," according to Heidegger, man's attempt to gain domination over the world by grounding it in a self-grounding ground takes the shape of formalizing language in "information theory." The quest for formalized language, says Heidegger, "is the metaphysics of the thorough-going technicalization of all languages to the sole functioning instrument of inter-planetary information."[48] When language has been formalized, it may then be regarded as a posit of man, on hand for his use in achieving mastery over the world. From the point of view of this project, natural language is treated as "not-yet-formalized language."[49]

> Even when information theory has to admit that formalized language must in the end always refer back to "natural language" in order to put into speech the saying of the technological stock [Bestandes] of what man has at his disposal by means of formalized language, even this situation signifies only a preliminary stage in the current self-interpretation of information theory (OWL 132, US 263).

The goal of language formalization, then, is to reduce all uses of natural language to some expanded version of the predicate calculus which orients itself on the basis of the model of the apophantic 'as' of assertions or statements. But Heidegger suggests that this metaphysical ideal of domination cannot grasp the essence of language. First, as we have seen, the subject-predicate structure of the apophantic 'as' cannot capture the irreducibly intensional structure of the hermeneutic 'as' of everydayness which is constituted by our teleological language. But secondly, even if our language of purposes and goals could be accounted for in terms of some sort of modal logic, there is no way that formalization could ever embrace the entire background of understanding embedded in our language. For we have seen that language is not an item of equipment at our disposal, but is rather a medium in which we dwell, a horizon that first makes possible our use of words as well as our *being* users of words. For this reason Heidegger says that "in order to be who we are, we human beings remain committed to and within the essence of language, and *can never step out of it and*

48. OWL 58, US 160.

49. OWL 132, US 263.

look at it from somewhere else. "[50] The natural language into which we are thrown is something that can never be fully dealt with by science because it is always the horizon in which all ontic formalizations and clarifications are conducted. There is no exit from the skein of language to a vantage point from which we can reduce all language to a posit of human beings.

Because language is the medium in which all discovery takes place, Heidegger says that it cannot be known "according to the traditional concept of knowledge defined in terms of cognition as representation" (*ibid.*). In other words, language is not an object; it is rather the condition for there *being* such things as objects. To try to achieve total clarity about language is to be guilty of the same confusion noted earlier: attempting to apply methods that are legitimate for studying objects (e.g., *regions* of language) to the horizon in which any inquiry at all is possible.

Heidegger's criticism of language formalization has consequences that are more far-reaching than their applicability to semiotics and linguistics. For on the constitutive view of language, the nonappearing content of the sciences — that which the sciences cannot deal with — is to be understood as itself linguistically articulated. Since the sciences are devoted to obtaining generalized laws covering decontextualized entities, their language must be extensional. The ideal formal language of a science consists of strings of uninterpreted signs which are then mapped onto states of affairs in the world. Heidegger points out, however, that this mapping operation, in which the formal language is interpreted, can be achieved only from within an informal, interpreted metalanguage which is already available. This metalanguage cannot itself be understood in terms of a formalization and semantics, since such a formalization would presuppose a wider metalanguage, which could only be formalized in a still wider metalanguage, and so forth into a vicious regress. At some level, then, we must acknowledge the existence of a metalanguage which remains informal and interpreted without recourse to an articulated semantics. This metalanguage embodies the all-embracing but generally tacit background understanding of Being-in-the-world. It is this language that we "can never step out of" in order to "look at it from somewhere else" (*ibid.*).

What Heidegger wants us to see is that the objectifying structure of scientific theorizing can never capture the essential richness of understanding embedded in our natural language. Though he

---

50. OWL 134, US 266. "und daher niemals aus ihm heraustreten können, um es noch von anderswoher zu umblicken" (my emphasis).

believes that language can never be fully mastered by what he calls the "technical-scientistic comprehension [Auffassung] of language," however, he thinks it can be deepened and widened in its powers of expression through a "speculative-hermeneutic *experience* of language."[51] In this "experience of language" philosophy does not try to master language, but instead lets language speak itself. In his own way of expanding our horizon of understanding through working within language, Heidegger says,

> we speak of language, but constantly seem to be speaking *about* language, while in fact we are already letting language, from within language, speak to us in language of itself, letting it say its essence (OWL 85, US 191).

By operating within the speculative-hermeneutic experience of language, philosophy can open a horizon of understanding from which it can deal with the nonappearing content of the sciences.

The final respect in which Heidegger claims that the sciences are limited in their possibilities is seen in their tendency toward "subjectivism." "The demand for an all-powerful principle of a ground that is to be proposed," Heidegger says, "tears modern man away from his rootedness [Bodenständigkeit]."[52] The Enlightenment ideal of freedom from prejudice and authority, together with the quest for an absolutely generalized objectivity through decontextualization, leads the scientific mode of existence to deny its essential situatedness in the world into which it is thrown. We have already seen that Heidegger regards the withdrawal into the Cartesian *ego cogito* as a necessary concomitant of scientific objectification. In modern technological "framing," he says,

> man has risen into the "I"-hood of the *ego cogito*. With this stance, all entities become objects. Entities, as objective, are absorbed into the immanence of subjectivity. The horizon no longer illuminates from out of itself (QCT 107, HW 241).

In trying to find himself in the immanence of the self-defining ground of the *ego cogito,* man loses his "homeness" and his ability "to build and well in the region of the essential."[53] The homelessness and uprootedness of Western technology has been

---

51. PT 24, PuT 39 (my emphasis).

52. SvG 60.

53. SvG 60.

spread around the globe, so that Being in all cultures is now "experienced in a Western fashion and represented on the epistemological models of European metaphysics and science."[54]

In the encroaching world-domination of Western technology, the subject "becomes the *center* to which entities as such are related."[55] The symptoms of homelessness are alienation, egocentrism, social fragmentation, and dissociation from nature and the environment. Man can be the "center" of the universe only by denying his *place* in the holistic contexts that make up the shared intelligible world. From the scientific understanding of man as an epistemological subject, there emerges an understanding of the world as a "picture" or "view" represented by the subject. Heidegger says that

> where the world becomes a view, entities as a whole are proposed as that with respect to which a man orients himself, which therefore he wishes to bring and have before himself and thus in a decisive sense re-present to himself. World-view [Weltbild], properly understood, therefore means not a view of the world, but the world understood as a view (AWV 278, HW 81).

In no other age, Heidegger points out, has man ever regarded the world as one view among others, subject to change, at man's disposal. The essential richness of the world can come to be regarded as merely an aspect or "view" only where the world is no longer a "dwelling" to man.

If the world is a "view," then it can be held up and contrasted with other possible views. It is a "conceptual scheme" that we have somehow devised for our own purposes. As a result, the relativism that Descartes's quest for certainty was to conquer comes to be recapitulated within the framework of the subjectivism of the Cartesian model. The enterprise of finding a secure foundation for our beliefs in a self-grounding ground ends in frustration. The tacit assumptions of modern science lead us to see our epistemic predicament as one in which we are presented with a pageant of world-views with no ultimate criterion for deciding which of these views correctly represents states of affairs as they are in themselves.

It is clear that Heidegger does not believe that his alternative

54. EGT 76. VA III 23.

55. AWV 278. HW 81 (my emphasis).

model of Being-in-the-world is relativistic in the same way as the model associated with modern science. The problem of relativism seems to arise only when our ordinary involvement in the world breaks down and we come to see our situation as one in which we are imposing different interpretations over present-at-hand "things." The realm of present-at-hand objects is supposed to provide us with a basis on which our differing interpretations can be calibrated. Without this system of calibration, it is thought, our interpretations would "hang in the air" and would not be "about" anything. The baffling aspect of relativism then appears when we reflect on the fact that, since we always encounter the world through the schematization of our interpretations, we can never gain access to the bedrock of reality as it is in itself, in order to determine whether *our* interpretation is the *correct* or *true* representation.

Heidegger's way of dealing with this picture should now be familiar. The relativist starts with a conception of alternative views which is legitimate within certain regional inquiries (e.g., competing theories in a science) and then tries to extend it to our everyday horizon of Being-in-the-world. But since the horizon of everydayness is the background against which all regional activities are conducted, the attempt to extrapolate from a model of inquiry that is valid for certain regions of our lives to the horizon that makes those regions possible is illegitimate. The relativist has no vantage point from which he can distance himself from his everyday horizon in order to treat it as one world-view or conceptual scheme among others. As we shall see in the next chapter, the relativist's position is self-defeating: he must maintain that he has a position from which he can compare radically different world-views while simultaneously regarding one of these world views as the limit of *his* world.[56]

In Heidegger's alternative model of our epistemic situation, the distinction between world-view and reality collapses. We always live within a shared intelligible world to which we are attuned by our common public language. Even in the limiting cases of theoretical reflection, the present-at-hand is discovered within a framework of projection that is parasitic on our everyday pre-ontological understanding. There is no escape from this background of understanding to a purely neutral standpoint from which we can describe or view radically different ways of understanding ourselves and our world. That we have the kind of

56. For this point I am indebted to Karsten Harries' *Between Logic and Poetry* (unpublished).

pre-ontological understanding we have is not something that can be ultimately justified or grounded in a self-grounding ground. But, as we have seen in this chapter, the idea that we *need* such justification or grounding is rooted in an illusion which arises only in the spurious attitude of pure reflection and in its construct, common sense.

V

The End of Traditional Philosophy

In the preceding chapters I have explored some of the consequences of Heidegger's thought for traditional epistemology
without reference to his explicit discussion of skepticism about the
external world. The results so far obtained may be summarized
under three headings:

A. *Descriptive*

In stage I of the Cartesian inquiry we are presented with a
common-sense picture of our ordinary beliefs and how we come to
arrive at them. According to this picture, in our everyday epistemic
predicaments we are seen as subjects coming to hold beliefs about
objects in the external world. These beliefs are supposed to be
grounded in inferences drawn from the perceived features of
things. It was suggested at the outset that, as long as our plain
situations are understood in this way, the stage II skeptical
challenge is in order and skepticism is a foregone conclusion. In
opposition to this traditional picture, Heidegger portrays our
everyday situations in terms of Being-in-the-world. As Being-in-
the-world, we are most primordially to be regarded as the Anyone,
involved in practical contexts in such a way that there is no distinction to be drawn between an isolated subject and transcendent objects that are to be known. In the description of everydayness, formulating beliefs about mere things has no clear role to play. The
fore-structure of understanding that makes our activities possible is
not composed of a web of beliefs about objects modeled on the
apophantic 'as' of statements or assertions. On the contrary, it consists of a generally tacit grasp of a network of internal relations
constituted by our intentional language and structured by the
hermeneutic 'as' of taking things as means to ends within our practical activities. Finally, Heidegger leads us to see that our most
primordial encounter with the world is not through the mediation
of mere seeing, but is rather through handling, manipulating, producing, and operating—that is, through *dealing* with the ready-to-
hand along the guidelines laid out by our social competence in a
publicly intelligible world. According to this alternative description
of our epistemic predicament, the common-sense picture presup-

posed by the Cartesian comes to be seen as a product of a *breakdown* in our everyday ways of Being-in-the-world.

B. *Foundationalist*

The Cartesian model assumes that the beliefs we might be said to hold in acting in the world must be grounded or justified if our confidence in acting is to be made fully intelligible. If we are to obtain intrinsic intelligibility as opposed to the theory-relative intelligibility of explanations, the ultimate ground for our beliefs must be found in the self-grounding ground of the *ego cogito* and its *cogitationes*. In Heidegger's picture of Being-in-the-world, on the other hand, we come to see the foundation for our beliefs as lying in the forms of life of the historical culture into which we are socialized in mastering a public language. The background of intelligibility that makes our ordinary beliefs and practices possible is something that is just "there"—it cannot be further grounded in terms of some intrinsically intelligible principle. From the standpoint of the tradition, then, the ground of our beliefs and practices appears to be an "abyss."

C. *Hermeneutic*

At the same time, however, while the background understanding that makes our lives possible must remain inchoate and implicit, the situations in which we find ourselves are always *already* intelligible to us to some extent. The pretext that motivates the Cartesian inquiry—the assumption that there is something fundamentally unintelligible about our lives which requires grounding—is seen to be an illusion. Any demand for explanation or justification presupposes a background of pre-ontological understanding that is simply *given* to us by virtue of our competence in being alive. When we see Being-in-the-world as structured by a meaning that is already understood through our shared mastery of a public language, the feeling that there is something unintelligible about our beliefs and practices tends to dissolve. And since there is no pretext for the Cartesian quest for certainty, foundationalism turns out to be pointless.

These consequences of Heidegger's fundamental ontology for our understanding of our plain epistemic situations set the stage for his brief discussion of skepticism about the external world. In this chapter, I will first discuss the treatment of skepticism in *Being and Time*. As we shall see, Heidegger regards the skeptic's position not as just confused or misguided but as fundamentally *mean-*

ingless. The skeptic's claims are, strictly speaking, "nonsense," since they can be uttered only by in effect denying the conditions for the possibility of any meaningful discourse whatsoever. In the course of examining Heidegger's critique of skepticism, however, a problem for his own project of fundamental ontology will emerge. For, as we have seen, Heidegger is not merely trying to solve a particular philosophical puzzle from within the accepted framework of philosophical activity. He is challenging the entire traditional conception of philosophy which leads to such "puzzles." His criticism of the Cartesian tradition is concerned with undermining the assumptions that underlie all of philosophy when this is understood as the quest for timeless, immutable truths. But if this is the case, then the question arises: Why is it that the quest for eternal truths of traditional philosophy is "nonsense" while fundamental ontology is in order and perfectly meaningful? Is it not the case that Heidegger's attempts to undermine the tradition also lead him to undermine his own position as a philosopher?

I call this kind of problem the *problem of reflexivity*. Although it will be seen that Heidegger can defend his position against certain forms of this objection, it will become clear in section 15 that the project of fundamental ontology as conceived of in *Being and Time* is untenable. In order to understand why Heidegger felt that fundamental ontology *could* succeed, it will be helpful to step back and reexamine Heidegger's plans for *Being and Time* as a whole. In section 16 I will consider the reasons why Heidegger says that "the question of Being" involves a "twofold task" (15), and I will attempt to clarify the over-all project of that early work as a form of transcendental historicism. When it becomes clear that the "transcendentalism" of *Being and Time* is indefensible and must be abandoned, it will be necessary to re-evaluate the achievement of this early work and try to show how it points to Heidegger's later thought. This will be the aim of section 17.

§14. *The Critique of Traditional Epistemology*

The Cartesian tradition portrays our ordinary lives in terms of a picture of disengaged subjects contemplating a world of objects. The practical affairs of everydayness are seen only as constraints that limit our ability to be careful and thorough in evaluating our beliefs. Philosophy is supposed to start from this everydayness, but, since it is free from the pressures of practical affairs, it is supposed to be able to reach a level of knowledge more objective than is feasible in our practical concerns. Heidegger reverses this traditional conception of our ordinary epistemic predicament. Practical affairs are not something superimposed over the pristine condition of the pure "I" set over against a collection of items. For Heidegger, being human is to be understood most primordially as "care" (Sorge). It is because Dasein is "ahead of itself" in its ordinary concerns that things can be encountered at all.

Whatever we discover in the world is discovered as an entity of a certain type only *through* our needs and interests. The disengaged encounter with the present-at-hand which is taken as primary in the Cartesian model is just a special case of this concernful, involved way of discovering the world. Heidegger says that

> when we ascertain something present-at-hand by mere intuition [anschauende Bestimmen], this activity has the character of care just as much as does "political action" or taking a rest and enjoying oneself. "Theory" and "practice" are possibilities of Being for an entity whose Being must be determined as care (193).

Since the Being of entities is determined by our interests and needs, there is no way to gain access to a realm of bare facts outside of our interests which will ground our beliefs.

If there are no grounds for our interpretations, however, the question arises how the *truth* of our beliefs can be established. The goal of the foundationalist tradition that has come down to us from Descartes is to find a procedure that will guarantee that our beliefs can be known to be true. Without such a guarantee that some of our beliefs are true, it is argued, there cannot even be relative degrees of probability in our beliefs. But if nothing can be known to be even probable, then it seems that there is no way to distinguish truth from error. It appears, then, that, if we accept Heidegger's way of dealing with skepticism, we must give up the notion of truth altogether. What starts out looking like a benign tolerance to different language-games ends up as an anarchistic inability to evaluate or criticize anything.

Heidegger's way of dealing with this problem is to radically rethink the traditional conception of "truth." The feeling that our ability to distinguish truth and falsehood has been lost originates in a conception of truth as a "correspondence" or "agreement" between some human product (e.g., ideas, propositions, theories) and some states of affairs in the world, the *adaequatio intellectus et rei*. Heidegger tries to lead us to see that this traditional understanding of truth is *derived from* a deeper and more primordial conception of truth.

To show that the correspondence theory of truth is derivative from and parasitic on a deeper sense of truth, Heidegger begins by examining traditional views which regard the "locus" of truth as the statement (or proposition, sentence, judgment, belief — the choice of terminology is irrelevant here). The prototypical example of the statement is the simple predication that asserts that some particular thing has a certain property or attribute. Heidegger draws on Aristotle's understanding of the statement as *apophansis,* as "letting something be seen" (32). On the correspondence theory of truth, the function of the statement is to let something be seen as it is: "To say that a statement *'is true'* signifies that it discovers the entity as it is in itself" (218). The statement is true if it agrees with the entity that is discovered in the statement.

Heidegger assumes that this conception of "truth" is correct and then goes on to ask how such an *agreement* of a statement with reality can be possible. The answer lies in the fact that letting things be seen and making statements is a mode of activity of Dasein: "Making a statement," Heidegger says, "is a way of Being toward the thing itself that is" (Sein zum seienden Ding selbst) (218). The statement is supposed to make manifest how things are, and, if it is trustworthy, then it provides us with evidence of the way things actually are in the world. But since the statement is taken as *evidence* of something being the case, Heidegger asks how a "statement demonstrates itself" (217) as true, and finds this to lie in actually examining the entity that the statement is about. The truth of the statement, "The picture on the wall is crooked," for instance, is confirmed by actually looking at the picture to see whether it is crooked. But this implies that things are discovered in statement-making only because Dasein is active in the world in discovering things. It is Dasein that makes statements and confirms them, and so statements can "let something be seen" only through the activities of Dasein. But this means, Heidegger suggests, that at a deeper level truth must be seen as inhering in the "being-discovering" (Entdeckend-sein) of Dasein itself (218). Since Dasein as the Anyone just is the field of disclosedness of shared meaningful expressions which makes discovery possible, "what is primarily 'true' — that is, discovering — is Dasein" (220).

Uttering statements, discovering entities, and confirming the agreement of utterance and reality — all these are possible only within the *clearing* of Dasein's disclosedness. Heidegger says that the most primordial understanding of truth is found in "the *oldest* tradition of ancient philosophy" (219), in the Greek word 'a-letēia', which he interprets as meaning, literally, "un-hiddenness." Whether or not this etymological association is accepted, the point that Heidegger is making is important. He wants us to see that "truth" in the sense of propositional truth is possible only against a background of "truth" in the sense of an "opening" or "clearing" of the intelligible world which arises from Dasein's *logos* and is deposited in the public language of a historical people. The paradigmatic case of truth in logic, that of elementary predication, is possible only in a world in which things have already been taken out of their hiddenness through Dasein's disclosing of the intelligible world.

Through Dasein's *care* structure, a field of disclosedness is opened which is "the most primordial phenomenon of truth" (220/1). Heideggers's claim is that the conception of truth as a relation between, roughly, word and world, makes sense only against a background in which the radical separation of knowing subject and items to be known is obliterated. What is primary is a historically unfolding "clearing" or "opening" which cannot be coherently set over against a reality distinct from that clearing. Within the field of shared understanding, mundane questions about what the world is really like and everyday distinctions of truth and error can proceed in ordinary ways. We can engage in such activities of questioning because we have mastered the techniques for evaluation and criticism passed down to us in our public language. What is ruled out in this conception is very general questions about whether *our* clearing "agrees with" or "corresponds to" some "reality" set over against this clearing. For there "is" reality only within the sphere of this disclosedness.

If truth is regarded as the primordial disclosedness of Dasein, then it follows that there can be no truth where there is no Dasein. Heidegger says, " '*There is*' ['Es gibt'] *truth only insofar as Dasein is and as long as Dasein is*" (226). The shared background of practices which makes possible the projection of totalities of significance is the foundation for discovering entities and for determining the truth and falsity of sentences within any regional projection. All decisions as to whether ghosts, neutrinos, or numbers exist must be made against this background. But the inchoate background of forms of life cannot itself be grounded — as we have already noted, " 'in itself' it is quite incomprehensible why entities are to be *discovered*, why *truth* and *Dasein* must be" (228).

If it is claimed that truth has no ground other than our forms of life, however, then it follows that the kinds of eternal truth that philosophers have traditionally sought must themselves be finite. In Heidegger's words,

> Newton's laws, the principle of contradiction, any truth whatever — these are true only as long as Dasein *is*. Before there was

> Dasein in general, there was no truth. . . . Before Newton's laws were discovered, they were not "true"; it does not follow that they were false (236).

Once the framework for Newton's laws has been opened, of course, the laws can be read back into the past and confirmed or disconfirmed. As retroactive in this way, they can be understood as in some sense "eternal." But here they must be seen as eternal only within the finite horizon of Dasein's projections and activities.

What Heidegger wants to guard against is the idea that there *could be* some privileged "God's eye view" of reality as it is "in itself," a view that is fundamentally denied to us finite mortals but can nevertheless be taken as an ideal or goal for our inquiries. There is no ultimate, final perspective toward which our discoveries are only approximations. Heidegger diagnoses this ideal of a final "eternal" truth by suggesting that it is a vestigial remnant of theology:

> Both the contention that there are "eternal truths" and the jumbling together of Dasein's phenomenally grounded "ideality" with an idealized absolute subject, belong to those residues of Christian theology within philosophical problematics which have not as yet been radically extruded (229).

Although Heidegger says that *"all truth is relative to Dasein's Being"* (227), this relativity should not be understood as a constraint or restriction on our powers and capacities. Heidegger wants us to accept our own finitude without even so much as entertaining the idea of an infinite mind to which we can only aspire. For Heidegger, as for Nietzsche, "God is dead": there can be no "absolute" perspective accessible to an ideal subject who sees things *sub specie aeternitatis.* The pseudo-problems of epistemology can be fully overcome only when we realize that there is nothing we must be *missing* when we say that all truth is relative to the projections of Dasein.

In saying that truth depends on Dasein's disclosedness Heidegger does not want to say that we *decide* what is true on the basis of our own "subjective discretion" (227). Though it is the case that our projections determine the Being of entities, Heidegger's position should not be understood as a type of intersubjective idealism. He says that, although Being is determined by Dasein, there are nevertheless *entities* independent of Dasein.

Entities *are,* quite independently of the experience, knowl-ledge and grasping by which they are disclosed, discovered and determined. But Being "is" only in the understanding of those entities to whose Being something like an understanding of Being belongs (183).

Care determines the Being and reality of entities, but it does not determine *that there are* entities. Thus Heidegger is led to assert somewhat paradoxically that "Being (not entities) is dependent upon the understanding of Being; that is to say, reality (not the real) is dependent upon care" (212).

But this puzzling statement surely seems to nullify the results we have achieved so far. For if there *are* "entities" and "the real" independent of us, then it seems fair to ask whether our understanding of Being or reality actually "fits" the way the real is in itself, outside of our understanding. And with this question, the whole maze of traditional skeptical puzzles seems to be revitalized. How are we to reconcile this claim with the results we have achieved so far?

The point that Heidegger is trying to make in saying that entities and the real are not dependent on Dasein seems to be that Dasein is always *thrown* into the world, and so *whether* entities can be encountered or not is not left up to Dasein's discretion. In *Kant and the Problem of Metaphysics* he says that "all projection — and, consequently, even all of man's 'creative' activity — is *thrown, i.e.,* determined by the dependence of Dasein on entities in totality [Seiende im ganzen], a dependence to which Dasein always submits."[1] But within the context of the discussion of care it does not seem that Heidegger has the right even to *try* to assert that entities can exist independent of Dasein. For, as we have seen, every way of encountering an entity, whether it be the ready-to-hand of practical affairs or the present-at-hand of theoretical reflection, is necessarily mediated by some schema of interpretation projected in Dasein's understanding. This means, however, that there is no way to obtain a direct, unmediated access to entities in order to pick them out and refer to them outside of any understanding of Being. Entities are always discovered within the "multiplicity" of the "grammar" of our ways of articulating the world. It should follow, then, that there is no way to talk about entities or the real *independent* of some articulated way of understanding Being.

To make this point in a different way, we saw that every way of identifying or discovering entities in the world is discursive. Even our prepredicative experience of a red color patch is discursive to

---

1. KPMe 244, KPMg 228.

the extent that seeing it as "red" is also seeing it as colored, as spatially located, as not green, not blue, not yellow, and so forth. In the formal mode, this implies that any attempt to *say* something about entities must already operate within the horizon of meaningfulness made accessible in the public world. But on this way of interpreting the results of *Being and Time,* when Heidegger says that entities and the real can "be" independent of Dasein, he is, in Wittgenstein's terminology, "running up against the limits of language."[2] His claim is incoherent because it tries to assert something about the Being of entities *outside of* any meaningful framework in which one can talk about or refer to entities. I can talk about hammers, neutrinos, mass-points, black holes, and the like only *within* horizons of understanding constituted by the public language I have come to master. If I try to talk about things outside of any horizon, however, language must fail me: my purported claim could be made only if the conditions for the possibility of any meaningful utterance had been suspended.

When Heidegger is most consistent, therefore, his claim is not that the real exists independent of Dasein, but that one can neither affirm nor deny the existence of entities outside of Dasein's projections. "When Dasein does not exist," Heidegger says, "it cannot be *said* that entities are, nor can it be *said* that they are not" (212; my emphasis). Both the Being and the non-Being of entities is dependent upon the linguistically constituted "clearing" which determines our sense of what it is to be. To imagine a state of affairs in which there would be no Dasein (and, hence, no understanding) would not be to imagine a situation in which there was an uninterpreted material substrate or a *Ding an sich* that existed by itself. For matter and things in themselves can *be* only where Dasein projects an understanding of Being.

Heidegger's position, when consistently worked out, is beyond both realism and idealism because it overcomes the distinction between interpretation and uninterpreted reality presupposed by both of these positions. Heidegger says that the conception of our epistemic predicament as Being-in-the-world agrees with realism in saying that "along with Dasein as Being-in-the-world, entities within-the-world have always already been disclosed" (207). And it agrees with idealism to the extent that it sees that "Being cannot be explained through entities and that reality is possible only in the

---

2. Friedrich Waismann reports that Wittgenstein leveled this criticism against Heidegger in his *Wittgenstein und der Wiener Kreis* (Oxford: Blackwell, 1967), pp. 68/9. The context makes it clear that Wittgenstein's criticism was far more extensive than my current application of it suggests.

understanding of Being" (207). But Heidegger's concept of "Being-in-the-world" circumvents the whole debate between realists and idealists because it nullifies the conception of the subject or consciousness that is supposed either to transcend its own sphere of immanence to know a transcendent object or to constitute objects within its own sphere of immanence. As a seamless whole, Being-in-the-world is prior to the discovery of immanence and transcendence; such notions as these are meaningful only against the background of Being-in-the-world.

The traditional problem of providing a *proof* for the existence of the external world gains its significance from the subject/object model of our epistemic predicament which makes up the shared ground of both realism and idealism. The question of a proof becomes a matter of determining "whether the real can be independent 'of consciousness' or whether there can be a transcendence of consciousness to the 'sphere' of the real" (202). This was Kant's problem, and we saw that he regarded it as a scandal of philosophy that the question of proving the existence of the world was not yet resolved. Heidegger believes that both the "problem" of the external world and its attempted solutions are, strictly speaking, *meaningless* when understood from the standpoint of the source of meaning in our lives. His argument rests on showing that skepticism as a human mode of comportment toward the world is incoherent and could succeed in its endeavors only by denying the conditions for the possibility of any mode of activity whatsoever.

In his discussion of the traditional problem of skepticism, Heidegger says that it is "impossible" even to frame the question of the existence of the external world:

> The "problem of reality" in the sense of the question whether an external world is present-at-hand and whether such a world can be proved, turns out to be an impossible one, . . . because the very entity which serves as its theme is one which, as it were, repudiates any such formulation of the question (206).

We have seen that all forms of meaningful activity gain their meaning from the background of intelligibility articulated by our practices and embodied in the expressions of a historical people. Every instance of Dasein is just a nexus of the meaning relations that structure Being-in-the-world. But if this is the case, then the skeptical mode of comportment toward the world could succeed in achieving the vantage point of an isolated "I" that sets out to prove the existence of the world only by abrogating the conditions for the possibility of its own meaningfulness as a human form of life.

Heidegger says that

> the question of whether there is a world at all and whether its
> Being can be proved is *without meaning* [ohne Sinn] if it is
> raised by Dasein as Being-in-the-world; and who else would
> raise it? (202; my emphasis).

The skeptic's doubts are self-defeating because the skeptic could
achieve the standpoint presupposed by his inquiry only by tacitly
denying that he is Being-in-the-world. And this denial carries with
it a denial of the Being of the questioner. If there has ever been a
skeptic, Heidegger says, "he has obliterated Dasein in the despera-
tion of suicide" (229).

The same point can also be made in the formal mode. If all uses
of language gain their meaning from the background of intelligibility which makes up the human world, then to attempt to use language in order to doubt or suspend belief in this world would be to
cancel the conditions for the meaningfulness of any use of language
at all. The very capacity to frame the question of the existence of
the external world presupposes that a world has been disclosed and
that entities have been discovered. The skeptic's claims, if they are
taken as having the full range of consequences they are supposed to
have, would be *nonsense,* lacking any meaning whatsoever.

When we are told that a range of propositions that seem perfectly
meaningful to us are in fact "nonsense," we have the right to ask
why it is that we seem to understand this language. The answer to
this question lies in the fact that we tend to assimilate the propositions of traditional philosophy to uses of language within certain
regions of our lives — language which is perfectly meaningful within
the boundaries of those regions but which cannot have the global
consequences that philosophy is supposed to have. In the theoretical attitude of chemistry, for instance, we can devise certain symbols for molecules and then ask whether or not the symbols happen
to "fit" the chemical structures in the substance we are examining.
In such cases, doubts and questioning are perfectly in order, since
they are guided by a framework of understanding that structures
our mode of involvement in the world of chemistry. Where the
skeptic goes wrong, however, is in trying to import the structure of
such mundane inquiries into the global enterprise of casting doubts
on the framework of beliefs that is supposed to make up our
understanding of the world in general. But if it is true that the
theoretical attitude is a "founded mode" of Being-in-the-world, its
inquiries are always parasitic on the field of meaning contained in
Being-in-the-world. It follows, then, that theoretical modes of

inquiry cannot have the extreme kinds of shocking and counterintuitive results that skepticism is supposed to have. We are now in a position to try to understand the source of the clash we feel between the aura of "plainness" that attaches itself to the skeptic's inquiry and the shocking results skepticism seems to have for our plain ways of understanding things. Skeptical doubts draw their apparent sense and legitimacy from ordinary situations in which mundane procedures of doubt are carried out about decontextualized entities. But the skeptic's attempt to employ these procedures in raising very general doubts about everydayness itself is incoherent: it tries to apply methods for examining beliefs within frameworks to the very horizon that makes any inquiry possible. It seems, then, that the skeptic's claims can be heard in two different ways. If they are heard as plain, regional doubts, they are indeed meaningful, but they cannot have the global consequences for our everyday beliefs they are supposed to have. If they are heard as philosophical, on the other hand, they are "nonsense" and only seem to be meaningful because they are assimilated to plain utterances that can have no sweeping consequences for our everyday epistemic situations.

§15. *The Prospects for a Fundamental Ontology*

Heidegger's critique of traditional epistemology has consequences that are more far-reaching than their application to skepticism alone might suggest. It calls into question any conception of philosophy that works from the assumption that there is a sphere of inquiry that can attain a vantage point from which reality can be investigated and systematized in such a way as to find the ultimate truth about how things are. For such a conception of philosophy would be possible only if there could be a standpoint outside of our ordinary Being-in-the-world from which the world could be examined. If Heidegger's account of our contextualization in the world is right, however, there is no such standpoint. Consequently the traditional idea that philosophers can gain access to some realm of eternal, immutable truths is undermined. If there is to be a human form of activity called "philosophy," it must, like any other mode of inquiry, be conducted from *within* the confines of our culturally and historically articulated horizon of understanding.

It appears, however, that this way of characterizing the results of Heidegger's analysis of Being-in-the-world leads to a problem for the project of fundamental ontology as conceived in *Being and Time*. We have already noted that there is a tension in *Being and*

Time between Heidegger's explicit *aim* of finding transcendental, essential structures that will serve as a foundation for an ontology in the widest sense, and the concrete *results* of the existential analytic which lead us to see that such findings will always be culturally and historically conditioned.[3] This tension seems to lead to a paradoxical result for the enterprise of *Being and Time* as a whole.

On the one hand, the critique of traditional epistemology gains much of its force from the insight that skeptical inquiries are incoherent because they can be conducted only by, in effect, denying their "thrownness" or "contextualization" within a horizon of understanding that is the condition for the possibility of any inquiry whatsoever. If all inquiries proceed only within the scaffolding of a linguistically and historically constituted horizon of pre-understanding, then any attempt to challenge that horizon from the vantage point of a pure, contemplative attitude must sink into incoherence. This consequence of the thought of *Being and Time* is largely negative and critical: it "diagnoses" skepticism and helps us to understand the source of its counterintuitive consequences.

On the other hand, however, *Being and Time* also has a *positive* goal in relation to which the critique of epistemology plays only a minor role. We saw that the description of everydayness and the account of Being-in-the-world are supposed to pave the way for uncovering "essential structures" of Dasein. These existentialia are the transcendental conditions for the possibility of any understanding of Being whatsoever. The essential structures of Dasein are brought to light in order to lay bare "the horizon for an interpretation of the meaning of Being in general" (15). This project of determining the meaning of Being is in turn subordinated to the broader task of developing a "science of *Being as such*" (230)—what Heidegger calls "ontology taken in its widest sense" (11).[4] The ultimate aim of *Being and Time* is to answer "the question of Being in general" (*Seinsfrage überhaupt*) (436). Seen in this way, the analysis of Dasein is only a *propaedeutic* for the over-arching goal of the work which is to develop a *metaphysica generalis,* a science of sciences.

If the published portion of *Being and Time* is to serve as a foundation for an ontology in the widest sense, however, it does not appear that the results of the first stages of fundamental ontology can be thought of as relative in any way. Heidegger says that "it must be possible to circumscribe [umgrenzt] the meaning of Being" (230). If we are to reach a final determination of "*the* meaning of

3. This problem was discussed at the end of section 5.

4. See above, section 6.

Being" through the analysis of Dasein, then this analytic must reveal the conditions for "the possibility of having *any* understanding of Being whatsoever" (231; my emphasis). But this project of analyzing Dasein in order to find "the *transcendental horizon* for the question of Being" (39; my emphasis) presupposes that the existential analytic will reveal timeless, immutable structures which will lay a firm foundation for ontology. Heidegger says that the existentialia discovered by the analysis of Dasein have a "transcendental 'generality' " that is "*ontological* and *a priori*. What it has in view is not a set of ontical properties which constantly keep emerging, but a composition of Being which is already underlying in every case" (199). It follows, then, that the findings of the existential analytic must be *transcultural* and *transhistorical* and not limited to any particular world-view. "The transcendental 'generality' of the phenomenon of care and of all fundamental *existentialia,*" Heidegger says, must "present a basis [Boden] on which *every* interpretation of Dasein which is ontical and belongs to a world-view must move" (199/200). What Heidegger is looking for is *the structure of interpreting itself* which underlies the shifting, defeasible interpretations belonging to any world-view.

If fundamental ontology is to fulfill its assigned task, then, it seems that the structures of Being-in-the-world that are uncovered by the existential analytic must be universally applicable in all cultures and historical epochs. Yet the "negative" side of *Being and Time,* according to which any inquiry must be seen as relative to the culture and historical period into which it is thrown, suggests that the outcome of Heidegger's "interpretation of interpreting" should itself be regarded as conditioned and relative. If there is no way to arrive at a final, correct representation of reality as it is in itself and if all interpretation — including the hermeneutic of Dasein — is contextualized in the pre-understanding of a particular historical culture, then there is no way to discover transcendental, essential structures of Dasein to serve as a foundation for a "science of Being as such."

On this way of reading the aims of *Being and Time,* it therefore appears that the tension in Heidegger's thought leads to a dilemma. Either it is true that cultural and historical factors determine our sense of what it is to be, in which case the results of *Being and Time* must themselves be seen as cultural and historical products. Or it is false, in which case the concrete conclusions of the work concerning Dasein are undermined, and Heidegger loses a large part of his grounds for criticizing the Cartesian model.

This paradoxical result may be called *the problem of reflexivity.* It is a puzzle that can arise for any philosophical position that calls in question the possibility of finding unconditioned grounds for our beliefs and practices. Since the critique of foundationalist philosophical positions must be made from the standpoint of a more or less fully worked-out philosophical position whose own theses are to be understood as universally valid, the critique can be reflected back onto the critical philosophy itself. The question then arises: Why is it that the criticized theses are overturned and discarded while the theses in which the critique is framed are immune from the criticism? As applied to *Being and Time,* the question is this: If Heidegger's philosophy is supposed to undermine traditional philosophy, why is it that his own philosophy is not at the same time undermined? In order to attempt to deal with the problem of reflexivity in *Being and Time,* it will be helpful to divide it into two distinct questions. The first question: If the ultimate ground for our beliefs and practices is the clearing articulated by the Anyone in the public language, how can the results of fundamental ontology attain universal and, indeed, transcendental validity? And the second question: If all truth is ultimately historical, how can the results of fundamental ontology be immutable and eternal?

The first question concerns the cultural and linguistic contextualization of any form of inquiry. We have seen that, for Heidegger, every mode of discourse gains its meaning from the public background of intelligibility opened by *logos* and deposited in the public language. The main thrust of Heidegger's critique of skepticism consists in the attempt to show that the skeptic's global doubts about our everyday beliefs and practices are self-defeating, since they undermine the conditions for the possibility of any meaningful discourse whatsoever. The results of the critique of skepticism can be generalized: since every inquiry must move *within* the circle of our linguistically constituted pre-ontological understanding of Being, there is no standpoint from which philosophy can make claims about the way things are that is unconditioned by the perspective built into our language. There is no "horizonless horizon" for a purified mode of inquiry liberated from the imprint of our everyday linguistic articulation of the world.

The problem of reflexivity arises when we go on to ask whether Heidegger's fundamental ontology does not *itself* presuppose the vantage point of such a horizonless horizon. In inquiring into the transcendental conditions for the possibility of any understanding of Being, doesn't he have to assume that he has a standpoint that is freed from the constraints of a particular language and culture? And if fundamental ontology must work from such a position, why is the language of fundamental ontology itself meaningful while the language of the Cartesian model is relegated to "nonsense?" We seem to be led to the conclusion that either fundamental ontology is a regional mode of discourse, in which case it is subject to the same limitations as other regional inquiries, or it is not bounded by any horizon, in which case it should be branded as "nonsense" for the same reasons that skepticism came to be regarded as meaningless. Heidegger's way of dealing with this puzzle has already been suggested above in section 13. In his view, the investigations of fundamental ontology neither operate within a regional framework nor presuppose a transcendental position outside of our everyday, public understanding. Rather, as the study of frameworks in general, fundamental ontology is solely concerned with working out what is already implicit in our ordinary pre-ontological understanding of Being. Since this pre-understanding is shaped and regulated by our shared, public language, the central task of fundamental ontology is to bring to light what is already contained in the "deep grammar" of our everyday language. Heidegger's project does not presuppose a standpoint *outside of* our everyday Being-in-the-world. Instead, it involves only a widening and deepening of the understanding of Being that is implicit in everydayness.

For this reason, fundamental ontology does not try to invent a "new" language, divorced from ordinary language, in which it is to express its ontological insights. Heidegger's goal is not to step outside our actual language, but to rework the horizon of our everyday language in order to free it from the misleading schematizations of the tradition. In the words of Erasmus Schöfer,

> Heidegger, in attempting to think the essence of Greek and Occidental philosophy, must distance himself from the linguistic imprint of that philosophy in order to reflect not in it, but about it. It is plain that he cannot indulge in the illusion that he is able to win back again a level of the German language which lay prior to and alongside the latinization of German, in order to make it once again practicable as language. Rather, Heidegger strives to disclose contents of language and thought which he can make productive in the mesh of modern German language, and which were previously closed off to the style and terminology of philosophical reflection (Schöfer 24/5).

By dialectically overhauling everyday language and ferreting out the hidden springs and sources of meaning of our common words, Heidegger hopes to develop an expanded horizon for the thoughts of fundamental ontology.

If the framework in which the investigations of fundamental ontology are conducted is a hermeneutically expanded form of the horizon of everyday language and not a regional framework, then it is clearly not subject to the criticisms that have been leveled at the Cartesian model and traditional philosophy in general. Heidegger is in a position to evaluate regional modes of discourse from the standpoint of the progressively widened language of our everyday lives. By stripping away the sediment of the tradition he intends to circumvent the "surface grammar" of the common-sense view which tempts us toward a picture of the world as collection of present-at-hand objects. From Heidegger's standpoint, everyday language itself in its "deep grammar" provides us with the equipment we need to get past the debris left by the history of Western metaphysics in order to attain a more primordial understanding of Being.

The crucial question, however, is not whether one can attain a vantage point that avoids being either regional or the spurious horizonless horizon of Cartesianism, but whether one can ever hope to attain a "transcendental" horizon in this way. In other words, can one expect to achieve anything like *the* horizon for the understanding of Being instead of *a* particular cultural horizon as embedded in a particular language? Is there any guarantee that the essential structures to be discovered in the existential analytic are not simply products of the linguistic organization of the world of a specific culture, even assuming this linguistic understanding has been interpreted to uncover its deep meaning?

The relativity of the understanding of Being to a language and a culture seems to become problematic only when we assume that different languages might constitute the world in different ways. We have already noted, however, that Heidegger has a way of handling this kind of cultural and linguistic relativism.[5] A full-blooded linguistic relativism can get off the ground only by assuming that we can make sense of distinct, incommensurable world-views that divide up reality in radically different ways. But such an assumption would be self-defeating. For one could maintain that there could be radically different world-views only by simultaneously assuming *both* that one can step outside of one's own world-view in order to identify and characterize different views, *and* that one of these world-views is the limit of one's own possibilities of understanding. Thus the relativist seems to be caught in a dilemma. If relativism is true, then our thoughts about other cultures and languages can make sense only within the framework of our own

5. At the end of section 13.

language, in which case one cannot coherently work out the relativist thesis. On the other hand, if relativism makes sense and a case can be made for it, then it must be false, since one *can,* in fact, transcend one's own world-view in order to comprehend other views.

The claim that language constitutes the world does not entail that we can make sense of the idea of radically different ways of understanding the world. If our interpretations of other cultures and languages are possible only within the framework of *our* linguistically articulated understanding of what it is to be, then there can be no exit from this horizon from which we can examine and compare radically different views. For this reason Gadamer says,

> The experience of the world in language is "absolute." It transcends all the relativities of the positing of Being, because it embraces all Being-in-itself, in whatever relationships (relativities) it appears (*Truth and Method* 408).

We can identify and discuss interesting differences between distinct languages only on the assumption that these languages are, in principle, intertranslatable and congruent in the ways they structure the world. Without this assumption, we would lack a basis for even *detecting* differences — or, for that matter, for identifying the activities of the creatures we were studying *as language.*

Furthermore it might be argued that the relativity of understanding to language will not lead to the prospect of radically different existentialia being discovered in different cultures. Although Heidegger admits that we can imagine worlds in which certain "accidental" structures of *our* world did not exist — for instance, readiness-to-hand and equipmentality[6] — it is not clear that we can make sense of the idea of a culture constituted in such a way that the existentialia could not be found. It is indeed the case, as we have seen, that there is no absolute ground for the existence of Dasein, truth, and disclosedness. And in this sense, Dasein may be thought of as contingent. But *given* the contingent fact of the existence of Dasein, it seems that our ability to discover certain structures is a necessary condition for our being able to identify any entity *as an instance of Dasein.* If we discovered entities with no situatedness, goal-directedness, or understanding of Being, that

---

6. "Perhaps even readiness-to-hand and equipment have nothing to contribute as ontological clues in interpreting the primitive world" (82).

were unable to take a stand on their "Being-toward-death" or were incapable of the expressions of Dasein-with, then we would not identify them as "Dasein." Entities without plans or goals, without care or disclosedness, would not be intelligible to us as human beings. We would not encounter them as humans who do things differently from us; they would be encountered as altogether different *kinds* of being. We would not understand *that they were human*.

This sketch of an argument gives us reason to doubt that Heidegger's project of fundamental ontology is necessarily incoherent when viewed in the light of his findings about the relativity of all understanding to the Anyone and language. For we find, first of all, that there is no way to make sense of the idea of different languages constituting the world in radically different ways. And, secondly, it seems plausible to claim that all imaginable languages must have the same deep grammar of pre-ontological understanding, and consequently that any hermeneutic of Dasein must reveal the same essential structures if it is to be intelligible to us *as* a hermeneutic *of Dasein*.

Nevertheless this way of dealing with the problem of linguistic relativism fails to take into account an important fact about languages, namely, that they are dynamic and constantly changing. Even if we cannot make sense of radically different world-views at this time, we know that our language has changed and will continue to change, in which case the prospect of finding a truly "transcendental" horizon for fundamental ontology again seems to become questionable.

It is this consciousness of mutability that leads to the second question that was distinguished in the problem of reflexivity: If all truth is historical, how can the results of fundamental ontology be timeless and immutable? If fundamental ontology is to achieve transcendental results, there must be something like a "closure" for the inquiry into the transcendental horizon for the understanding of Being. That is, if it is to be possible to "circumscribe the meaning of Being" once and for all, then there must be a point at which the meaning of Being has been fully and finally comprehended, and it must be possible to determine *when* this has been accomplished. But if all understanding is historical and constantly unfolding, it does not seem that such a closure can be achieved. The interpretation of interpreting itself which makes up the existential analytic will, like any interpretation, be an open-ended process, and the determination of Dasein's essential structures will remain tentative and defeasible. It seems, then, that fundamental ontology and "the science of Being as such" is undermined by the prospect of historical relativism.

In Chapter II we found that one of Heidegger's main goals in *Being and Time* was to overcome the historicism of the nineteenth century by identifying "historicity" as an essential principle of Dasein's Being. 'Historicity' refers to the temporal axis of Dasein's Being when it is regarded not as an object but as the *happening* of a life as a whole. Heidegger defines 'historicity' as "the temporalization structure of temporality" (332) through which Dasein *"is stretched along and stretches itself along"* (375) between birth and death. As "temporalizing as such" (375), historicity captures the dynamic structure of Dasein's way of taking up the possibilities into which it is "delivered over" by projecting itself onto its ownmost possibility of Being-a-whole.

Understood in this way, historicity has nothing to do with Dasein's being located in the stream of events of world-history. "The proposition, 'Dasein is historical,' " Heidegger says, "is . . . far removed from the mere ontical establishment of the fact that Dasein occurs in 'world-history' " (332). This aspect of the concept of "historicity" is designed to enable us to avoid the kinds of historicism found in Dilthey. In Karl Löwith's words,

> Heidegger carried Dilthey's historical relativism to its limit in that he traced it back to the unconditioned historicity of Dasein which is always owned and finite. A Dasein that is not only "in" time and incidentally "has" a history, but essentially *exists* temporally and historically, is no longer relative to time and history. This existentially absolutized historicity, which is made fast in "Being-towards the end," is supposed to first make possible the "vulgar" history of the world and make it intelligible.[7]

History as a stream of events is possible only on the basis of Dasein's historicity as "fate" and as the "co-happening" of a people's "destiny."

At the same time, however, Dasein is also understood as "historical" in the sense of being *in* history. Heidegger says that because Dasein is historical in the primordial sense of being a happening, it is always taking up the possibilities of the heritage into which it is thrown. Dasein's "stretching itself along" is always achieved in a concrete form as a gloss on the basic themes of its historical culture as these are made accessible in the language of the Anyone.

Thus it appears that the concept of "historicity" has two distinct meanings. On the one hand, it refers to a transcendental structure

---

7. *Heidegger: Denker in dürftiger Zeit* (Frankfurt a.M.: Fischer, 1953), pp. 46/7.

of Dasein's Being. In this sense it is to be understood as a foundational "principle" of temporality which underlies and makes intelligible different modes of Dasein's Being toward the world. On the other hand, however, this "transcendental" sense of "historicity" implies that Dasein must also be understood as contextualized in the course of a concrete history. But this means that the positive *results* of fundamental ontology must also be understood as contextualized in history. Fundamental ontology is a historical product.

Now it is not at all clear that these two concepts of "historicity" are at home with each other.[8] If historicity is taken as a suprahistorical, "transcendental structure" of Dasein's Being which makes possible the understanding of Being, then it does not appear that the inquiry into the nature of Dasein which discovers this structure can be "historical" in the ordinary sense of this term. Since Dasein's historicity is found to be a timeless, unchanging truth about the Being of Dasein, it must be incorporated into *any* philosophical position that is concerned with finding the truth about being human. On this way of understanding the concept of historicity, fundamental ontology can be saved from the charge of historical relativism only by forfeiting all the concrete results obtained in *Being and Time* concerning Dasein's contextualization in history. If historicity is taken as implying that Dasein *is* historically contextualized, however, then it seems that fundamental ontology itself is a historical product. But on this alternative the conclusion seems unavoidable that the concept of historicity is also a historical product and cannot be seen as identifying a "transcendental " structure that can serve as a foundation for an ontology in the widest sense. The existentialia discovered by fundamental ontology must be understood as derived from the historical context in which *Being and Time* originates. If this is the case, however, then the results of fundamental ontology must be understood as reflecting the current situation of the interpreter. Given a different historical situation, quite different essential structures might be discovered. It would seem to follow, then, that there could be no closure for the question of Being.

Heidegger might try to extricate himself from this dilemma by saying that although the concept of historicity is not *supra*historical, it is nevertheless *trans*historical. We noted that Heidegger believes that there are sources, springs, and roots of our

8. This point has been made by Otto Pöggeler in "Heidegger Today," *The Southern Journal of Philosophy,* VIII (Winter 1970): 273-308, pp. 299-300, and "Heidegger's Topology of Being" in Joseph J. Kockelmans, ed., *On Heidegger and Language* (Evanston, Ill.: Northwestern, 1972), pp. 121/2.

understanding of Being which have originated in the dawn of Western history and which continue to flow through history as a deep, underlying current. These sources were to be disclosed by the historical reduction which was to be the theme of the second part of the work, the "destruction" of the history of ontology. Heidegger thinks that all our "degenerate" traditional schematizations and conceptualizations have sprung from these inherited ontological sources. As he says,

> The ontological source [Ursprung] of Dasein's Being is not "inferior" to what springs from it, but towers above it from the outset; in the field of ontology, any "springing-from" is degeneration. If we penetrate to the "source" ontologically, we do not come to things that are ontically obvious for "common sense"; but the questionable character of everything obvious opens up for us (334).

Assuming that there is a single strand of meaning that runs through Western history, then, Heidegger's own concept of historicity would be designed to capture, in the weave of modern language, the deep understanding of human temporality that arose in earliest times and has been concealed by the tradition. On this view, Heidegger's choice of words and means of expression are historically determined, but the deep grammar of the concept expressed in this way is drawn from the transhistorical content of Western thought.

Fundamental ontology might therefore be characterized as a form of "transcendental historicism."[9] It takes seriously the insight of the nineteenth-century historicists that all possibilities of understanding are embedded in history and that there is no tribunal of reason that can ultimately ground and legitimate those possibilities. But it is also "transcendental" in the limited sense of holding that there are esssential possibilities extending beneath the flow of

9. The traditional concept of "historicism" embraces two central theses: (1) the claim that the human world is in a constant state of flux, that all cultural phenomena are historically conditioned, that our only guide to understanding is history, and that the interpreter himself stands in the stream of history; and (2) the idea that history is made up of unique and unrepeatable acts and events, so that the historical can be understood only in its "individuality." [See Georg G. Iggers, *The German Conception of History* (Middletown, Conn.: Wesleyan, 1968), esp. pp. 5-9, 287-290.] It will become apparent in the next section that only the first of these theses is applicable to Heidegger's conception of history. To say that his historicism is "transcendental" means that history is woven into a unified flow in which the individuality of agents, periods, and epochs gains its meaning only within a greater totality.

history which are the basis for our understanding of Being. The goal of fundamental ontology, then, is to overcome the superficial understanding of Being that arises in common sense and the tradition in order to "retrieve" the deeper, more primordial meanings of our heritage. The essential structures uncovered by this approach are "transcendental" in the attenuated sense of capturing the conditional necessity of the content of Western thought. It is, on this view, a contingent fact that there is a historical Dasein. But once this fact is given, then what counts as Being will have a certain necessity within the context of Dasein's historical and cultural understanding.

On this way of reading the aims of *Being and Time,* we can understand why Heidegger says that

> if we are inquiring into the meaning of Being, our investigation does not then become a "deep" one, nor does it puzzle out what stands behind Being. It asks about Being itself insofar as Being *enters into the understandability of Dasein* (152; my emphasis).

The question of Being can be dealt with only from within the field of intelligibility of Dasein as this is passed down to us by history in our public language. The content of our understanding cannot be sought in any deeper ground than the contingent fact that there happens to be an understanding of Being. But within this horizon of intelligibility, essential structures and a transcendental horizon can be disclosed and a certain sort of closure can be attained.

It should be evident, however, that this sort of transcendental historicism is fraught with difficulties. In the first place, it seems that the idea that we can discover the *final* underlying meaning of history is at odds with Heidegger's own conclusions about the contextualization of historical science. Heidegger says that "we need not discuss the fact that historiography, like any science, is, as a kind of Being of Dasein, factically 'dependent' at any time on the 'prevailing world-view' " (392). Since every interpretation is rooted in a fore-structure of understanding mediated by the prevailing view of the Anyone, it seems that historical interpretations will change with the shifting interests and concerns of historians. When Heidegger says that "the *'selection'* of what is to become a possible object for historiography *has already been met with* in the factical existentiell choice of Dasein's historicity" (395), he implies that what can count as relevant for historical science is always determined in advance by the "undiscussed assumption" (150) of historians.

But this seems to indicate that there can be no such thing as finding the final meaning of history. We cannot imagine a "last history of Greece," for instance, not because we cannot imagine a time when all the data are in, but because our understanding of what is *important* about the Greeks constantly unfolds with our interests and goals. If historiography is always situated and thrown into a cultural context which shapes its reading of history, then it is not clear how fundamental ontology can use history in order to arrive at a final and conclusive determination of the meaning of Being implicit in the West.

We saw that Heidegger seems to think that, in order to distinguish betweem superficial and deep interpretations of the meaning of Being, it is sufficient to become authentic. Authenticity is supposed to provide us with a criterion for deciding between competing interpretations and for determining when the spiral of interpretations has arrived at the final answer to the question of the meaning of Being. Aside from the fact that the dichotomy between authenticity and inauthenticity seems to provide us with an unjustifiably Manichean picture of the possibilities of understanding, however, it is not at all obvious how achieving authenticity is supposed to determine the closure and correctness of the interpretation of what it is to be. Heidegger says that authenticity will lead us into a "sober understanding" of the "basic possibilities for Dasein" (310). It reveals to us our "ownmost possibilities" (264) and it drives out "every accidental and 'provisional' possibility" (384). But there is no clue as to what these "basic possibilities" are. Although resoluteness might bring us face to face with our unique responsibility for making something of our lives, it does not seem to provide us with any indication as to which of the concrete possibilities circulating in the Anyone are the ultimate or basic sources for our understanding of Being.

We are told that the "transparency" of authenticity will enable us to detect and diagnose the distortions of the tradition. Authentic transparency leads to a "clearing-away of concealments and obscurities" (129) and enables us to understand the causes for our tendency to misinterpret Being. By becoming authentic, Dasein is also supposed to see the interrelationship of time and Being. Heidegger's claim is that, once we understand ourselves as finite happenings, we will free ourselves from the idea that *we* are to be understood as the objective presence of the present-at-hand, and we will thereby be led to a more primordial understanding of the temporality of Being in general.

Nevertheless, the suggestion that authentic transparency will determine the closure and correctness of the interpretation of Being runs into difficulties when it is set off against Heidegger's claim that we are always essentially characterized as falling and thrownness. Given this way of understanding our human situation, there does not appear to be any room for a *total* or *complete* transparency for Dasein. Heidegger says that "to be closed off and covered up belongs to Dasein's *facticity*" (222). But if there is no ultimate clarity or final intelligibility for Dasein, it does not seem that the "existentiell truth" of authenticity can provide us with a firm foundation for ontology.

Yet even if it were the case that authenticity guaranteed complete transparency, this would only push the problem of finding a criterion back a step. For it would then become necessary to find a criterion that would enable us to decide between competing claims to authenticity. Heidegger believes that once Dasein has become authentic it can "decide for itself" whether the analyses of fundamental ontology are correct or not (315).[10] What is missing here, however, is any account of how we can distinguish true insight from self-deception in the phenomenon of becoming authentic. How can we distinguish the assurance that arises in this transformation from the same types of certainty that are experienced in religious conversions or under the influence of hallucinogens?

Heidegger hoped simply to by-pass the epistemological tradition and its concern with rational grounding and justification. Seeing that there is no pure, untainted vantage point for epistemology in the broad sense, he turns directly to an attempt to work out "the Being of beings." But it seems that epistemological questions come back to haunt him. Given Heidegger's account of the contextualization of human activities, there is no way to find a firm foundation for ontology in the widest sense. In the end we are left with neither a criterion that will justify Heidegger's interpretation over others nor a closure for the historically shifting cycle of interpretations. Once we understand that philosophy itself must always stand within a "hermeneutic circle," the Heideggerian project seems to be left in the predicament of Neurath's boat, constantly being rebuilt plank by plank while riding the high seas. From the standpoint of such a conception of philosophy, there is no prospect of establishing a *fundamental* ontology to serve either as a secure foundation for the regional sciences or as a basis for arriving at a final answer to the question of Being. The idea of a "science of Being as such" collapses.

10. See above, section 6.

§16. *The "Twofold Task" and the End of Metaphysics*

In the closing pages of the published portion of *Being and Time* we can sense Heidegger's uncertainty and indecisiveness about his project. He suggests that "the *preparatory* existential analytic of Dasein" has been only a *path* toward working out the question of Being and that this approach remains provisional and tentative until "Being in general" has been conceptualized:

> Our way of exhibiting the constitution of Dasein's Being remains only a *path*. Our *aim* is to work out the question of Being in general. The *thematic* analytic of existence, however, first needs the light of the idea of Being in general, which must be clarified beforehand. . . . Whether this is the *only* path or even the right one at all, can be decided only *after one has gone along it* (436/7).

The unpublished parts of *Being and Time* were supposed to work out the idea of Being in general in order to provide a "light" for developing a "thematic analytic of existence." The circularity of the program is obvious: the "preparatory" existential analytic (the description of everydayness) serves as a basis for working out the idea of Being in general, and this in turn is the basis for a "thematic" analysis of existence.

But the problematic nature of this project is also evident: if the findings of the preparatory analytic are relative to a particular historical context, then the idea of Being in general which is derived from that analytic will also be relativized, and the thematic analytic of existence will lack a firm basis. The whole enterprise of *Being and Time* seems to float in the air with no supports. Heidegger sounds disingenuous when he says that "the *conflict* as to the interpretation of Being cannot be settled, *because it has not yet been enkindled*" (437). For the question is whether there is any prospect of settling the conflict once it *has* been enkindled. The fact that the work remains uncompleted suggests that Heidegger felt that the path marked out by *Being and Time* was not sufficiently promising to traverse in full.

The methodological difficulties *Being and Time* falls into result from Heidegger's hermeneutic approach to the question of Being. Since, for Heidegger, there is no access to an uninterpreted given independent of our pre-ontological understanding of Being, the question of Being must ask about "Being itself insofar as it enters into the understandability of Dasein" (152). But if Dasein's current pre-understanding is itself shot through with distortions and deceptions, the "phenomenology of understanding" has to be coupled with a hermeneutic stage in which the deep underlying meaning of our everyday interpretations of ourselves and the world is worked out. In other words, there is for Heidegger no unmediated access to the things themselves, no immediacy or direct "presence" of a Cartesian self-grounding ground. Our understanding is always discursive, never intuitive. Heidegger seems to want to mask this consequence of his thought when he speaks of securing our theme "in terms of the things themselves" (153) or of working from a "basic experience of the 'object' to be disclosed" (232). But the prospect of recourse to things themselves and basic experiences is vitiated by the fact that all our ways of encountering things are embedded within the horizon of understanding of a historical culture. With no exit available from the shared background of linguistically articulated interpretations, there is no way to find a firm foundation for fundamental ontology.

Although the project of fundamental ontology seems to end in frustration, it is clear that, during the period when he was composing the work, Heidegger felt that it could succeed. In order to understand why fundamental ontology fails, it will be helpful to step back and examine Heidegger's plan for the whole of *Being and Time*. In particular, it will be worth while to consider why Heidegger says that the question of Being involves a "twofold task" (15) and how the unpublished parts were to realize these tasks. If we can understand how Heidegger envisioned the work as a whole and why his project necessarily fails, we will be able to cast light on the "turn" (Kehre) in his thought after *Being and Time* and also prepare the way for a re-evaluation of the enduring achievements of that early work.

The architectonic for *Being and Time* as a whole is summarized in the second Introduction, which is entitled "The Twofold Task of Working Out the Question of Being" (15). According to this account of the program, there are two interdependent tasks involved in approaching the question of Being. The first is called "the ontological analytic of Dasein as laying bare the horizon for an interpretation of the meaning of Being in general" (15), and the second is "the task of destroying the history of ontology" (19). The first task was to have been completed in Part One of *Being and Time,* and the second was the aim of Part Two. It is important to realize that Heidegger saw both of these tasks as essential to the project of working out the question of Being. The two parts were supposed to buttress and reinforce each other. Neither by itself could be sufficient to fulfill the ends of philosophy as Heidegger understood this enterprise.

The first part of *Being and Time* has the form of a transcendental argument. The "preparatory existential analytic" begins with an existentiell account of oneself in everyday situations. The description of Dasein "in its average *everydayness*" (16) prepares the way for identifying the essential structures that make possible Dasein's modes of existence. The goal of this first stage of the project is "the interpretation of Dasein in terms of temporality, and the explication of time as the *transcendental horizon* for the question of Being" (41; my emphasis). Heidegger wants to show that Dasein always understands Being in terms of time:

> . . . Whenever Dasein tacitly understands and interprets something like Being, it does so with *time* as it standpoint. Time must be brought to light — and genuinely conceived — as the horizon for all understanding of Being and for any way of interpreting it (17).

In order to identify the transcendental horizon for interpreting the meaning of Being, Heidegger first shows that Dasein's understanding is characterized by "temporality" (Zeitlichkeit). Because Dasein is an activity of temporalizing, it opens a clearing in which entities can come to appearance in their Being. What it is to be an entity is constituted by the "horizontal schemata" of Dasein's ecstatic temporalizing.

In the third division of Part I, which was to have been called "Time and Being," Heidegger intended to show that Dasein's way of ecstatically projecting Being is itself "made possible by some primordial way in which ecstatical temporality temporalizes" (437). This deepest form of temporality is identified with the Latinate "Temporalität." Heidegger says that "*Temporalität* is the most primordial temporalizing of temporality as such."[11]

> . . . The way in which Being and its modes and characteristics have their meaning determined primordially in terms of time, is what we shall call its *"Temporal"* [temporale] determinateness. Thus the fundamental ontological task of interpreting Being as such includes working out the *Temporality of Being* [Temporalität des Seins] (19).

The account of the Temporality of Being reveals the most primordial horizon for understanding the Being of entities.

From this account of the "transcendental" part of the project, we can see why Heidegger later claimed that *Being and Time*

---

11. GP 429.

"abandons subjectivity"[12] and maintained that "every kind of anthropology and all subjectivity of man as subject is . . . left behind in that work."[13] From the perspective of the over-all plan for Part One of *Being and Time,* all the "variations of Being" (333), its "various modes and derivatives" (18), are supposed to be conceptualized in terms of a primordial Temporality that is both prior to and a condition for the possibility of Dasein's temporalizing. A sketch of the program for the final division of the first part of *Being and Time* is found in Heidegger's 1927 lectures, published as *Die Grundprobleme der Phänomenologie.* In these lectures, the account of the different modes of Being in terms of Temporality is structurally similar to a Kantian "schematism," but it is stripped of all its ties to subjectivity. What constitutes the Being of entities is not the activity of a transcendental ego; it is instead the activity of a primordial Temporality.

The transcendental part of *Being and Time* is supposed to provide an answer to the question of the *meaning* of Being: "In the exposition of the problematic of Temporality [Temporalität] the question of the meaning of Being will first be concretely answered" (19). The answer arrived at in the transcendental stage tells us that the "genealogy of the possible ways of Being" (11) and the account of the different "modifications and derivations" of Being (18) must be worked out within the horizon of time. But Heidegger suggests that it would be wrong to overestimate the results of this first task. At the end of this stage of the inquiry we are provided with a "horizon" for engaging in ontological research, but the inquiry does not terminate here:

> In its ownmost meaning this answer tells us that concrete ontological research has the assignment of *beginning* with an investigative inquiry which keeps within the horizon we have laid bare — *and this is all it tells us* (19; my emphasis).

The transcendental part brings us to the realization that our inquiry has the "assignment" of moving within the horizon of time. Heidegger says that the answer is "to provide the assigned clue or guideline [Leitfadenanweisung] for our research" (19), but it does not yet seem to undertake that research.

Where is the concrete work of ontological research to be carried out? Contrary to what is commonly assumed, there is reason to

12. LH 280, WM 159.

13. BW 141, WM 97.

believe that this research is really undertaken only in the second "task" of *Being and Time:* "the task of destroying the history of ontology."[14] This second task involved in the question of Being corresponds to what I referred to in Chapter II as the "dialectical stage." Heidegger claims that the "assignment" to carry out the "destruction" follows from the nature of Dasein itself. When the Being of Dasein is found to be characterized by temporality and historicity, it becomes clear that every mode of Dasein's activity is essentially contextualized in history. The same holds true for the activity of inquiring into the meaning of Being: it is contextualized within the course of the history of ontology and is inescapably dependent on that history for its possible results. As Heidegger says,

> From the ownmost ontological meaning of inquiry itself as historical, it follows that the working out of the question of Being has the assignment [Anweisung] of inquiring into the history of that inquiry itself—that is, of becoming historiographical—in order to bring itself into the positive appropriation of the past, into the full possession of its own most proper possibilities of inquiry (20/1).

The inquiry into the meaning of Being has the assignment of appropriating the history of ontological inquiry, precisely because it understands itself as a *product* of that history.

The second part of *Being and Time* is called the "phenomenological destruction of the history of ontology *with the problematic of Temporality as our clue* [Leitfaden]" (39; my emphasis). Using the results of the first stage as its clue or guideline, the historical stage is supposed to de-structure the history of ontology, "staking out the positive possibilities of that tradition," until it arrives "at those primordial experiences in which we achieved our first ways of determining the nature of Being—the ways that have

---

14. The central role of history in the over-all plan of *Being and Time* is often overlooked, partly because the shift to "historicity" at the end of the work does not seem to be clearly tied in to what precedes it. Thus Michael Zimmerman writes, "It seems as if the entire analysis of Dasein's 'historicality' was only 'tacked on' to the end of *Being and Time* and seems not to have played a vital role in the articulation of the leading idea of the work itself." ["The Foundering of *Being and Time*," *Philosophy Today,* XIX (Summer 1975): 100–107, p. 104]. Two excellent works that bring to prominence the historical part of *Being and Time* are David Hoy's "History, Historicity, and Historiography in *Being and Time*," in Murray, ed., *Heidegger and Modern Philosophy,* and Werner Marx's *Heidegger and the Tradition* (Evanston, Ill.: Northwestern, 1971), trans. Theodore Kisiel and Murray Greene, esp. pp. 101–113.

guided us ever since" (22). The destruction has both a diagnostic and a dialectical role to play. On the one hand, it diagnoses the misconceptions and confusions that run through the tradition and shows their roots in "Greek ontology and its history which, in its numerous filiations and distortions, determines the conceptual character of philosophy even today" (21). On the other hand, it brings to light the underlying conception of time, which is concealed by the tradition and in fact makes that tradition possible. In fulfilling both these roles, the historical interpretations carried out in the destruction will "keep within the horizon we have laid bare" in the transcendental stage — that is, it will make use of the deeper sense of Temporality uncovered in Part One in its readings of the history of ontology.

From this account of the over-all plan for *Being and Time* it is evident that it would be wrong to think of the projected second part of that work as an erudite appendix in which Heidegger intended to compare his new "theory" with those of his predecessors. The answer to the question of Being, Heidegger says, should not be thought of as a "free-floating result" or as a " 'standpoint' which may perhaps differ from previous types of treatment" (19). Since *Being and Time* is embedded in the history of ontology and dependent on that history for its findings, it must be seen as an unfolding of possibilities already implicit in the tradition. Understanding itself as a dialogue with the tradition, its goal is to retrieve the hidden "wellsprings" of understanding built into the tradition and to "bring us the insight that the specific mode of Being of previous ontology, and the destined turnings [Geschicke] of its inquiries, its findings and its failures, have been necessitated in the very character of Dasein" (19). Far from being a historical appendix, then, the destruction contains the concrete ontological research that makes up fundamental ontology. By tracing through the "decisive stages" of the history of ontology (23), it enables us to "remember" the sources and origins of the pre-ontological understanding that constitutes our everyday "forgetful" interpretations of ourselves and our world.

If the ultimate content of *Being and Time* is historical, then Heidegger's account of "the ontological genesis of the science of history" (392) at the end of the work must be seen as a propaedeutics for the historical stage, a recipe or prescription for authentic historical research. The account of historiography, Heidegger says, "will serve to prepare us for the clarification of the task of destroying the history of philosophy through historiography" (392). By working out "historiography in its primordial and authentic possibilities" (393), Heidegger wants to lay out the appropriate approach to the history of ontology and prepare us to become authentic historians. For only when we have been properly cultivated for the historical task can we "remember" in an appropriate way. To understand Heidegger's plan for Part Two of *Being and Time,* then, it is necessary to sketch out his conception of authentic historiography.

Historiography and historicity are ultimately rooted in Dasein's tripartite temporal structure. We saw when that Dasein is regarded as an event or happening, it must be seen as essentially goal-directed. Dasein exists as a purposive thrust toward its future—its realization of itself as Being-a-whole. By virtue of its teleological structure it opens a clearing, or *Spielraum,* in which entities can count or matter in some determinate way. In "coming toward" itself as futural, Dasein also "comes back" to what it is as "having been." Its openness discloses the range of possibilities in which it is situated and which provide the resources for its choices. On the basis of this temporal movement, Dasein is already-in the world. Since the "ex-stasis" of futurity is primary in Dasein's temporal axis, Heidegger says that "the character of having-been arises, in a certain way, from the future" (326). Only because Dasein is a situated projection can it be lost in the forgetfulness of mere "presencing"or "making-present" (Gegenwärtigen) in its everyday concerns.

The priority of the future also characterizes Dasein's authentic historicity. Heidegger says that "history has its roots so essentially in the future that death . . . throws anticipatory existence back upon its *factical* thrownness" (386) in such a way that it can take over its inherited possibilities in a resolute stance as "fate." But we have noted that Dasein's personal existence as fate is always tied up with the "destiny" of its generation and people. Its goals and aims always dovetail into the broader framework of the goal-directedness of its community. When Dasein explicitly understands itself as implicated in this shared project, it also understands its life as a commentary on its heritage and as a dialogue with what has come before. Its task of owning up to itself involves appropriating its *heritage* as the sole resource for its Being. Authentic Dasein therefore exists as a repetition or retrieval of "the possibilities of the Dasein who has-been-there [des dagewesenen Daseins]" (385): it resolutely takes a stand on its own Being by taking over possibilities it inherits from its predecessors, and in doing so it acts *"for 'its time' "* (385).

After explicating Dasein's historicity and its essential futurity, Heidegger goes on to examine the nature of the historical sciences. Historiography is rooted in Dasein's historicity, he says, and it therefore has the same *"ontological structure"* (392) as historicity.

This has two consequences for the ontological genesis of the historical sciences. It means, first of all, that the historian can be concerned with the "Dasein who has been there" as the theme for his inquiry only because, as historicity, he is already open to what has been as the reservoir of possibilities for his Being. But it also means that "even *historiographical* disclosure temporalizes itself *in terms of the future*" (395). Heidegger says that "historiography does not take its departure from the 'present' and from what is 'actual' only today in order to grope its way back from there to something that is past" (395). Instead, the historian understands the past in terms of the goals and ideals he projects *for the future.*

In section 6 we saw that Heidegger regards the historian's projections of futural values and goals as a condition for the possibility of selecting historical data: the historical is identified in terms of what contributes to the realization of certain aims of history. In *Being and Time* he suggests that the historicity of the historian's existence also determines how the theme of history is to be understood. "In a retrieving repetition," Heidegger says, "the Dasein who has-been-there is understood in its authentic possibility which has been" (394). In other words, we interpret the lives of our forebears as coherent goal-directedness in trying to make something of their lives as a whole. But since the Dasein who has come before is an "existentiell possibility in which fate, destiny and world-history have been factically determined" (394), to grasp our predecessors as authentic is also to understand them as participants in a world-historical destiny that we share with them.

The authentic historian therefore understands his own goals and values as interwoven with the projections of the object he studies. On the basis of this understanding of goals as essentially communal, the historian interprets his predecessors as fellow-travelers in the attempt to realize a common cultural sending. From this account of historiography it follows that the concern with understanding the past does not arise from a mere antiquarian curiosity about the lives of those who have come before. On the contrary, since the aim of historiography is to retrieve and repeat earlier possibilities for the purposes of a shared historical undertaking, the historian's task is to *appropriate* those possibilities and *apply* them in his projections toward the future.

In authentic historiography, the existence of those who have come before is "disclosed in such a manner that, in repetition, the 'force' of the possible gets struck home into one's [own] factical existence" with the result that the earlier possibility "comes toward that existence in its futural character" (395). Heidegger attempts to resolve the debate between the historical school and Hegelians as to whether the historical is something unique or is part of a universal project. The goal of historiography is not to uncover "that which has happened once and for all," he says. Nor is it concerned with universal laws that "float above" history. Rather, authentic historiography "makes manifest the universal in the once-for-all" (395): that is, it reveals the universal destiny implicit in every individual life. The historian's primary goal, then, is to achieve "belongingness" to his heritage and to *apply* history to his current context.[15]

Historiography therefore has the same tripartite structure as historicity. In projecting himself onto his destiny, the historian takes up his heritage and applies it to the present. On the basis of this tripartite articulation of historiography, Heidegger tries to show that there is an underlying ontological unity in the three kinds of history distinguished by Nietzsche in *The Use and Abuse of History:* the "monumental," the "antiquarian," and the "critical."[16] First, as futural, the historian projects the "monumental" possibilities of human existence as those which stand out as the ideals of his culture. Secondly, in projecting his destiny the historian is brought back to the heritage that is to be retrieved. He sees himself as having the task of "reverently preserving the existence that has-been-there in which the possibility seized upon has become manifest" (396). Authentic historiography is therefore "antiquarian." Finally, since the historian has an obligation to the present, he must be able to apply his findings to his current situation. He calls his contemporaries away from their forgetful "presencing" and calls them back to the task of appropriating their heritage in terms of the greater venture of their destiny. Authentic historiography is therefore "critical" of the present: "Authentic historiography becomes a way of depresencing the Today [Entgegenwärtigung des Heute], that is, of painfully detaching oneself from the falling publicness of the Today" (397).

Heidegger's goal in developing the implications of Nietzsche's classification of the types of history is to prepare us for undertaking the task of destroying the history of ontology. In the historical reduction of Part Two, we are to project the "monumental possibilities" opened by the great thinkers of history, while "reverently preserving" the possibilities they have handed down to

---

15. The importance of "belongingness" (Zugehörigkeit) and "application" (Verwendung) in historical knowledge has been developed by Hans-Georg Gadamer in *Truth and Method,* Part II.

16. Nietzsche, pp. 20ff.

us, in order to do "violence" (311) to the complacency of the Today. The goal is not to report objectively on the series of events that
have led up to the present, but to *appropriate* what has been in projecting toward a destiny we share with our forebears.

But historiography also has a hermeneutic structure. For this
reason Heidegger says that, for the historical sciences, "the main
point is the cultivation of the *hermeneutical situation* which . . .
opens itself to the retrieving disclosure of what has been there"
(397; my emphasis). It will be recalled that the hermeneutical situation was defined as "the totality of 'presuppositions' " which makes
up the fore-structure of understanding guiding our interpretations
(232).[17] Since historiographical interpretations have a hermeneutic
structure, they must anticipate some sense of the whole of world-
history and select their materials on the basis of their "undiscussed
assumption" (150) about the meaning of the whole. If the analysis
of authentic historiography is supposed to pave the way for the
destruction of the history of ontology, then it must provide an appropriate set of "presuppositions" to guide the inquiry.

What is the "presupposition" that makes up the "hermeneutical
situation" of the historical part of *Being and Time?* The answer is
to be found in the results of the transcendental stage of the work:
what is presupposed in the destruction is the conception of the
Temporality of Being uncovered in Part One, that is, in the Ontological Analytic of Dasein. We saw that the first half of *Being
and Time* was supposed to open up the "transcendental horizon for
the question of Being" (39). Its task is to provide us with a "clue" or
"guideline" for concrete ontological research. It now appears that
the clue that was to become available in Part One served the function of providing a basis for the task of Part Two: "the task of interpreting the basis of the ancient ontology in the light of the
problematic of Temporality" (25).

Heidegger seems to think that, once we are cultivated as authentic historians, we will be able to shatter traditional prejudices and
remember the concealed meaning of Being in our heritage. As
authentic historians, we will be "critical" of the Today and "the
prevalent way of treating the history of ontology, whether it is
headed toward doxography, toward intellectual history, or toward
a history of problems" (22/3). Disregarding the prevalent
understanding of history, the destruction "attempts to set in motion a thoughtful dialogue between thinkers,"[18] reading past

17. See above, section 6.

18. KPMe xxv, KPMg xvii.

ontologists in such a way as to de-construct the thinker's words to find the destined goals underlying them.

It is noteworthy that, according to the Table of Contents for *Being and Time,* the destruction was supposed to move systematically backwards through the "decisive stages" of the tradition, beginning with Kant and then proceeding through Descartes to Aristotle (40). The method is clearly that of a historical reduction or regression which fits the image of peeling off the encrusted layers of tradition in order to retrieve the hidden fountainhead of understanding at the source of the history of ontology. But, Heidegger says, the destruction "does not take its departure from the 'present' and from what is 'actual' only today": it originates instead in the *future,* from a projected meaning for world-history as a totality. As Heidegger was later to formulate this historical goal, in posing the question of Being,

> our concern is to restore man's historical Dasein — and that always means that of our ownmost *future* Dasein — to the totality of history determined for us, to rejoin us with the strength and potency [Macht] of the primordial Being which is to be disclosed (IM 34, EM 32; my emphasis).

In Heidegger's view, then, the only way to achieve the ends of philosophy is through the study of history. Posing the question of Being and tracing the history of the way this question has been posed are inseparable. Heidegger thoroughly agrees with Count Yorck, who says that "there is no longer any actual philosophizing which would not be historiographic. The separation between systematic philosophy and historical presentation is wrong in its essence" (402).[19] Like count Yorck, he thinks that "the failure to historicize one's philosophizing is methodologically like a residue of [traditional] metaphysics" (402). Since philosophizing is always embedded in and indebted to history, there can be no vantage point outside of history for metaphysical speculation. Metaphysics, like any human activity, is at its core a dialogue with the past.

When *Being and Time* is understood in the light of its over-all aims and architectonic, it becomes clear why Heidegger thought that his transcendental historicism would succeed where both historicism and traditional ahistorical transcendental philosophy

19. Heidegger says that his account of history in derived from Dilthey's work "which gets illumined in a more penetrating fashion by the ideas of Count Yorck von Wartenburg" (397). In section 77 of *Being and Time* he quotes extensively from Count Yorck's letters to Dilthey in the *Briefwechsel zwischen Wilhelm Dilthey und dem Grafen Paul Yorck von Wartenburg 1877-1897,* Halle, 1923.

had failed. Since philosophy itself is characterized by historicity, the question of the meaning of Being must ultimately be historical — that is, it asks about the history of that question. But since historiography is hermeneutical in nature, it must be guided by presuppositions about the underlying meaning of the whole history of ontology. This leads to the question of how we are to find the right sorts of presuppositions to guide our historical inquiry. Here the preparatory analytic of Dasein comes into play. By analyzing our vague average understanding of Being in everydayness, we will be able to arrive at a conception of the relation of Being to time that will serve as a clue or guideline for reading the history of ontology.

On this conception of the over-all project of *Being and Time,* the two tasks that make up the "twofold task in working out the question of Being" mutually support each other. The historical stage is possible only if we have cultivated our hermeneutical situation as historians. This is achieved through a transcendental analysis of everydayness which reveals its horizon of understanding. The transcendental analysis provides us with a principle for destructuring the thought of the ontologists who have come before. As well-cultivated historians, we will work our way back through the history of ontology, diagnosing the misconceptions and failures of our predecessors and disclosing the hidden insights underlying their thought. Finally, the historical investigation will confirm what was uncovered in the transcendental stage by displaying the "birth certificates" for our "basic ontological concepts" (22). Both tasks are necessary for the project as a whole. The transcendental analysis tells us what to look for in reading the history of ontology, and the historical stage authenticates the findings of the transcendental stage by showing their historical origins.

What is disclosed in this approach to the question of Being is not a Cartesian self-grounding ground that makes the whole of history finally intelligible in some way. Rather, what it provides is a "*genealogy* of the different possible ways of Being" (11; my emphasis) that displays their origins in history and reveals the basis for our current, everyday interpretations. Fundamental ontology is fundamental not in the sense of uncovering ahistorical foundations for our beliefs and practices, but in the sense of making historical diversity intelligible. The final genealogy of Being is supposed to be "primordial" in the dual sense of this word. It both identifies the conditions for the possibility of any understanding of Being in its modes and variations and recaptures the "earliest" or "oldest" articulation of Being in our heritage. We saw in Chapter II that Heidegger regards these two meanings of 'primordial' as amounting to the same thing: in the words of "The Essence of Truth," "The primordial disclosure of Being as a whole, . . . and the beginning of Western history, are the same and contemporaneous."[20] But why there should have been such a disclosure or such a history remains ungrounded, an "abyss" (Ab-grund).

At the time of the composition of the published portion of *Being and Time,* Heidegger believed that by fusing the transcendental and historical approaches he could overcome the difficulties inherent in each. Though he saw that neither approach could stand by itself, he hoped that combined they would gird each other up. But it seems that he later came to realize that the two tasks in fact tend to undermine each other: the findings of the transcendental stage shatter the prospects of finding *the* underlying meaning of history, and the historicity of the question of Being defeats the project of finding a transcendental horizon or essential structures to ground a fundamental ontology. The hybird approach to metaphysics, which was supposed to produce a stronger crossbreed, in fact issues in a nonviable mongrel. The reason why Heidegger came to see *Being and Time* as an illuminating failure can be clarified by considering the consequences of each of the tasks that were to have made up the finished product.

First, the analytic of Dasein that paves the way for the transcendental stage of the inquiry reveals certain essential structures of Dasein, including Dasein's situatedness in a concrete cultural world. To be human is to be contextualized within a background of intelligibility which is articulated by historically conditioned forms of life as these are mediated by our common language. We have seen that this backdrop of cultural meanings provides us with the scaffolding of possible roles and self-interpretations through which we can come to take some concrete stand in the world. But it has also become clear that our situatedness within a framework of forms of life has the consequence that we can never achieve total clarity or transparency about our context. When Heidegger says that "Dasein is equiprimordially both in the truth and in untruth" (223), he means that, although Dasein *is* disclosedness insofar as it opens a world, it is also always essentially closed off to the extent that, as falling, it tends to cover up and disguise entities in its everyday interpretations. Our understanding is always infected by distortions mediated to us by the common sense of the Anyone and by the tradition. There is no exit from these misinterpretations that will enable us to reach total clarity.

20. BW 129, WM 85.

If Dasein is situated in this way, however, the prospects for working out anything like *the* history of ontology become clouded. Since Dasein is always "in untruth," there is no perspective from which the historian can identify historical facts for a final, authoritative account of history. Historical understanding will always be dependent on the goals and ideals circulating in the current world in which the historian lives. Insofar as this framework of interests and goals seems to be mutable, there is no reason to think that one can arrive at an interpretation of history that will ground a science of Being as such. As a result, the findings of the transcendental stage appear to defeat the possibility of achieving the goals of the historical stage.

Turning now to the consequences of the historical stage, it seems unlikely that there will be any way to uncover transcendental conditions for the possibility of encountering beings, given the historicity of all forms of inquiry. We saw that Heidegger hoped to overcome this historicist impasse with a radicalized conception of history. According to this view of history, the whole of Western thought is seen as having an underlying thread of meaning that is retrievable through a dialectical method. The goal of authentic historiography is to uncover "transcendental" truth, where this is now understood in the attenuated sense of being "transhistorical."

But it appears that Heidegger's conception of history as containing a primal ur-text of meaning is undermined by his account of Dasein's historicity. For even though the notion of a totality of meaning may be a "regulative idea" for the possibility of a hermeneutic approach to history, the fact that this projected totality originates in mutable cultural values implies that the conception of the meaning of history as a whole might shift. We have seen that, as participants in history, we constantly reshape and transform our destiny in our essential decisions. In fact, the whole tenor of Heidegger's conception of historicity tends toward the view that history, far from being a series of commentaries on a static primal text, should instead be seen as an unfolding flow in which historical agents are constantly reinterpreting the meaning of what has come before for the purposes of the future. As Werner Marx has pointed out, in *Being and Time* Dasein is conceived of as an entity which "transmits to itself the possibilities of the community which 'still perdure' as 'heritage'," and in transmitting them it *transmutes* them, thereby transforming itself.[21]

If this is the true significance of the notion of historicity, however, then the belief that historiography can reveal "transcendental"

---

21. *Heidegger and the Tradition,* pp. 105/6.

knowledge in any sense is unjustified. The idea that there are immutable, universal structures that account for the wide variety of forms of life in different cultures and historical epochs seems untenable. Once the fundamental historicity of understanding and interpretation has been struck home, it becomes apparent that there is no way to discover a structure of interpreting itself that supports our shifting interpretations. As Otto Pöggeler suggests, Heidegger's realization of the full implications of historicity led him to abandon his hopes of ever being able to arrive at a final analysis of Dasein:

> The Being of man, too, (as *Being and Time* attempts to grasp it in its "existentialia") could be in a similar way the being of man in a certain epoch and not determine him for once and for all ("Heidegger Today" 282).

If our understanding is always caught up in the flow of history, then our understanding of understanding itself is also caught in that current. There can be no transcendental ground for the destruction of the history of ontology or for the question of Being in general.

It is important to see what motivated Heidegger's attempt to develop a transcendental historicism, if we are to understand why fundamental ontology could not succeed. Under the influence of Dilthey and the historical school, Heidegger had come to realize that the Kantian project of finding timeless, transcendental structures of man on the basis of an analysis of our *current* ways of interpreting ourselves was doomed to failure. There is no "a priori" knowledge in the sense of what can be known to pure reason independent of any social or historical conditioning. The Kantian dream of discovering an ahistorical framework for any inquiry is motivated by the goals of epistemology in its broadest sense: the goal of providing a final ground or foundation for our beliefs and practices. Heidegger's recognition of the temporality and historicity of our Being defeats the hope of finding such a foundation. Since we are a "happening" caught up in history, the question of Being is characterized by historicity: "the basic position and attitude of our questioning is in itself historical; it stands and maintains itself in happening, inquiring out of happening for the sake of this happening."[22] Fundamental ontology is part of the world-historical happening of Western thought and, therefore, cannot be conceived of as the attempt to find ahistorical, transcendental structures that lie outside of that happening.

22. IM 37, EM 34.

But Heidegger still hoped to find a center and meaning in the discursivity of history by regarding history as a story or narrative with a unified thread of meaning between beginning and end. History is regarded as a text whose ultimate meaning as a whole is determined by the future:

> History as happening is an acting and being acted on which, *determined from out of the future* and taking over what has been, passes through the *present* (IM 36, EM 34; my emphasis on the first phrase).

Since the meaning of the whole is implicit in the beginning, Heidegger believed he could find a historical correlate of the traditional notion of the "a priori" in the primordial origins, springs, sources, and roots of Western thought. The aim of fundamental ontology is therefore to retrieve the beginnings of our destiny, the heritage that continues to flow beneath our everyday forms of life. In the words of the *Introduction to Metaphysics,* to pose the question of Being

> means nothing less than to retrieve [wieder-holen] the beginning [Anfang] of our historical-spiritual Dasein in order to transform it into a new beginning. . . . But we do not retrieve a beginning by reducing it to something past and now known, which need merely be imitated, but rather by rebeginning the beginning *more primordially,* and indeed with all of the strangeness, darkness, and insecurity that attend a true beginning (IM 32, EM 29/30).

The goal of the question of Being is to "win back our roots [Bodenständigkeit] in history" (*ibid.*) by retrieving the *archē* that is the impetus of our sending as a whole.

Thus, Heidegger's appreciation of the historicity of the question of Being leads him to absolutize history and treat it as a "primal text" whose concealed meaning lies below the tumult and clamor of our commentaries. This faith in the ultimate truth inhering in our origins and wellsprings of understanding—this Heideggerian "archaicism"—is later found in his glorification of the peasant's oneness with the land and the Greek temple in "The Origin of the Work of Art." It motivates his interest in the Pre-Socratics and still inspires the notions of "autochthony" and "homeness" (Heimat) in the later writings. And it informs his preoccupation with etymologies and what I have called the "deep grammar" of language throughout his works. The dream of recapturing a time of purity, spontaneity, and belongingness to Being has its roots in a desire to recover an elemental unity in the midst of transience and dispersal—a centripetal force in a centrifugal world.[23] The unifying thread of meaning is found not in Platonic forms, consciousness in general, or transcendental subjectivity, but in the *story* of history—the *logos* that weaves together the *archē* of our heritage and the *telos* of our destiny into a coherent, meaningful narrative.

It should be evident, however, that this attempt to retain a limited sort of transcendentality in the notion of an underlying core of meaning in history cannot be justified. In fact, it seems to belong to the same kind of "residues of Christian theology within philosophical problematics" that Heidegger wanted to eliminate from fundamental ontology (229): it is the product of a secularized religious nostalgia that presupposes the soteriology of Western thought. The longing for origins, according to Mircea Eliade, stems from roots that are essentially religious:

> The nostalgia for origins is equivalent to a *religious* nostalgia. . . . It is a nostalgia for the *perfection of beginnings* that chiefly explains the periodical return *in illo tempore*. In Christian terms, it could be called a nostalgia for paradise.[24]

The conception of history as a happening or event with an underlying point and purpose, which contains the promise of deliverance from the falling of our decadent world, makes sense only if we buy into the redemption myth of Christianity.

The natural response to Heidegger's archaicism is the kind of skepticism found in the recent works of such "post-structuralists" as Foucault and Derrida. Foucault, for example, reminds us of Nietzsche's diagnosis of the faith in "the lofty origin" as " 'no more than a metaphysical extension which arises from the belief that things are most precious and essential at the moment of birth.' "[25] "The pursuit of the origin," according to Foucault, "assumes the existence of immobile forms that precede the external world of accident and succession" (*ibid.* 142). Far from being an attempt to preserve historicity, the yearning for an *archē* appears as a denial of historicity,—a rejection of change, movement, unfolding. It

---

23. This trim metaphor is borrowed from J. Ogilvie.

24. *The Sacred and the Profane*, trans. Willard R. Trask (New York: Harcourt, Brace & World, 1959), p. 92.

25. Michel Foucault, "Nietzsche, Genealogy, History," in *Language, Countermemory, Practice*, ed., Donald F. Bouchard, (Ithaca, N.Y.: Cornell, 1977), p. 143.

seeks a timeless mythic guide and model for our lives, an *essence* underlying all mere existence.

> This search is directed to "that which was already there," the image of a primordial truth fully adequate to its nature, and it necessitates the removal of every mask to disclose an original identity. However, if the genealogist refuses to extend his faith in metaphysics, if he listens to history, he finds that there is "something altogether different" behind things: not a timeless and essential secret, but the secret that they have no essence or that their essence was fabricated in a piecemeal fashion from alien forms (*ibid.* 142).[26]

"What is found at the historical beginning of things," Foucault suggests, "is not the inviolable identity of their origin; it is the dissension of other things. It is disparity" (*ibid.*).

Derrida also criticizes the kind of "logocentrism" implicit in Heidegger's archaicism. In his view, the attempt to find a center underlying all free play in history is still part of the "metaphysics of presence":

> From the basis of what we therefore call the center (and which, because it can be either inside or outside, is as readily called the origin as the end, as readily *arche* as *telos*), the repetitions, the substitutions, the transformations, and the permutations are always *taken* from a history of meaning—that is, a history, period—whose origin may always be revealed or whose end may always be anticipated in the form of presence. This is why one could perhaps say that the movement of any archeology, like that of any eschatology, is an accomplice of this reduction of the structurality of structure and always attempts to conceive of structure from the basis of a full presence which is out of play.[27]

Although Heidegger has overcome the Cartesian dream of finding an immediate "presence" in the direct, immediate intuition of a given, he is unable to give up the craving for a center of all structures, an unmoving fulcrum around which all movement occurs.

26. I am grateful to Forest Pyle for drawing my attention to this passage.

27. Jacques Derrida, "Structure, Sign and Play in the Discourse of the Human Sciences" in *The Structuralist Controversy,* ed., Richard Macksey and Eugenio Donato (Baltimore: Johns Hopkins, 1972), p. 248.

In section 6 I tried to show how Heidegger's conception of history as a meaningful totality arises from his hermeneutic understanding of history. If history is to be a narrative, it must have a meaning; if it has a meaning, then we must project a meaning for the whole — in other words, we must read historical events as contributing to the development and effectiveness of universal history. But universal history in turn presupposes *values* projected by the historian on the basis of which he selects his data. The narrative conception of history is therefore tied up with assumptions about the validity of our current cultural values.

This argument for an over-all meaning in history can be challenged by questioning either its initial premise or its conclusion. The French "annalist" school of historians, for instance, has raised doubts about the assumption that history in fact must have a narrative structure. And the claim that our current values are in order has led some critics to argue that the hermeneutic conception of history as a meaningful narrative is an instrument of repression insofar as it is used to *legitimate* existing values and close off possibilities of criticizing current institutions. Hayden White has recently suggested that narrativity "is intimately related to, if not a function of, the impulse to moralize reality, that is, to identify it with the social system that is the source of any morality that we can imagine."[28] If this is the case, however, it might be argued that narrativity and the hermeneutic conception of history are ideological devices which should be challenged in the interests of achieving liberty from social institutions that are stagnant or unjust. And if the very notion of narrativity is challenged in this way, then Heidegger's archaicism loses its sole support.

When the mythic and apocalyptic vision of history in *Being and Time* is challenged, the prospect of finding underlying grounds or a center of structure in history dissolves. Philosophy can no longer be regarded as "hermeneutic" in the sense of interpreting the text of everydayness and the tradition in order to find its hidden "meaning" and "ground" (35). There is no longer any reason to believe that beneath the chatter of our mundane lives we will hear the murmurings of a primal text or deep grammar that legitimates our existence and assures us of having a place in some nobler enterprise of a historical sending. As in Gadamer's *Truth and Method,* history comes to be seen as a text whose very identity and being resides in its "history of effectiveness" (Wirkungsgeschichte) as it is taken up and applied for practical purposes by each generation.

---

28. "The Value of Narrativity in the Representation of Reality," *Critical Inquiry,* VII (Autumn 1980): 5–27, p. 18.

In this Gadamerian picture of history, our dialogue with the past is not so much the pursuit of a concealed *archē* as it is creative reinterpretation which carries forward the flow of tradition without any pretence that there is an ultimate, final truth that unifies the whole. Heidegger's distinction between "tradition" and "heritage" seems to fall away in this conception of history: there is no way to disentangle the distorted commentaries from the original text that supposedly underlies it.

In his later writings Heidegger came to see the preoccupation with finding *the* meaning of Being or *the* hidden ground of Being as itself an expression of the "will to power" which is the essence of technology. Instead of seeing history as the story of *man's* disclosing and concealing of Being, the later works are concerned with the history of Being as the "gift" of Being in its revelation and concealment. The question of Being tends to be explicitly historical in the later writings. In *Der Satz vom Grund* (1955/6), for instance, Heidegger interprets the project of finding the relation between Being and grounds as follows:

> The question of the extent to which Being and *ratio* belong together can only be asked from the standpoint of the destiny of Being and can be answered by thinking back through the destiny of Being. Now, however, we experience the destiny of Being from the outset only in traversing through the history of Western thought. This begins with the thought of the Greeks (SvG 176).

But the goal of this sort of inquiry is not to find the wellsprings of all understanding in the Greeks. It is content with simply engaging in a dialogue with the past: "Each epoch of philosophy has its own necessity," Heidegger writes, "we simply have to acknowledge the fact that a philosophy is the way it is. It is not our business to prefer one to the other."[29]

The question of Being, which has been taken up with such confidence in *Being and Time,* seems to end in frustration. Heidegger's later writings proclaim the end of philosophy: "the development of philosophy into the independent sciences . . . is the legitimate completion [Vollendung] of philosophy."[30] The sole "heir" of philosophy is now a "reflective" or "meditative" thinking (besinnliches Denken) which is closer to poetry than to science. Philosophy moves away from the ideal of finding the "correct

29. TB 56, SD 62.

30. TB 58, SD 64.

representation" of Being toward evocations and intimations of the "mystery" of Being. The titles of Heidegger's last books — for example, *Dead Ends (Holzwege), Path Markers, Underway* . . . — show the open-ended and inconclusive nature of philosophical thought. Instead of the search for a center of all structures we find "releasement" (Gelassenheit) from the craving for a center and meditations on the epochal search for such a center.

§17. *Re-evaluation of the Achievement of* Being and Time

Kant thought it was a "scandal of philosophy" that no one had yet succeeded in proving the existence of objects in the external world. We saw at the outset that Heidegger responds by claiming that the *real* scandal of philosophy was that anyone would think that such a proof was needed. For the demand for such a proof makes sense only against a background of uncritical assumptions about the nature of our ordinary epistemic situations and about the conditions for making our everyday activities fully intelligible. The seemingly innocent and commonsensical demand for a proof is in fact buttressed by a great deal of sophisticated metaphysical stage setting which has been done before the skeptic ever makes his appearance. Both the narrow puzzle of skepticism and the attempt at "overcoming metaphysics" through epistemology in the broad sense are metaphysical at their core. As Heidegger says in a later essay, " 'Epistemology' and what goes under that name is at bottom metaphysics and ontology, which is based on truth as the certainty of guaranteed representation."[31]

In section 5 we traced the path that led Heidegger away from the prevailing epistemological orientaion of the nineteenth century to a "return to metaphysics." *Being and Time* was supposed to by-pass the subject/object model and the rationalist presuppositions of the Cartesian tradition in order to turn an unjaundiced eye on the nature of our relation to the world. The search for intelligibility is disengaged from the Cartesian quest for certainty. Instead of seeking the kind of global and intrinsic intelligibility promised by the Cartesian model, Heidegger attempts to bring to light the plain sources of intelligibility already implicit in our everyday lives, and then tries to show the roots of this pre-understanding in our temporal happening and in the history of the West.

It has become clear in this chapter, however, that the more ambitious goals of *Being and Time* necessarily end in failure. The

---

31. EP 88, VA I 67.

findings that were the basis for criticizing the Cartesian model also
tend to undermine the prospects for metaphysics in general. The
dream of achieving *"transcendental* knowledge" and *"veritas
transcendentalis"* (38) concerning Being seems to dissolve when the
situatedness and historicity of inquiry in general is brought to light.
In the "Introduction to 'What Is Metaphysics?' " of 1949 Heidegger
concedes that the error of *Being and Time* lies in the very notion of
fundamental ontology, which is "still a kind of ontology" and
"revolves around an indirect or direct conception of 'transcendence.' "[32] From the standpoint of the later writings, the preoccupation with finding essential structures and transcendental
horizons comes to be seen as still trapped in what Heidegger calls
"onto-theologic": the attempt to think Being as the "ground-giving
unity" for entities as a totality.[33]

In retrospect it seems that *Being and Time* fails because it is still
caught in the kind of "representational-calculative thinking"[34] that
characterizes the tradition. It attempts to free us from our myopic
understanding of Being as that which is representable for a subject
by offering a new and better model of our situation in the world.
But it is precisely the preoccupation with finding a "correct model"
or "correct representation" which is at fault. The search for a new
model as an alternative to the Cartesian model presupposes that
there is some common endeavor which fundamental ontology and
the tradition share—identifying the grounds for our intelligibility—but which fundamental ontology does *better*.[35] But
this presupposition only seems to validate the very tradition it
wants to overcome. By setting up a new model in contrast to that of
the tradition, *Being and Time* tends to perpetuate a traditional set
of puzzles, only now couched in a new vocabulary and style.
Heidegger later came to see that denying or repudiating subjectivism only reaffirms the validity of the traditional polarities and
oppositions that set philosophical puzzles in motion in the first

---

32. WM 209. Translated by Walter Kaufmann as "The Way Back into the Ground
of Metaphysics" in his *Existentialism from Dostoevsky to Sartre* (Cleveland: Merid-
ian, 1965), p. 219.

33. *Identity and Difference,* trans. Joan Stambaugh (New York: Harper & Row,
1969), p. 58. *Identität und Differenz* (Pfullingen: Neske, 1957), p. 55.

34. BW 377, SD 65.

35. The danger of regarding Heidegger's major achievement as offering us a
"new" metaphysical theory has been brought out by Richard Rorty in his "Overcoming the Tradition: Heidegger and Dewey," in Murray, ed., *Heidegger and the Tradition.*

place. As he says in the second *Nietzsche* volume, the new model of *Being and Time,*

> without intending it, is faced with the threat of itself becoming, once again, a perpetuation of subjectivity and of becoming itself a hindrance to the decisive steps still to be taken.
> . . . Any turn toward "objectivism" and "realism" is still subjectivism: the question about Being as such stands beyond the reach of the subject-object relation.[36]

If the question of Being is to be adequately dealt with, it must be posed outside of the grids that structure traditional philosophical debates.

Once the more ambitious goals of *Being and Time* are abandoned, what remains of the critique of the Cartesian model? Is it possible to disentangle the more limited but enduring achievements of that work from the grandiose aims of founding a "science of all sciences?" I would like to conclude by considering two components of *Being and Time* which seem important and persuasive independent of the bolder intentions of that work. These are, first, Heidegger's phenomenology of everydayness and his attempt to show that the Cartesian model is a "founded mode" of Being-in-the-world; and, second, his emphasis on the historicity of all human endeavors. If these achievements are to be understood as lying outside the tradition, it will also be necessary to suggest a way of interpreting *Being and Time* in such a way that it is no longer seen as giving us a "correct representation" of some set of facts.

The first component of *Being and Time* that seems to retain its value even after the demise of fundamental ontology is the phenomenology of everydayness. I pointed out in Chapter II that the description of everydayness and the attempt to work out a "natural conception of the world" play only a subordinate role in the over-all plan for *Being and Time.* The role of the descriptive stage is to provide a text-analogue that will serve as a basis for a cycle of deep interpretations aimed ultimately at answering "the question of Being in general." In this sense the account of everydayness is only a springboard that enables us to leap to higher things. Once it has served its purpose, it is supposed to fade into the background.

Yet in many ways the description of Being-in-the-world remains one of the most original and impressive contributions of *Being and Time.* In opposition to the tradition's preoccupation with the con-

---

36. *Nietzsche II* (Pfullingen: Neske, 1961) 194/5.

templative attitude, Heidegger attempts to characterize our situation in ordinary practical contexts of agency. Starting from such banal examples as hammering in a workshop, lifting a door latch, and operating a car's turn signal, he unfolds a picture of daily life that presents an alternative to the Cartesian model's narrow and one-sided perspective. We come to see ourselves not as subjects passively registering sense impressions, but as agents dealing with equipment in skillful ways. Far from being a *res cogitans,* the self appears as goal-directed activity caught up in a mesh of means/ends relations, acting with know-how and competence in a familiar life-world.

In Heidegger's portrayal of everydayness as a web of internal relations, the Cartesian subject and objects drop out as superfluous and pointless. The common-sense conception of a substantial "I" distinct from a world of mere things, spinning a web of beliefs out of gossamer data, has nothing to contribute to our understanding of ourselves in our everyday involvements. What makes our activities possible, according to Heidegger, is not a web of beliefs we have formulated about things in the world, but our prereflective attunement and competence in coping with our world. Before we can ever reach the detached, disengaged attitude of pure reflection, we must have already gained mastery over the ready-to-hand in our practical dealings in the world.

Heidegger's description of Being-in-the-world also leads us to see ourselves as originally located in a shared, public "we-world." Before finding ourselves as isolated, forlorn subjects, we are placeholders in a spectrum of social systems that intersect in us and open up the range of possibilities from which we can gain a concrete content for our lives. Understood as the Anyone, Dasein comes to be seen as meaningful expression against the background of meaning of an intelligible life-world. We have found that this background of meaningfulness is constituted by our public language and has deep historical roots. It is essentially *transpersonal,* and it provides the field against which we first become human.

The portrait of Dasein as Being-in-the-world helps to restore an older sense of the life-world as an ordered, holistic totality — as a cosmos. The world we encounter in our everyday lives is not a space-time coordinate system filled with a collection of homogeneous objects; it is a coherent, teleological order with an orientation and a focus. This world is immediately intelligible to us because it contains expressions of communal interests, needs, and goals. When we see that the world is already intelligible to us in this way, the idea that the Cartesian model has an important role to play in providing rational clarification for our everyday practices is deflated. The aura of unintelligibility that seemed to surround our practices is diagnosed as the product of a *breakdown* in our ordinary involvements and not something built into the human condition. From the standpoint of Heidegger's description of our plain situations, the frameworks that generate certain futile pseudo-problems are shattered, and the traditional puzzles of philosophy tend to dissolve.

The kinds of description and diagnosis that Heidegger presents derive their impact and plausibility from the concrete, detailed ways they are worked out. It is important to see that this impact remains even if no claim is made about the "essential structures" of worldhood and of agency in general. In other places and at other times there might be humans whose self-understanding is so radically different as to obviate the whole range of questions we have been dealing with. But Heidegger's phenomenology seems to stand up as an impressive and forceful interpretation of our current modes of self-understanding. The description of Being-in-the-world retains its importance even when the transcendental pretence of *Being and Time* is abandoned.

It might be asked how the rejection of transcendentalism affects the diagnoses of science and the Cartesian model discussed in the last chapter. The main thrust of Heidegger's critique of the tradition consists in his attempt to show that science and Cartesian foundationalism are derived from and dependent on everyday Being-in-the-world. These diagnoses have the form of transcendental arguments: they are supposed to show that our pre-ontological understanding is a condition for the possibility of scientific and epistemological accounts of our everyday beliefs and practices, and that those accounts therefore cannot be thought of as the basis for making our everyday situations fully intelligible. But if the transcendentalism of *Being and Time* is abandoned, what is the status of such arguments?

Richard Rorty has dealt with the question of the validity of transcendental arguments in "Verificationism and Transcendental Arguments."[37] In that essay he points out that, given the situatedness and historicity of our practices, there can be no sound inference from our *current* ways of speaking and acting to immutable truths about the conditions for the possibility of language and action in general (*ibid.* 6). There is no legitimate philosophical undertaking of finding essential structures of man or of the world. But Rorty nevertheless maintains that certain sorts of "parasitism" arguments might be in order. It might be possible to show that

37. *Noûs,* V (February 1971): 3–14.

humans can engage in one sort of activity only if they can already perform another sort of activity, with the result that it is legitimate to claim that the former is "parasitic" on the latter. The private-language argument, for instance, might be taken as showing that the identification of sensations is parasitic on the mastery of a public language. From this kind of argument, however, it is not possible to draw any conclusions about the necessary structures of human experience or about the actual nature of the world. Parasitism arguments can reveal only a hierarchy of dependencies.

Rorty claims that "the only good 'transcendental' argument is a 'parasitism' argument" (*ibid.* 5). It seems that Heidegger's diagnoses of science and Cartesianism may be interpreted as "parasitism" arguments in this sense. If his critique of the tradition is sound, it should show that our everyday pre-ontological under-standing of the world is more primordial than science or epistemology (using the word 'primordial' now without its historical connotation). The attitudes of scientific theorizing and pure contemplation are parasitic on the natural attitude of involved Being-in-the-world. And, if this is the case, then the claim that Cartesianism is incoherent may still be justified: there is no pure, horizonless vantage point from which we can provide grounds and justifications for our beliefs and practices. In this sense, then, theory and passive contemplation are "founded modes" of our con-cernful involvement in the world.

To say that Being-in-the-world is more primordial than theoretical reflection or pure contemplation does not entail that it is the *most* primordial way of being for humans. It is possible for Heidegger to speak of theory and knowing as founded modes without having to assume that he has found ultimate foundations or universal, essential structures. The ontological genesis of the theoretical attitude traced in Chapter IV shows us how the theoretical attitude naturally emerges in the course of practical life and how it remains parasitic on Being-in-the-world. But whether Being-in-the-world is the "ultimate" way of being for man, or whether the whole interplay of theory and practice is fundamental to us, remains up in the air. Heidegger's critique of common sense and the tradition retains its full force regardless of whether he has found any "transcendental" truths about the being of man.

The phenomenology of everydayness and the kinds of parasitism arguments that make up the critique of the theoretical attitude therefore work to deflate the cluster of ideas presupposed from the outset in the Cartesian model. First, the subject/object picture of our ordinary epistemic predicament appears as a derivative mode of the holistic web of internal relations that make up Being-in-the-world. And, second, the atomistic and reductivistic methods of providing justifications come to be seen as parasitic on the tacit background of our everyday pre-ontological understanding. The kind of intrinsic and global intelligibility for our lives that the Cartesian model was supposed to provide turns out to be neither realizable nor necessary. Since every encounter with the world is mediated by a prior projection of a ground plan or blueprint of how things will count, there can be no such thing as an untainted standpoint of theory or pure contemplation. The descriptions and diagnoses developed in *Being and Time* and expanded in the later writings seem to yield these conclusions even when the transcendentalism of the early work falls away.

A second component of *Being and Time* that seems valuable even after the more ambitious goals of the work are abandoned is Heidegger's emphasis on history and the historicity of all human activities. The conception of man as an event or happening caught up in the flow of a shared historical project lights up the transitoriness of human endeavors while emphasizing our deep responsibility to the unfolding historical current in which we are implicated. The priority given to historicity has both negative and positive consequences. On the negative side, Heidegger's historical diagnoses serve to remind us that certain basic assumptions that seem obvious and self-evident to common sense are products of fairly recent historical shifts in Western thought. When we recognize our contemporary world-view as historically conditioned, many of the problems that seem pressing to common sense come to be seen as the by-product of conceptual grids with no privileged position in the whole of Western history.

On the positive side, the historical emphasis in *Being and Time* awakens us to the fact that our lives are embedded in a broader historical project and that we are deeply indebted to our history. To realize this indebtedness is to recognize our burden of responsibility and obligation to the historical context in which we find ourselves. But the appreciation of our historicity also has a liberating effect. For historical understanding also opens up a boundless range of possibilities for reinterpreting and re-evaluating our current situation. Heidegger's attempt to recapture an earlier "prephilosophical understanding" (219) embodied in such words as *aletheia, logos,* and *physis* is designed to expand our horizons of understanding by revealing alternative possibilities for interpretation which are deeply ingrained in our culture.

When properly understood, the concern with retrieving forgotten possibilities expresses not so much a nostalgia for an Eden that never was as a confidence about what we can achieve once we overcome our tendency to forgetfulness. In Heidegger's view, the "planetary imperialism of technologically organized man"[38] cannot be overcome by a new discovery or by a decision made by individuals. It can be overcome only by thinking through the history of Western thought and remaining open to change.

> Man cannot relinquish this destiny of his modern essence from out of himself; nor can he break from it through an authoritative decision. In thinking ahead, however, man can reflect that the Being-a-subject of mankind has never been the sole possibility of the originating essence of historical man, nor will it ever become so. A fleeting shadow of a cloud over a concealed land—that is the darkening gloom which truth as the certainty of subjectivity (prepared in advance by Christianity's certainty of salvation) casts over an event [Ereignis] that subjectivity still refuses to experience (QCT 152, HW 102).

Modern subjectivism and technology can be brought to their culmination only by a historical thinking which is at the same time a "thinking ahead."

What can no longer be sustained in *Being and Time* is the idea that historicity provides us with some sort of timeless, ahistorical principle that can provide a basis for a final answer to the question of Being. Heidegger's recognition of the transience of understanding represented an important break with the tradition of Western metaphysics, but his attempt to make transience itself into an atemporal principle shows that he had not yet fully extricated himself from that tradition. In this sense *Being and Time* is still caught up in "onto-theologic." When the foundationalist aims of that work are abandoned, however, historicity comes to refer not to some sort of timeless temporalization structure of temporality, but rather to the transience and contextualization of all human activities.

If Heidegger's phenomenology and conception of historicity are to stand outside of the tradition of "representational-calculative thinking," it is necessary to avoid construing the results of *Being and Time* as providing us with a "correct representation" of ourselves and the world. This means that there must be a way of interpreting the *truth* of the characterization of Dasein as historical Being-in-the-world in such a way that it is stripped not only of its traditional ties to truth as *certitudo,* but also of its ties to truth as *adaequatio.* The question of the "truth" of *Being and Time* becomes especially pressing when we consider the paradox of

---

38. QCT 152, HW 102.

reflexivity. If Heidegger is claiming that all our beliefs are transient and contextualized, we can ask about the status of this claim as well: Is it also transient, a product of a passing historical world-view?

There is evidence in *Being and Time* that Heidegger is struggling to work out a new conception of "truth" appropriate to the question of Being. He wants to avoid having his work interpreted as a point of view or a standpoint which correctly represents the facts where others have been mistaken. And he shows his distrust of statements or assertions when he says that a phenomenological concept "may be debased if it is communicated in the form of a statement" (36). It is clear that the findings of *Being and Time* were supposed to have the structure of the hermeneutic 'as' rather than that of the apophantic 'as' of statement-making. Yet the enterprise of working out a fundamental ontology to ground the sciences seems to have misled Heidegger into attempting to find a correct representation about the Being of entities. In a later essay, he says that his thought was led astray from a "decisive insight" in *Being and Time* to the extent that he was still tempted to regard "truth" in terms of *adaequatio:* "it was inadequate and misleading," he says, "to call *alētheia* in the sense of opening, truth."[39]

The new conception of truth he was struggling toward makes its appearance in the discussion of truth in the historical sciences. Heidegger says that "the possibility and structure of *truth in historiography* are to be expounded in terms of the *authentic disclosedness* ('truth') *of historical existence*" (397). What kind of truth is being conceptualized in this claim? We found in the last section that the "authentic disclosedness of historical existence" has nothing to do with ascertaining the *facts* about what has happened in the past. Rather, it pertains to a certain sort of life-relation to one's heritage. As authentically historical, Dasein retrieves the "quiet *force*" of the possibilities it has inherited: in its resolute stance, the history of what has been is disclosed in such a way that "the 'force' of the possible gets struck home into one's factical existence" (395). To be authentically historical, then, is to transmit the "force" of the past into the future by fully appropriating it for the present. Authentic truth here seems to be a matter not of what one knows, but instead of how one lives.

When Heidegger says that truth in the historical sciences is based on this "authentic disclosedness ('truth') of historical existence," he is suggesting that there is a unique kind of truth appropriate to historiography. He agrees with the contention of Count Yorck that

39. BW 389, SD 77.

the methods and goals of the historical sciences should be different from those of the natural sciences. According to Count Yorck, historiography is essentially *practical* in its orientation: "The practical aim of our standpoint," he writes to Dilthey, "is *pedagogical* in the broadest and deepest sense of the word" (402; my emphasis). In opposition to Ranke, who is concerned with objectively presenting historical events "as they really were," Yorck says that the aim of historiography is "to make possible the cultivation of individuality in seeing and looking" (403). The goal of historical study is to cultivate individuals, to enhance their lives and deepen their sense of values. History, on this view, is not merely a story; it is a mode of understanding which can affect the order of life itself.

Heidegger fully agrees with Yorck's claim that the scientific understanding appropriate to the human sciences is distinct from that suitable for the natural sciences. If we are to appreciate the genuine role of historiography, Yorck says, we must "raise up 'Life' into the kind of scientific understanding appropriate to it" (402). Historical science cannot be content with collecting data about the past and seeking causal connections among events. This sort of "aesthetico-mechanistic" approach is misguided, according to Yorck, because it ignores the "vitality" [Lebendigkeit] with which the past continues to surge through us as we transmit and transform its possibilities. Because history is a part of us, "that which penetrates into the ground of vitality eludes an exoteric presentation" (402). There is no way to distance oneself from history, no way to objectify it and examine it as one would stones and trees. Instead, the scientific understanding suitable to historiography is a matter of engagement, participation, and commitment. Like Nietzsche, Yorck feels that history is understood only when it is *applied* to the practical needs of life here and now.

For this reason Yorck says, "Truth is never an element [Element]" (403). Truth is not a rudimentary first principle that is one and the same for every science. "Truth" in the historical sciences is measured by how it forms, enriches, and expands our life-horizons. The criterion of truth is not that of correspondence or correct representation; it is determined by the way that "the force of the possible" is appropriated in our own existence. Truth is decided by its impact on our lives: it concerns not correct beliefs, but what makes *conscience* "powerful" (403).

Heidegger's phenomenology of Dasein might be thought of as "true" in a sense of this word similar to that which Count Yorck is trying to develop for historiography. As in the case of historiography, the characterization of Dasein is not an exoteric presentation of some external state of affairs. Instead, it is something in which we are all already engaged: the attempt to be clear and explicit about our sense of what it is to be. Here the measure of the truth of Heidegger's phenomenology is not whether it offers us a correct representation of who and what we are. The measure of truth lies in the way our lives are enriched and deepened through these descriptions. This conception of truth is implicit in Heidegger's interpretation of truth as "a-lētheia" — as "*un*hiddenness," "*un*-concealment." At the deepest level, prior to the correspondence of statements to facts in the world, truth is envisaged as the emergence of a clearing or opening that releases entities from hiddenness.

An analogue of this conception of truth as a process of illumination and opening can be found in psychotherapy. It would be naive to think that the goal of the psychoanalytic dialogue is to arrive at a "correct representation" of the patient's mental state or of the precise sequence of events that led to his neurosis. On the contrary, its aim is to deepen, widen, enrich, and clarify his self-understanding, to allow him to see a broader range of connections, and to liberate him from pointless obsessions by making him more open toward the world. Analysis is successful, according to Roy Schafer, when the patient "comes to construct narratives of personal agency ever more readily, independently, convincingly and securely," when he is able to "reallocate attributions of activity and passivity," when he discovers an "increased possibility of change, of new and beneficial action in the world," but in such a way that this conception of change "excludes randomness or personally ahistorical or discontinuous consequences, such as total and abrupt reversals of values and behavior."[40] The notion of truth as correct representation has no clear role to play in this process. The language of "disclosing," "clearing," and "lighting up" is much more appropriate here than that of "correspondence." Successful therapy is measured by its consequences for one's life.

In a similar way the field of disclosedness opened by Heidegger's description of Dasein might be detached from the issue of whether it corresponds to some set of facts. The description is measured not by criteria of correctness, but by criteria pertaining to its consequences for our lives. For example, does it give us a deeper and broader sense of who we are? does it enable us to assume our existence with renewed clarity and vigor? does it liberate us from obsessive and futile puzzles? does it enable us to see connections among a wide range of phenomena? does it bring us into accord

40. "Narration in the Psychoanalytic Dialogue," *Critical Inquiry* (*"On Narrative"*), VII (Autumn 1980): 29–53, see especially pages 42 and 50/51.

with deep and pervasive resonances of our heritage? does it offer us a richer and more illuminating vocabulary for describing and interpreting ourselves? These criteria point less to the question of finding a better "model" or "representation" than they do to transforming our lives.

If the truth of *Being and Time* is to be measured by the way it deepens and intensifies our lives, then the traditional problems of historical relativity and the reflexive paradox lose their force. Since truth is displaced from correct representation and relocated in our existential ways of appropriating and applying what has been opened up, our shifting understanding of ourselves and our world would present no difficulties for the *truth* of those interpretations. But it seems that, to the extent that Heidegger's characterization of Dasein is understood as achieving this kind of truth, it can no longer be seen as providing a basis for a fundamental ontology or a science of Being as such.

Interpreting the question of Being as rooted ultimately in this sort of truth would transform our understanding of what is at issue in that question. What we should expect is no longer a final, conclusive answer to the question of being, but rather a new mode of openness in the asking—a new *way of life* instead of a new metaphysical model or theory. The question of Being, which Heidegger says "belongs to the metaphysical essence of Dasein,"[41] can be dealt with only by bringing about a transformation in that metaphysical essence, that is, a transformation in our self-understanding of what is at stake in our questioning. That this kind of shift was part of the original plan for *Being and Time* is indicated by the third part of Heidegger's definition of "fundamental ontology" quoted above in Chapter II. According to his 1928 lectures, fundamental ontology includes (1) "the interpretation of Dasein as temporality [Zeitlichkeit]"; (2) "the temporal [temporale] exposition of the problem of Being" and (3) "the development of the self-understanding of this problematic, its task and limits—the overturn."[42]

In his later writings Heidegger makes explicit the need for such a transformation. "What is at stake," he says, "is a transformation [Verwandlung] in man's Being itself, . . . man in his relation to Being, i.e., in the turn [Kehre]."[43] The essay "on the Essence

41. LL 197.

42. LL 196 (my emphasis). See above, p. 66.

43. Letter to Richardson in the Preface of William J. Richardson, *Heidegger: Through Phenomenology to Thought* (The Hague: Nijhoff, 1963), p. xx(xxi). In this

of Truth" of 1930 also calls for a "transformation of thinking."[44] And in the "Introduction to 'What Is Metaphysics?' " Heidegger says that a transformation of metaphysics is possible only if there is a change in human nature:

> As long as man remains the *animal rationale* he is also the *animal metaphysicum*. As long as man understands himself as the rational animal, metaphysics belongs, as Kant said, to the nature of man. But if our thinking should succeed in its efforts to go back into the ground of metaphysics, it might well help to bring about a change in human nature, accompanied by a transformation of metaphysics.[45]

As long as we understand ourselves as rational animals whose task is to find a correct representation of entities and their Being qua rational ground, metaphysics will continue to revolve senselessly in the same grooves. If we are to transform the question of Being, we have to change ourselves.

---

passage Heidegger is quoting from notes for a lecture course delivered in 1937/8.

44. BW 127, WM 83.

45. WM 197. "The Way Back into the Ground of Metaphysics," p. 209.

Index